D0146393

THE PHILIPPINES

WESTVIEW PROFILES
NATIONS OF CONTEMPORARY ASIA
Mervyn Adams Seldon, Series Editor

†*The Philippines: A Singular and a Plural Place,* Second Edition, Revised and Updated, David Joel Steinberg

†*Japan: Profile of a Postindustrial Power,* Third Edition, Revised and Updated, Ardath W. Burks

Taiwan: Nation-State or Province? John F. Copper

Singapore: The Legacy of Lee Kuan Yew, R. S. Milne and Diane K. Mauzy

The Republic of Korea: Economic Transformation and Social Change, David I. Steinberg

Thailand: Buddhist Kingdom as Modern Nation-State, Charles F. Keyes

Laos: Keystone of Indochina, Arthur J. Dommen

Malaysia: Tradition, Modernity, and Islam, R. S. Milne and Diane K. Mauzy

Pakistan: A Nation in the Making, Shahid Javed Burki

†*Vietnam: Nation in Revolution,* William J. Duiker

†Available in hardcover and paperback.

THE PHILIPPINES

A Singular and a Plural Place

SECOND EDITION, REVISED AND UPDATED

David Joel Steinberg

Westview Press
BOULDER, SAN FRANCISCO, & OXFORD

Westview Profiles/Nations of Contemporary Asia

Cover photos: (top) Opposition candidate Corazon Aquino and running mate Salvador Laurel at a Manila rally; (bottom) a Catholic nun talks with marines near rebel-controlled camps, Manila. (Photos courtesy of Tom Gralish and *The Philadelphia Inquirer*)

Published in 1990 in the United States of America by Westview Press, Inc., 5500 Central Avenue, Boulder, Colorado 80301, and in the United Kingdom by Westview Press, 36 Lonsdale Road, Summertown, Oxford OX2 7EW

Library of Congress Cataloging-in-Publication Data
Steinberg, David Joel.
The Philippines, a singular and a plural place / David Joel Steinberg.—2nd ed., rev. and updated.
p. cm.—(Westview profiles. Nations of contemporary Asia)
Includes bibliographical references (p.).
ISBN 0-8133-0766-X
ISBN 0-8133-8060-X (pbk.)
1. Philippines. I. Title. II. Series.
DS655.S74 1990
959.9—dc20 90-34436
CIP

Printed and bound in the United States of America

The paper used in this publication meets the requirements of the American National Standard for Permanence of Paper for Printed Library Materials Z39.48-1984.

10 9 8 7 6 5 4 3 2 1

To Joan,
who lights up
my life

Contents

Illustrations

Preface to the Second Edition

The Philippines is a singular and plural noun. The name *Philippines* refers both to an island archipelago and to a country of over 60 million people. It identifies a unified nation with a single people, the Filipinos, and also a highly fragmented, plural society divided between Muslims and Christians, peasants and city dwellers, uplanders and lowlanders, rich and poor, and between the people of one ethnic, linguistic, or geographic region and those of another. To understand the Philippines, one must understand the conflict between the centripetal force of consensus and national identity and the centrifugal force of division and instability.

Although many institutions have been inherited from a colonial past, their resemblance to foreign models masks the subtle ways in which they have been domesticated into a distinct social fabric. Things may not be what they seem to a visitor. The Filipino's fluency in English, a tradition of pleasing and of avoiding disagreement, innate good manners, and warm charm all help to hide the real inner core of the society. The foreign propensity to discount Philippine institutions as superficial has influenced Filipino self-perception. At a press conference in 1982, Imelda Marcos posed the ambivalence far more candidly than she probably meant: "The Philippines is in a strategic position—it is both East and West, right and left, rich and poor." After a pause she continued, "We are neither here nor there." To study this people in indigenous terms should need no apology or justification, and yet the sad fact is that many people and societies in the past and the present have treated the Filipinos with condescension.

Ignorance, as always, is one cause of that condescension. A lack of close attention even from those who are not ignorant is another. A third is the temptation to assume that Manila is the whole archipelago, that the elite is the voice of the people, and that concepts such as modernity, progress, and development are good because they are familiar, Western, and trendy. It is all too easy to miss the indigenous signals because of all the international static.

The Philippines: A Singular and a Plural Place is an introduction to this fascinating country. An extended essay based on more than thirty years of study and observation of the Philippines, it is not intended to be a definitive treatise. This book is a charcoal profile, not an oil portrait. It attempts to sketch some of the key factors and experiences that have given the Philippines its particular identity.

The first edition was published in 1982. At that time, Ferdinand Marcos was firmly entrenched in Manila, and Benigno Aquino was in exile in Boston. I had long, fascinating meetings with Aquino, who used my library of Philippine materials extensively. So much has happened since then. This book required massive revision to remain of value. Almost half of the current volume is completely new, and substantial portions of the older text have been revised. Certain portions of material have been drawn from my own previous writings on the Philippines. I am grateful to the University of Michigan Press, the University of Hawaii Press, and the editors of *Pacific Affairs* and the *New York Times* for permission to reuse in altered form what first appeared in their publications.

My personal and professional debts over three decades are enormous. I am grateful to David Timberman for reading and advising me on this edition of the text. Jaime Zobel de Ayala has graciously permitted me to use some of his exceptional portrait photography. Many in the Philippines have shared with me their wisdom and insights: From President Corazon Aquino through all sectors of society, Filipinos have welcomed me, teaching me about their beautiful land. As a member of the International Observer team, I witnessed the fateful election between Marcos and Aquino, and I have heard the roar of democracy and listened to the silent vigil of a nation yearning to be free.

I am solely responsible for the interpretative analysis and any errors in fact. This edition was typed and retyped by my extraordinary secretary and friend, Gail Allan. She now knows more about the Philippines than she ever thought she would, but she never once complained about the burden I imposed upon her.

David Joel Steinberg

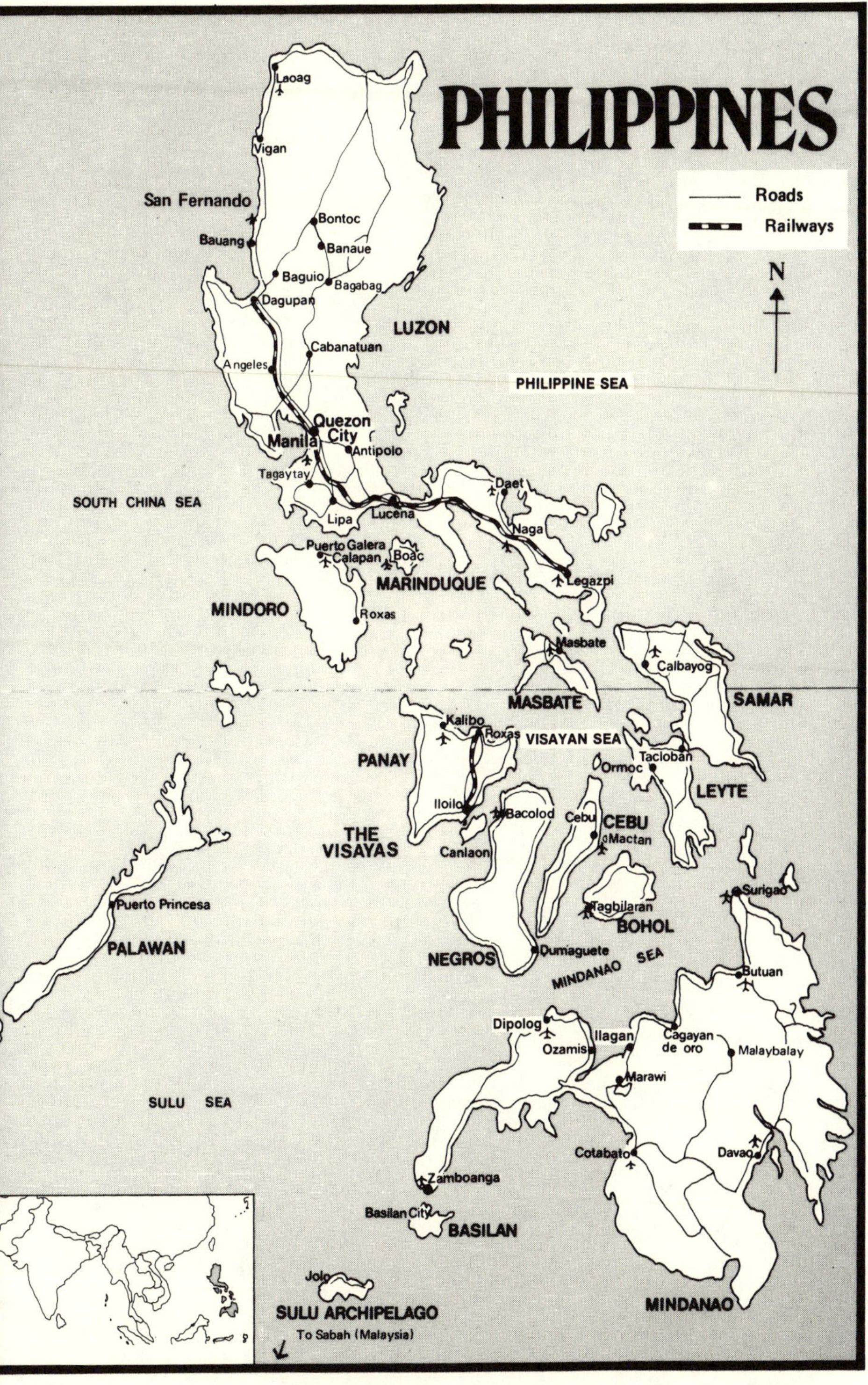
PHILIPPINES
Roads
Railways
N
Laoag
Vigan
San Fernando
Bauang
Bontoc
Banaue
Baguio
Bagabag
Dagupan
LUZON
Cabanatuan
Angeles
PHILIPPINE SEA
Quezon City
Manila
Antipolo
Tagaytay
SOUTH CHINA SEA
Daet
Lipa
Lucena
Naga
Puerto Galera
Calapan
Boac
MARINDUQUE
Legazpi
MINDORO
Roxas
Masbate
Calbayog
MASBATE
SAMAR
Kalibo
Roxas
VISAYAN SEA
PANAY
Tacloban
Ormoc
LEYTE
Iloilo
Bacolod
Cebu
CEBU
THE VISAYAS
Canlaon
Mactan
Surigao
Puerto Princesa
Tagbilaran
BOHOL
PALAWAN
NEGROS
Dumaguete
MINDANAO SEA
Butuan
Dipolog
Ilagan
Cagayan de oro
Ozamis
Malaybalay
Marawi
SULU SEA
Cotabato
Davao
Zamboanga
Basilan City
BASILAN
Jolo
SULU ARCHIPELAGO
To Sabah (Malaysia)
MINDANAO

1

The Rules of the Road

The jeepney can serve as the symbol of the Filipinos' journey into modernization. At the end of World War II, the drab, totally utilitarian American army jeep was just about the only type of vehicle moving on the shelled, destroyed roads of the archipelago. These mass-produced instruments of war were stripped down and rebuilt by the Filipinos, who converted them into minibuses capable of holding between ten and fifteen passengers. They lacked comfort but got people around cheaply and quickly. They became and still are the mass transit system not only of Manila but also of the thousands of rural barrios (villages). Decorated with tassels, bits of plastic stripping, foil, mirrors, paint, and virtually anything else that can be attached to the chassis, the jeepneys are a folk art extension of their individual Filipino owners and a vivid example of the way Filipino society has stamped industrialization with a native label. Graced with religious iconography and prayers for divine protection, named with elegance and occasional precision (the Tondo Terror, the Atom Bomb, or Maria's Lover), and covered with devotionals to unknown maidens and/or to the Virgin Mary, the jeepneys bear a kind of noisy witness to the secular faith usually known as "development." But it is not the vehicle but the driver and passengers who are the keys to understanding the Philippines.

Western cultural bias assumes implicitly, but incorrectly, that there are universal truths governing, among other things, the way people drive and the way in which people perceive the space through which they move. Teodoro Valencia, a veteran Manila columnist, commented many years ago that "Manila is the only modern city where it is prohibited to park on the side of the road but not in the middle of the busiest street to change a tire or repair a car." Visitors to the Philippines never cease to wonder at the way in which traffic moves, or doesn't move, and at the way in which people ignore "the rules of the road." A newcomer to Manila is amazed when a jeepney driver, after a quick hand signal out of his open-sided jeepney, suddenly cuts across traffic

A typical jeepney in Manila. (Courtesy of the Philippine Ministry of Tourism)

as if there were no one else on the road. Similarly, it is a common sight to see a disabled jeepney sitting in the middle of an intersection because it has broken down. Although it may have a full complement of passengers, rarely does anyone attempt to push the jeepney to the side of the road in order to permit a free flow of traffic.

Anthropologist Richard L. Stone described this phenomenon as "the private, transitory possession (or ownership) of public property." What Stone argued is that a Filipino sees the space over which he moves in the same terms as stationary space. The space on which he stands is his own, even if in the West if would be called "public domain." Thus, the hand stuck out of the side of a jeepney indicates a trajectory over which the jeepney driver intends to move and a claim to that future space into which he is turning, and a driver whose jeepney breaks down feels little sense of obligation to move his jeep aside, because until he can get his jeep moving again, that intersection belongs to him. This is not simply the erratic attitude of those people who make their living by driving; if that were the case, the passengers in the broken-down jeepney or in the many jeepneys backed up behind would provide, through shouting, noise, or pushing, the necessary impetus to move the jeepney and to assert the public's right to public space.

That mundane example offers an insight into the larger concepts of how Filipinos view private and public, how they perceive an appointment in the public sector or the "sanctity" of personal property. The squatter, and there are millions of them in Manila, builds a shanty out of corrugated tin and bamboo and sees the land on which he builds as his own. The sidewalk vendor or the beggar who opens for business on a crowded street views that pavement as if he owned the lease to the land.

The line between what is public and what is personal is far less clearcut than in the West. Filipinos often see a career in the public sector as a familial opportunity. The obligations of kinship have encouraged nepotism. So much has politics been a way of life that it has often been impossible to distinguish the lines between the bureaucrat and the politician, the politician and the technocrat. This interpenetration of functions has altered the Western-imposed concept of a civil service. Since the holding of office guarantees power and therefore the opportunity for wealth, the scramble to get appointed has cheapened the meaning of service.

In 1949 Senate president Jose Avelino was one of the few officeholders actually censured for gross violations of the law. Turning to President Elpidio Quirino at Malacañan Palace, Avelino asked, "Why did you have to order an investigation, Honorable Mr. President? If you cannot permit abuses, you must at least tolerate them. What are we in power for? We are not hypocrites. Why should we pretend to be saints when in reality we are not? . . . When Jesus Christ died on the Cross, He made a distinction between a good crook and the bad crooks. We can prepare to be good crooks." In the Philippines, few politicians have died poor.

In his pursuit of gain for himself and his family, the capitalist entrepreneur in the Philippines is doing what entrepreneurs everywhere are expected to do; the public servant, however, in his pursuits often seems to be acting in ways that other societies define as corrupt. Venality cannot be condoned nor dishonest behavior excused in the name of social mores, but concepts of good and bad, public and private, and honest and dishonest are no more universal than are patterns of driving. They are shaped by the matrix of values developed in each culture and society across the world. One cannot understand the Philippines without exploring and accepting those values.

KINSHIP AND OTHER RELATIONSHIPS

Relationships in the Philippines are defined in a "we-they" framework to a greater degree than in the West. A Filipino's loyalty is to the plural identity of his family. The web of kinship and fictive-kinship creates the social environment. The Filipino knows far more about the extended family from which he comes and far more about the network in which he operates than does a mobile American who believes that relationships, even with one's immediate family, can be turned on or off like a spigot. Like ripples on a pond, a Filipino's sense of obligation lessens by gradual degrees as people are further removed from his nuclear family and close associates.

This sense of concentric circles has always been especially important in regard to the obligations of social interaction. Students of Philippine culture have used the phrase "smooth interpersonal relationships" (*pakikisama*) to describe one of the salient characteristics of Philippine life. Philippine relationships have depended on the notion of debt of gratitude or reciprocity of obligation (*utang na loob*), and Filipinos are acutely sensitive to the burden of paying back those favors done for them by others (*puhunan*). The accusation that an individual is insensitive and thoughtless (*walang hiya*) is damning. There is no way that a child can ever repay his obligation to his parents, for example, and the Biblical injunction "to honor thy father and thy mother" is far more a reality in the Philippines than in most contemporary Western societies.

Women in Philippine society have always had a special position. The pre-Spanish *indio* (Malay) society was seemingly free from sexism as children traced kinship bilaterally, and women held power on all levels. Even today, for example, almost all spirit mediums (*baylan*) are women, and they minister to the people through the ancient, animistic rites that form a cultural stratum of the Philippines. The Spanish legacy added an element of courtly respect. The wife was traditionally the decision maker of the family, participating in all key questions of economics as well as of social issues, and she usually kept, invested, and monitored the family money; often represented the family in any bargaining; and certainly shaped all decisions from behind the scenes. As a mother, she had almost total say in decisions concerning the children, including the critical issue of marriage choice.

Corazon Aquino is one of the world's best-known and most respected women. Imelda Marcos was governor of metropolitan Manila; minister of human settlements; promoter of Philippine tourism; buyer of gems; and participant at conferences, coronations, and the United Nations. Aurora Quezon, Luz Magsaysay, Senator Eva Estrada Kalaw, and many others are proof that President Aquino is within, not outside of, tradition. She is a paradigm of what a woman in Philippine society can achieve.

Since each Filipino child traces his or her lineage bilaterally and since each child usually has a large number of siblings, a youngster moves through the world with a wide network of family. The interlocking of this extended but still intimate family is tended—like the irrigation system of dikes and paddy—with care. In addition, through the bridge of ritual kinship, the base has traditionally been further broadened, although urbanization and rural mobility are weakening this institution. Both sought-after acquaintances and close friends can become fictive-kin by fusing the pre-Spanish custom of blood compacts and the Roman Catholic concept of ritual God-parenthood (*compadrazgo*). In 1521, Ferdinand Magellan sealed his new alliance with the Cebu chief Humabon by serving as *compadre* (godfather). Manuel Quezon, the leader of the nationalist movement prior to World War II and the first president of the Philippine Commonwealth, similarly sealed his relationship with Douglas MacArthur, then field marshal of the Philippine forces, when Arthur MacArthur, the general's son, became Quezon's godson (*inaanak*). By asking a friend or the landlord of someone of economic or social or political importance to serve as *compadre* or as *comadre*, a parent can proclaim to the world at large that the bonds of loyalty now link that individual with the child. Sometimes fate plays odd tricks. Carmelo Barbero, a longtime undersecretary of defense under Marcos, invited Benigno Aquino to be *compadre* and Imelda Marcos to be *comadre* of one of his children. Years later the relationships had soured, but whenever Aquino saw Imelda Marcos, even during their rare sessions at the Waldorf Astoria in New York while Aquino was in exile, they would always discuss the Barbero child.

Frequently in the past, this system was used to establish a kind of life insurance for the child in case anything happened to the parents, and sometimes it has been used to provide a means of upward social mobility for the child, since the parents search for their most powerful friend or acquaintance to accept this religious and cultural obligation of responsibility. Much can depend on this reciprocity, and the child (like Isaac) is the tangible symbol, the living proof of the linkage. The sacrament of marriage similarly ties families together, forging obligations that extend far beyond the immediate in-laws and often involving the farming of lands and the choice of location where the new family will establish itself.

SOCIAL VALUES

Extending beyond real and fictive family are bonds that tie an individual to others from the same town and province, linguistic group, and geographic area of the country. Classmates and fellow alumni of a given university are halfway to kin, Filipinos defining relationships through shared past experiences. Ferdinand Marcos and Benigno Aquino are always described as brothers ("brod") belonging to the same fraternity,

Upsilon Sigma Phi, even though Aquino was a full generation younger than Marcos. Others who come from the same region or speak the same language have a special claim on each other.

The patron-client relationships that link a tenant to a landlord, a ward politician to a regional officeholder, a *sari-sari* (local store) owner to a Chinese distributor in Manila, help to define the reciprocal obligations of social hierarchies. The little man and woman knows what he or she has to do to remain in favor with the boss, and the patron understands how to protect, support, and sustain the network below. From the sales manager to the salesperson, the governor to the local tax collector, the banker to the client all function in both a modern and a traditional frame of reference. *Pakikisama* and *utang na loob* mean that accounts do not get changed casually, suppliers do not abandon middlemen quickly, and politicians do not forget what patronage means.

The modern, capitalist Philippines encompasses a traditional, pre-modern world, built solidly on these personal elements. Personalism helps to define decisions that otherwise would appear to be irrational. Hierarchies tie the lowliest peasant to the wealthiest entrepreneur, landlord, or politician. But if personalism helps define normative behavior in social organizations, how do Filipinos respond to a nameless bureaucracy, a social situation of conflict, or times when there is not a patron available or willing to help?

People in the Philippines use "fixers." Applicants bribe bureaucrats to get driver's licenses, export licenses, building permits, and myriad other official documents of approval. The fixer is the go-between, the medium by which the process happens. Just like the specialist on the stock exchange, the fixer sets the market, determining how much a given service is worth. Since the public sector grossly underpays its employees, the fixer also, in effect, creates an indirect form of taxation, a gray market to make the civil service work. Foreign merchant ships routinely expect to distribute thousands of dollars of alcohol and cigarettes to harbor pilots, customs officials, and stevedoring companies in order to ensure that the ships' papers are found in order, that the laborers are at the ships' sides, or that the vessels are not slapped with quarantines.

Corruption, if that is the appropriate term, is endemic. But from the individual Filipino's point of view, it is the means by which an individual can work his way through the complexities of modern society. It is a system easily abused. A near-sighted driver who has had his eye test fixed is a menace on the roads. A real estate developer who bribes the building inspector in order to use cheap cement puts his tenants at risk at the next earthquake. A defense attorney who buys a judge has destroyed justice, a sense of fairness in the system, and the integrity of the courts.

By a thousand big and little strokes, the society, the economy, the nation itself gets distorted. The newspapers annually publish a roster of who has paid the largest income tax in the preceding year; that list has virtually no relationship to those who made the most money. Timber exports are reported at approximately $200 million, but it is widely understood that this is more than a billion-dollar-a-year export industry. There is a multibillion dollar goldmining and smuggling operation in Mindanao, with much of the gold transshipped to Hong Kong or Macao. Virtually none of this enormous underground business pays any tax to the local or central governmental authorities, except in the form of bribes.

"Anomalies" have become institutionalized modes of behavior. The roots go back into the Spanish era when, for example, a departing governor was forced to stand trial before he could return home. The presumption was that he had stolen massively. His replacement had to decide whether the theft was beyond what was appropriate. In the twentieth century, black-market operations, wartime buy-and-sell schemes, import and export quota licenses, crony capitalism, and special favors from politicians who expected a kickback—all are symptoms of a structure in which the individual or family believes it has a legitimate right to take advantage of the system for the family's benefit.

And yet the society is preoccupied with law if not with justice. Everyone in Manila seems to be a lawyer and many actually are. The Philippines has a long tradition of Roman and canonical law, with a substantial overlay of U.S. constitutional and case law jurisprudence, on a common law (*adat*) base. Ferdinand Marcos was obsessed with legalisms and with manipulating constitutions to assure that he could do what he wanted. Smart lawyers win for wealthy clients, and politicians deliver favors in Congress by statute and preferential, pork-barrel legislation.

Despite a widespread awareness that the deck is stacked against them, Filipinos constantly petition in person the powerful and seek redress by litigation. A court case permits a personalization of a dispute, an opportunity to adjudicate directly, so that even a plaintiff who loses feels that he or she had a chance. Abstractions and institutions recede; face-to-face encounter creates a humanized interaction, a form of combat that is part theater and part law.

When he was a young man, Ferdinand Marcos was accused of murdering a political opponent of his father. Many years later, when Marcos had been elected president, his son asked him if he had shot the man. Marcos responded by asking if his son thought he would be in the presidential palace if he done such a thing. Foreigners took that observation as a denial of guilt; Filipinos interpreted it as an admission. In order to get to the top, it is widely understood that the Ten

Commandments may have to be bent or suspended. Guilt, in the moral sense, is rarely publicly expressed, even after conviction. Religious confession may be a route to absolution; public repentance is virtually never uttered.

Personalism, smooth interpersonal relationships, and hierarchical structures are safety lids for the society. Filipinos are usually both friendly and tolerant. But the society also tolerates moments of violence. To run amok is an understandable behavior if an individual has been wronged or provoked sufficiently. Crimes of passion abound and revenge is, in Philippine terms, often an acceptable explanation of criminal behavior. Temporary, explosive anger at a personal affront is a way Filipinos frequently express existential rage. Political violence, especially just prior to elections, is widely accepted and usually unpunished. Foreigners often comment on the number of guns Filipinos carry in the tradition of the American frontier. Yet it is also true that one can travel to the rural barrios or wander alone in the dense slums of Manila and be far safer than in New York, Yokohama, or Rome.

Compassion, a pity for the living, and resignation (*bahala na*) suffuse Philippine culture. The little man, the *tao*, may feel trapped by fate and poverty, but he also has a faith and world view that sustain him. Life is good even though it is hard. The social pressures—in Marxist terms, the contradictions—that outsiders see as leading to revolution and social upheaval do not drive the Filipinos to the barricades easily. The have-nots seem to tolerate the class prejudices, the hierarchies, and the inequities far more than would be the case elsewhere in the world.

Why do not the masses arise more often? Why do not Filipinos overthrow a corrupt elite, greedy capitalists, or insensitive employers? The socioeconomic causes are there, but as the leaders of the New People's Army (NPA) and their predecessors have discovered, it is hard to ignite a revolt and hard to sustain the passions to keep it aflame. The "people power" revolution against the Marcos government was a remarkable expression of active nonviolence (*lakas-awa*). Filipinos can be provoked; they have fought with heroism against conquering U.S. and, later, Japanese imperialists. But they seem more at peace with their culture and with their society, whatever its distortions, than most outsiders think they should be. This negative judgment of Filipino behavior by outsiders is but another expression of cultural neocolonialism.

The East is not inscrutable, but it is different. The Philippines, despite its superficially strong Western overlay, is a Southeast Asian nation, and the Filipinos are a Southeast Asian people. This is easily forgotten because it is easy to overemphasize the Western aspects in Philippine life. The name of the brilliantly successful Chinese mestizo Washington Sycip suggests something about the cultural environment in which his parents lived. The panoply of Philippine first names—Perfecta, Divina, Diosdado Apple Pie and her sister Cherry—reveal the impact of borrowings from abroad. The elegant sections of Makati, Forbes Park, and the other opulent communities of Manila are monuments to conspicuous consumption and Western materialism that outdo Beverly Hills or Saint-Tropez. At Big Ten alumni dinners the gridiron fight songs are sung with a gusto that echoes crisp autumn Saturdays in the U.S. Midwest.

And yet, the jeepney with its driver is a paradigm, underscoring how Filipino genius can adopt and adapt an initially alien product into something familiar. The symbolic and actual rules of the road are different, and the people riding inside that jeepney are different as well. The multicultural and alien heritage, which has influenced so much of the Philippine past and present, is a complex legacy. It drafted the road map by which Philippine life goes forward, but the Filipino people have altered the signposts and changed the destination as they have traveled along their route.

2

This Very Beautiful Pearl of the Orient Sea

The Philippines is one of nature's glories, and the archipelago has a splendor that catches a new visitor by surprise. The fabled sunsets across Manila Bay are so dramatic that the garish color photos used for postcards pale against nature. The rich green of the tropical rain forest, the dance of sunlight on the South China Sea, the fragile promise of newly planted wet rice, and the majesty of cumulus clouds piled tens of thousands of feet into the sky are only a few of the many facets of natural beauty on display in the Philippine Islands.

There are some 800 species of orchids and some 8,500 species of flowering plants. The skies are filled with more than 500 species of birds; underfoot are more than 100 kinds of lizards from the little gecko flicking at insects with its tongue on the walls of a home to crocodiles and iguanas in the swamps. The place looks as if it had been created for the *National Geographic Magazine.*

The beauty of the Philippines has never been lost on the Filipinos themselves. The title of this chapter comes from a passage by Apolinario Mabini, one of the remarkable nationalist leaders at the turn of the century. Its context is that in 1898, Mabini was lamenting that the newly emergent American imperialism would lead the United States to covet the Philippines because of the richness of its physical resources and its potential as a colony. Mabini went on to note that the Filipinos "covet it more, not only because God has given it to us, but also because we have shed so much blood for it." From the beginning, the dramatic beauty of the place has suffused Philippine nationalism with a sense of pride, as well as offering a series of visual images on which to build. The Sampaguita, with its exaggerated aroma of pungent sweetness, is, appropriately, the national flower.

Mayon volcano in the Bikol region. (Courtesy of the Philippine Ministry of Tourism)

THE PHYSICAL ENVIRONMENT

Nature has not been as bountiful as it is beautiful. The Philippines looks more opulent than it is. It has had chronic difficulty in feeding its population. Natural disasters—typhoons, earthquakes, volcanic eruptions—have plagued the peoples who live in and love the islands. Ever since Ferdinand Magellan arrived in 1521 in search of the fabled spices of the East, only to discover that the Spice Islands were well to the south of the Philippines, attempts to harvest nature's apparent bounty have been qualified. Today the search is for oil. Perhaps it will be discovered in significant quantity off Palawan, but the Philippines looks and smells more like an Eden than it is.

Stretching like a thin arc of cirrus clouds from just below the Tropic of Cancer toward the equator, the archipelago is a volcanic spine of islands fanning out from the Asian mainland. There are 7,107 islands scattered across 500,000 square miles, and the country has a land area of 114,672 square miles and stretches almost 1,150 miles. Although the total land area is approximately the same as that of Italy, only 1,000 of the islands are populated. Only 462 islands are one square mile or larger; 11 islands contain 94 percent of the total land mass. The three stars on the Philippine flag identify the island of Luzon, with 40,541 square miles, or about 35 percent of the land area; the island of Mindanao, with 36,680 square miles; and a cluster of intermediate-size islands in the Visayas including Cebu, Palawan, Samar, Negros, Leyte, Panay, and Bohol. Geographical fragmentation is one of the central facts of Philippine life.

Water not only atomizes the country, it also dominates the life cycle, determining to a much greater extent than in a temperate climate where people live and where plants grow. Marine waters that are within the national boundaries cover 639,112 square miles, and there are 2,000 local species of fish. In the last few years, prawn farming has become a major new industry throughout the archipelago, offering the promise of a new protein source and export product. There are 600,000 Filipino fishermen, about half in coastal fishing, and their annual catch is about 1.4 million metric tons. Still, almost all of the coral reefs have been damaged by cyanide dumped into the water to force fish to the surface. Dynamiting to catch fish has also drastically depleted the rich stock in Philippine waters. Man has savagely abused nature.

In addition to providing fish, a key source of protein, the seas surrounding the islands determine the rain cycle. The Asian monsoon has been romanticized in Western literature; its reality, if more prosaic, is more important. During the summer months in the Northern hemisphere, the land mass, especially the great Asian continental mass, heats up far more than the surrounding oceans. In the winter months, the land mass cools to a temperature lower than that of seawater. Since hot air rises and since the earth is rotating on its axis, this heating and cooling factor determines the prevailing wind flow, and that, in turn, determines whether the wind carries moisture from the sea onto the land or dry air from the land out across the sea. The impact of this phenomenon varies from place to place, depending on the location of mountain ranges, the size and position of an island, and other topographical and climatological features.

The monsoons—which mark the onset of the rainy or the dry season—are relatively predictable in any given area. In Manila, the rains come from June to November, the cool dry season is from December to February, and the hot dry season is from March to May. Except in Mindanao, which tends to have a relatively even rainfall distribution throughout the year, the cycle of nature is shaped by this monsoonal pattern.

The temperature rarely rises above 100 degrees Fahrenheit, and the lowest recorded temperature is barely below 60 degrees Fahrenheit. There is very high average humidity, and the volume of rain is extraordinary when it comes. Annual rainfall can exceed from 160 to 200 inches a year in certain parts of the archipelago. This tropical inundation means that the land is bombarded, which creates serious problems of soil erosion and leaching. Increasingly, wide belts of the Philippines are

Rice terraces. (Courtesy of the National Media Production Center)

covered with a tough but commercially useless cogon grass called *talahib.* The heavy rainfall also means that the rivers, although relatively short in distance, carry substantial quantities of water and silt down from the mountains to the river mouths, creating important alluvial deposits at the expense of the hinterland. In such a climate, there is rapid decay of dead plant matter, and as a result, a tropical rain forest often looks lush even though the topsoil level is extremely shallow. The rapid decay rate permits the strongest plants to survive by gaining their nutrients from those that do not make it.

WET RICE

Wet rice cultivation is, in effect, a form of hydroponics. The rice paddies are basins that hold the seed, fertilizer, and water required for growth. The baked-dry field itself may supply virtually no nourishment to the plant. Everything the plant needs to thrive must be supplied by the water—either from rainfall or from irrigation—and fertilizer inputs.

It is possible to double- or even triple-crop rice in one calendar year when sufficient irrigation is possible. Most Filipino rice farmers, however, rely on the monsoons to supply the necessary water and get

Transplanting wet rice. (Courtesy of the Philippine Ministry of Tourism)

only one crop per year. The rice cycle must be carefully timed to the onset of the rainy season so that in the key early phase of the growth cycle, there is rainwater to flood the rice field, which permits the germination and growth of the specially transplanted rice stalks. As the cycle nears completion, it is essential that the fields drain in order that the grain may ripen in a dry, not swampy, soil. The farmer must pray that nature cooperates, for if it continues to rain through the period when the rice should be maturing toward harvest, the grain will never burst properly. In areas that have access to artificial supplies of water through irrigation, the critical factor is the strength and viability of the dikes, for the farmer needs to be able to flood a field at one stage and then to drain the water back out of the field at another.

The farmer's paddy and dikes represent a critical capital investment; like his plow and water buffalo (carabao), they are a means of success and a symbol of survival. The cultivation of wet rice, a back-breaking, arduous task, is extremely labor intensive. It requires hard work, the fortune of nature, and strains of seed that resist natural pests, droughts, and floods. The peasant must be conservative since his survival and that of his family depend on the success of the next crop. Improving yields per unit of land, therefore, not only requires the development of new and higher-producing strains of rice, it also requires that the peasant's

Carabaos tilling a paddy. (Courtesy of the Philippine Ministry of Tourism)

caution be overcome by proof that the new seed or technique will work as well in the countryside as it did at an agricultural station.

The pressure to raise production and increase the yield per field is intense, because the Philippines is one of the fastest-growing countries in the world. In 1950, its population was approximately 20 million. Today, it is over 60 million, and at the current rate, it will exceed 90 million by the end of the century. Well over half the population is under twenty years of age. Population density, especially in urban and fertile areas, has increasingly strained traditional patterns of inheritance and exacerbated landlord-tenant relations.

Peasant unrest has been greatest in the rich, rice-producing provinces of central Luzon, which are known as the rice bowl, although increasingly the landless agricultural proletariat of Negros has become the most explosive force in rural society. For many decades, the Philippines operated a land frontier, especially on Mindanao, permitting migration away from the dense zones into relatively virgin land areas. Now, however, expansion—the cell-like re-creation of traditional farms on new land—is far more difficult, as the farmland population density is twice as high as that of Thailand. Questions of ownership, of equity, of landlord-tenant relations, and of social values enormously compound the problem. The government planner and the economic expert face the classic conundrum posed by the Red Queen to Alice in *Through the Looking-Glass:* "It takes all the running you can do to keep in the same place. If you want to get somewhere else, you must run at least twice as fast as that."

The Philippines became an importer of rice in the mid-nineteenth century to feed a spurt in population as modern technology and public health measures reduced the infant mortality rate, extended the life expectancy of the average Filipino, and eliminated natural plagues that had previously limited population growth. Also, the amount of land in cultivation for rice decreased as new crops, grown for the export market, were substituted.

In 1870, for example, 48.35 percent of the crop land was estimated to be in rice, but in 1902, that figure had dropped substantially. The statistics, dubious in 1902 and even more so in 1870, still substantially understate the magnitude of the problem, because it was the very best land that was shifted from rice cultivation to one of the other crops, and the amount of acreage planted in the four top export crops rose in 1870–1902 from 26 percent of all crop land to 36 percent. Some of this expansion took place on the Philippine frontier, including Negros and Mindanao, but much of it took place at the expense of tropical rain forests or rice lands. The Philippines regularly purchased rice from Saigon, Rangoon, Calcutta, and the southern part of the United States and was unable to feed itself throughout the American era and into independence. By the end of the first decade of U.S. rule in the Philippines, the United States had spent 120 million pesos from the insular treasury to purchase rice abroad; a report of the Philippine Commission noted that if half of that money had been spent for irrigation systems, it "would have put the country today in the position of exporting rice instead of importing it." That comment remained applicable for the next sixty years.

The population explosion over the past century has thus forced generations of governments to devote constant attention to food production. Traditionally, crop yields in the Philippines have been among the lowest in Asia, for example, approximately one-fourth of the yield per unit of land in Japan. Earlier efforts have compounded the problem, producing, among others, the serious problem of soil erosion—81 percent of the island of Cebu has been badly eroded. There are also chronic problems in the flow of credit and in the capacity to store and ship the grain.

Some signs indicate that modern technology can increase productivity faster than a growing population can consume the food. Through a massive international effort, funded initially by the Rockefeller and Ford Foundations, the International Rice Research Institute (IRRI) has developed a vast rice seed bank near the University of the Philippines School of Agriculture at Los Baños in Luzon from which new, faster-growing, and disease-resistant hybrid strains have been developed. The strains are known as "miracle rice," and different strains—IRRI-5, IRRI-8, and more recently IRRI-36, among others—are now being grown in the Philippines and all over the world. Among the extraordinary qualities of these new strains is the capacity to ripen earlier, even when the skies are still cloudy from the monsoon, but the new strains do require more water and capital input than the traditional strains. More land is being multiple-cropped, and each harvest is yielding more rice.

SUGAR, HEMP, AND COCONUT

Until the introduction of machine-powered sugar centrals (refineries), the development of narrow-gauge railroads to carry the sugarcane, and the emergence of oceangoing steamships in the nineteenth century, sugar was a marginal crop. The capital for the erection of the sugar centrals came almost exclusively from foreigners, especially Chinese, English, and Spanish interests. Foreign entrepreneurs, bankers, and factors established operations in Manila and Iloilo to help finance and manage the new export industry and to market the increasing amount of Philippine sugar across the world. Sugar helped to enrich the mestizo planter community, financing a new respectability and solidifying their position in society. These planters, many of whose children became the leaders of the nation, were created by this new industry.

Negros, which had been a virtually uninhabited, sleepy backwater, became a new center of wealth and power. In 1856, the island of Negros produced, using old-fashioned methods, approximately 4,000 piculs of sugar (about half a million pounds). In 1857, Nicholas Loney, an Englishman working for Ker and Company, moved from Manila to Iloilo and began the commercialization of the export crop by offering modern machinery to be paid for out of future profits. By 1861, there were thirteen mills on the island of Panay; in 1864, the island was exporting 14 million pounds of sugar. Loney noted that the "most extensive tracts of fertile soil easily cleared, and well-situated for shipments of produce," were to be found on Negros. By 1893, there were 274 steam-operated sugar mills, and the agricultural revolution had so changed Negros that its population had grown tenfold. The number of municipalities grew from six to thirty-four, and by the end of the Spanish period, the Spanish had created two provincial governments, Negros Occidental and Negros Oriental, on the one island.

The export of sugar became the biggest business in the Philippines, rising from 47,025 tons in 1879 to 121,471 tons in 1910 and 1,016,568 tons in 1932. In 1977, the nation exported 2.6 million tons. By 1984, it fell to 1.2 million tons. In 1985, it dropped to 600,000 tons, caused partially by the collapse of the Marcos regime and partially by the gyrations of the world market. Twelve percent of the total population became dependent either directly or indirectly on the sugar industry. During the depression, Philippine sugar was protected in the U.S. market, so the 1,016,568 tons produced in 1932 had a worth of 119,602,829 pesos ($60 million). During the same period, 65 percent of the sugar centrals located on the island of Java were closed, and 3 million tons of Javanese sugar went unsold because it could find no market. Much of the modernization of the Philippines took place around this export crop. The development of deep-water ports, railroad and telegraph lines, and sophisticated harbor facilities followed the demands of this bulk crop and its movement.

Tariff policy was a critical determinant of profit in an export industry like sugar. Spanish policy had almost always been restrictive and protectionist, although toward the end of their period of colonial rule, the Spanish followed market forces and permitted free trade. During the twentieth century, U.S. tariff policy reshaped the Philippines because Philippine products were permitted special access to the U.S. marketplace; after 1913, virtual free trade existed between the Philippines and the United States, and Filipino sugar, tobacco, and copra gained important positions in the U.S. market. Hemp already had a privileged position and was unaffected by the new tariffs. Total trade with the United States rose from $34 million in 1899 to $251 million in 1940, and the percentage of Philippine exports that went to the United States rose from 16 percent to 81 percent over the same period.

Although free trade generated a constant surplus for the insular treasury and made fortunes for people involved in agricultural export, it ignored future economic consequences. As early as 1909, Manuel Quezon noted that free trade "would create a most serious situation in Philippine economic life, especially when the time came for granting" independence. In the post–World War II reality of an independent national entity, the issues of access to or exclusion from major export markets have been of critical importance in Philippine economic planning. Dependent colonial status permitted a secure market, but being an independent political identity has tossed the Philippine economy about like a cork in a storm. Just as the Javanese sugar industry was virtually destroyed by the savage effects of the worldwide depression, so the Philippine cultivator, entrepreneur, and middleman have been buffeted today by the economic uncertainties of a world market in which future and current prices fluctuate wildly.

As sugar shaped the history and destiny of Negros, the development of the hemp and abaca export markets has dominated Bikol, the strip of land running along the lower portion of Luzon. Tobacco has altered the area of northern Luzon and pineapples, northern Mindanao. Approximately one-third of all pineapples produced for the U.S. market are grown on Mindanao, and the Del Monte plantation is a fiefdom unto itself.

In contemporary Philippine life, one export crop often thrives while another suffers. The world price of sugar has gyrated, as has the price for coconut products. In 1979, coconut oil export earnings were about $750 million, which was 18 percent of the total export income and meant that coconut oil was the top single export earner for the country. In 1980, however, the world price dropped from forty cents to twenty-four cents a pound, and earnings for 1980 fell to $400–$500 million, even though the production of coconut oil rose from 738,000 tons in 1979 to 1 million tons in 1980. This kind of gyration from one year to the next has little meaning until it is set in a human context. Fourteen million people, perhaps one-third of the total population, derive some of their livelihood from the coconut industry. More than 70 percent of the coconut growers farm on fewer than ten acres of land, and these small farmers may see their earnings slashed by 50 percent or more. Coconut oil, copra, and other coconut products compete in a world market in which coconut products are but one possible source of supply for cooking oil and soaps, as peanuts, soybeans and many other crops all produce oil that may be used for cooking. The recent anxiety in the West over the impact of saturated fats in the diet is also driving down the world price of coconut oil as oils high in polyunsaturated fats (corn and sunflower oils, for example) are being substituted for coconut oil in more processed foods.

Dependence on export markets and the vagaries of worldwide production, drought or an overabundance of rain, agricultural pests, and poor harvests have been compounded by two additional factors since World War II. The first, the more significant force during the first decade or so, was the distortion of Philippine economic development caused by the ending of U.S. colonial rule. During the American era, the Philippines developed export industries that were aimed solely at the U.S. market; in the post–World War II period of national independence, the Americans clung to colonial economic privileges while they denied Philippine producers opportunities that hitherto had been available to them. In 1946, the Americans extracted a number of preferential provisions, tying them to the 1946 Rehabilitation Act and the Trade Act of 1946, better known as the Bell Act. The Bell Act required that the

Filipinos revise their constitution to give Americans parity with Filipinos in the economic development of natural resources. The Americans also gave independence without fully permitting the Filipinos to control their own currency, since the peso was tied to the dollar at a fixed rate of two to one. The Filipinos have slowly renegotiated or let expire most of those agreements with the United States. The 1954 Laurel-Langley agreement, the 1962 floating of the Philippine peso, and the renegotiation of agreements regarding military bases are all part of that historical process.

The postwar period has been marked by rising tariff barriers against Philippine products. The sugar and coconut blocs in the islands fought rear-guard actions to retain privileged positions in the U.S. market, but their partial victories were achieved at the price of economic nationalism. In contrast to the colonial era, the Philippines now has a chronic deficit of payments with the United States. American rehabilitation and military aid partially offset this deficit during the early postwar years, but eventually import controls had to be implemented to curb the flow of U.S. goods into the Philippines. The special interests and economic power of the elite have created an economy in which the Philippines is too vulnerable to U.S. domestic political pressure, to U.S. (and now Japanese) business cycles, and to the price fluctuations of a limited number of commodities. In 1988, to cite one example, sugar imports to the United States were cut by 25 percent because a 1982 subsidy program mandated a formula to protect domestic sugar producers, primarily those in beet sugar. Although the U.S. secretary of agriculture, Richard Lyng, was required by law to take this step, he openly regretted having to punish Filipino producers among others.

The second major factor, one that has played a significant role since 1973, has been the Philippines' need for imported petroleum to meet 90 percent of its energy requirements. In 1973 petroleum imports represented only 12 percent of total imports; by 1979 they were 29.1 percent. Although vast sums have been spent over recent decades in the exploration for oil, especially offshore, the Philippines has yet to find the oil and natural gas fields that have made Brunei and Indonesia so much money. Dependence on Muslim sources for petroleum makes the Philippine government highly sensitive to Muslim attitudes in its struggle with the Muslim minority in the south, and rising oil costs have exceeded export earnings on raw materials and semifinished products, forcing the government to borrow abroad to maintain the needs of a nation that has rising expectations and a population that is growing rapidly at 2.8 percent a year, the highest rate in East Asia.

LAND OWNERSHIP AND THE DISTRIBUTION OF RURAL WEALTH

Questions of land ownership, the peasants' share of production, and income distribution as the cycle of food is grown, harvested, transported, and sold are crucial. Integrally interwoven with these questions are those of access to land and of tenancy.

When the Spaniards arrived in the archipelago more than 400 years ago, they altered the existing usage of land by establishing the European concept of private ownership—prior to their arrival, land had been held communally. Since there was ample land for the very small population of the time, there was virtually no pressure on land. The Spanish assumed that the cultivators of a given parcel were also the owners, and they froze that use by conferring ownership rights. The Spanish also preempted for the crown all lands not specifically identified as belonging to an individual or a village.

The famed Bayanihan dance troupe of the Philippines takes its name from the communal activity of the village at harvesttime. *Bayanihan* denotes team spirit, an atmosphere of unselfish cooperation, and a sharing of labor and spirit for the common good. This symbol of the shared involvement in the rice cycle is at sharp variance with the reality of land ownership and economic self-interest. There has long been a tension between those people who own or control land and those who work on it or are employed by the landowners.

Very often the sense of local community has coincided with hostility to government abuses, and taxes have been one key area of contention. Among the many tax obligations levied by the Spanish on the natives were the *polo,* a forced-labor obligation of forty days for all males between sixteen and sixty; the *tributo,* a head tax, which was frequently abused; the tithes to the church; the *donativo de zamboanga,* a periodic special levy to help fight the Muslims; the *vandala,* a forced delivery system by which certain goods had to be delivered to the government at set prices; and an assortment of municipal and local obligations. The burdens of these repressive taxes fell excessively on the peasant, who paid the same *tributo,* for example, as the landlord. Since the tax burden was unresponsive to crop yield and the crown usually took its "royal fifth," the peasant was constantly under pressure, occasionally desperate enough to rebel against Spanish authority, and frequently driven into debt and into becoming a tenant on his own land.

Nineteenth-century economic development led the Spanish to restructure the tax base, and urban and industrial taxes were created. Eventually a graduated personal tax was established, forced labor (the *polo*) was reduced, and tariffs were used to generate income. But the Spanish were unwilling to impose any rural land tax, primarily because of friar opposition. The friars owned a vast percentage of the land under cultivation and were unwilling to fund the colonial treasury's needs. When the friars first acquired their lands, much of the property was still virgin and uncultivated. Thus, the friars gave concessions to individuals known as *inquilinos* to clear and improve the land. These *inquilinos* were allowed a certain number of years rent free and were thereafter charged a rent-in-kind by the friars. The *inquilinos,* in turn, sublet their concessions to sharecroppers (*kasama*) for about 50 percent of each sharecropper's yield. In practice, the system was frequently abused, and the peasant sharecropper often paid to the *inquilino* far more than the theoretical 50 percent. The friars, who needed the rents from their estates to maintain their mission work, failed to reform the repressive quality of this institution and to realize that this brutal landholding system was defeating much of their purpose in the Philippines.

When the Americans arrived, they came with the conviction that the Philippines had to be self-financing and that through collection procedures and new taxes, sufficient revenues could be generated to fund the necessary infrastructure and to generate growth. Among the major sources of new revenue projected by the Americans was the sale of public land. Based on American precedent, it was hoped that the expansion out to the Philippine frontier would generate the economic capital required, while also solving the deeply entrenched problems of tenancy and sharecropping. With this plan in mind, William Howard Taft went to Rome to negotiate with the Vatican for the sale of the friar lands. Taft, a progressive, believed in the Jeffersonian use of public lands, and that attitude continued into the independence period, when Ramon Magsaysay believed that a massive resettlement scheme on the Mindanao frontier would be the solution to peasant unrest in central Luzon.

The U.S. colonial land policy was predicated on the American experience and on the belief that the Philippines was underpopulated. The assumptions were that the archipelago could support many more people if the tens of millions of acres of public land were developed, that there was a labor shortage in the society, and that the problems of tenancy would be solved by free land and universal education. The American object, therefore, "in purchasing the friar lands was to get them into the hands of the actual tenants, many of whom were and are very poor." Although the Americans were aware that "unscrupulous persons of means" utilized their educational advantage "to win cases which they ought to lose," they did not believe that the colonial government needed to intervene, especially since any tenant could apply for land through the Homesteading Act. Since the insular government had approximately 16 million acres of reserve agricultural land, it failed to appreciate that homesteading in an Asian, wet-rice, peasant society might not succeed. Land was not merely real estate as in the United States, something that could be measured by money; it was a unique social, political, and economic force. Filipino agricultural expansion followed what anthropologists describe as a mitotic pattern, a cell-like division of old structures on new land. Instead of setting out to escape to a new and brighter future like the homesteader in the United States, the Filipino peasant carried his past with him when he moved. After ten years of homesteading, only about 10,000 Filipinos had actually filed for and moved out onto new land, and many of those filings were dummy applications because the tenant was forced by his landlord to apply for land.

The Americans never imposed a policy of land reform, even though the opportunity was theoretically there. In part, the reason was political. The Americans made a tacit deal with the elite to maintain existing social patterns in exchange for collaboration. Since the United States intended to work through the existing social structure, it was unwilling to undercut the basis of the elite's wealth by striking at land ownership. The Americans believed that economic progress and education would emancipate the peasant.

Rafael Palma, one of the early leaders of the Philippine nationalist movement, took pride in chronicling in his memoirs how he defended the Lichauco family estate, El Porvenir, in Pangasinan in central Luzon against a tenant suit and how he triumphed for the Roxas family in front of the Philippine Supreme Court. It was soon obvious that the U.S. land policy had failed to redress the inequalities of the Philippine land system. Loss of land through foreclosure increased throughout the twentieth century and spawned an ugly fissure in the social fabric. The tenant rebellions of the Sakdalistas, the Hukbalahap (People's Anti-Japanese Army), and the New People's Army (NPA) provide grim evidence of this missed opportunity.

The malignancy of tenancy has proved hard to solve. Population growth, a longer life expectancy, fragmentation of ownership through inheritance, rural usury, an increase in absentee landlordism, the collapse of the traditional landlord-tenant relationship in favor of impersonal economic obligations, and a growing peasant awareness of economic inequalities because of education, political agitation, and the media have combined to make land reform one of the sensitive issues for Philippine society. Land ownership remains the most desired means for economic investment for rich and poor. The U.S. colonial practice of permitting the elite to gain power through land acquisition created a situation prior to martial law in which land reform was impossible because the privileged elite controlled the government and was the government. In 1951, a U.S. land reform expert, Robert Hardy, concluded that the "pernicious land tenure system" had thwarted "all efforts for technological improvement in agriculture." Subsequent land reform efforts, including the Economic Development Core (EDCOR), the 1955 Land Reform Act, the 1963 Land Reform Act, the Marcos efforts of the 1970s, and the 1988 Comprehensive Agrarian Reform Plan (CARP) have failed to address these inequities adequately.

OTHER CROPS AND RESOURCES

Of the total land area, some 35 percent is under cultivation. Rice is grown on 8.9 million acres, maize on 8.2 million, coconut on 5.7 million, and sugarcane on 1.5 million. Exporting agricultural products has a long history in the Philippines, starting with such firms as the tobacco company Tabacalera. Del Monte has been growing pineapples on Mindanao since the early part of the twentieth century, and the Japanese were actively involved in developing the timber resources on Mindanao prior to World War II. The role and the scope of these agribusinesses have increased dramatically over the past decades, and today the tropical rain forests of the Philippines are one of the country's key sources of export income. The hardwoods—including the many strains of Philippine mahogany, molave, narra, and ironwood—represent one of the great natural resources of the Philippines. Their cutting and milling is literally and figuratively changing the landscape and causing environmental havoc for future generations. Vast fortunes have been made, new areas of the country have been opened, islands have been stripped bare or depleted, minorities and hill people have been driven away, and ancillary services—including milling towns, lumber camps, and port facilities—have all sprouted on many of the islands of the archipelago. If the rate of cutting continues, there will be an acute shortage of timber for domestic use by the year 2000. A quarter of a century ago, 15 million square miles were covered by rain forests; today only 1.2 million square miles of forest still stand. The rampant entrepreneurial development of the logging and timber industry, especially for export to Japan and the United States, has altered the ecology of the Philippines, created serious problems of soil erosion, and done lasting damage to the nation's watershed. Although, belatedly, the government has attempted to encourage reforestation, it is rarely practiced correctly. The billion-dollar-a-year timber export industry is one of the most corrupt in the country. The government collects less than 20 percent of the taxes it should get, and kickbacks, dummy corporations, bribery, and violent crime make it a national disgrace.

Coconut trees at dusk. (Courtesy of the Philippine Ministry of Tourism)

Logging in the hardwood forests. (Courtesy of the Philippine Ministry of Tourism)

Major extractive mining industries have been established in the country, involving the development of the nickel, iron, chromite, manganese, and copper reserves. The Philippines has the world's largest deposits of chromite, and it is the sixth-largest producer of gold in the world. Over the last decade there has been a major gold rush in Mindanao that has gone almost totally unregulated or taxed. It is estimated to be worth billions, although there is no way to quantify it accurately. Just under 20 percent of the export trade comes from such mineral exports, including about 225,000 metric tons of copper annually. Of the 49.4 million acres of mineral land, only 34.6 million have been geologically surveyed.

Long before the arrival of the Europeans, the natives were bartering or exporting rare and exotic products for foreign goods. The Chinese have been involved in the Philippine trade for a millennium, and one early name of the islands, Mai, is a Chinese one. Over the past decades, archaeologists have discovered a very large number of beautiful Chinese porcelain pots and dishes in pre-Christian graves. Some of these pots are of such an early date or are of such exquisite quality that the definition of Chinese export porcelainware has had to be reformulated. In return for their porcelainware, the Chinese wanted Philippine exotica, including shark's-fin, rare woods, metals, and produce. Off the shores of Mindanao and elsewhere, local divers have been harvesting natural pearls for centuries. Philippine hemp, including Manila rope, has long been prized by all mariners for its strength and suppleness.

The resources of the archipelago and the quality of the environment have shaped the history and the life of the Philippine people. There is a link between the ornate, perhaps even gaudy, ornamentation of Philippine dress and the brilliant sunrises and sunsets. The national male dress of the Philippines is the *barong tagalog*. This shirt, which is perfectly suited for the tropics, is elaborately embroidered and takes the place of the Western coat and tie. Indeed, at formal occasions in the Philippines, the shirt is worn buttoned to the neck without a tie, as a symbolic reminder of the days when the Spanish authorities proscribed any *indios*, as the natives were known, from wearing a tie. The shirts are made out of native fibers, including piña and ramie. The fabrics, especially those made from banana fiber, are magnificent.

MANILA

The international traveler approaching the Philippines by air is offered a spectacular view. As the plane drops, it passes over rugged but barren ridges of volcanic mountains. These majestic peaks, set off by brilliant blue sky and cumulus clouds, suddenly fall away as the plane moves across fertile rice paddies in the provinces of Pampanga and Tarlac. Especially during the transplanting season, when the fields are flooded with lush green young rice shoots, this is a breathtaking vision of tropical splendor. As the plane comes into its final approach, it passes over the polluted, enormous freshwater lake, Laguna de Bay; leaves behind dusty roads, picturesque water buffalo, and bamboo houses; and descends over the vast urban sprawl that is the city of Manila. As the plane's landing gear goes down, the visitor looks over a city of enormous density filled with a maze of small streets; tin-sheeted, wood, or bamboo huts and houses; factories; and marketplaces. Patches of green and occasional banana trees give a crazy quilt effect. Manila from the air is dense and choked with exhaust fumes and industrial smog. It has the appearance of a city that "just growed" like Topsy.

After the plane touches ground, the passenger is swept into the sterile, interchangeable environment of all international airports, but following the trip through customs, the passenger suddenly comes out into seemingly endless crowds of well wishers, the humid warmth of the Philippine climate, and the frenetic chaos of taxi drivers and porters. There are taxis of indeterminate age and Japanese origin for the trip to a hotel or another destination.

The first impression of Manila is that it is an affluent city because of the gleaming modern airport facility, the manicured lushness of flowering shrubs and trees and elegant lawns, and the showy boulevards. Very soon, however, the traveler leaves the controlled and empty space of the airport area and its adjacent, prepackaged tourist zone and sees the other Manila—buses belching black smoke, jeepneys careening around potholes, sidwalk vendors hawking their wares. The vision is fascinating. This is clearly a modern city. Television antennae rise from the most ramshackle shacks by the road's edge; cars choke the streets, and perhaps passengers as well, with their fumes; neon signs, vast supermarkets, high-rise industrial complexes, and real estate developments appear like oases in a desert of poverty and urban sprawl. Yet Manila is also clearly something very different, something almost impenetrable, something that the visitor can sense but not know—a place of packed humanity living lives of noisy desperation.

Manila is a world apart from the countryside around and behind it. The Tagalog word for the interior, for the mountains, is *bundok*. The interior is a place from which many come but to which few return. It is the traditional home of folk verities, but it is also a place of ambivalence. For most people in the city, the mental map of the rest of the archipelago is much like the famed (and often-parodied) *New Yorker* vision of the rest of the United States, distorted out of shape by the exaggerated self-view of the city.

Roxas Boulevard, Manila Bay. (Courtesy of the National Media Production Center)

The relationship between this great urban center and the countryside is psychologically important, economically evident, and politically critical. Manila is both dependent upon and condescending toward the countryside that makes up the bulk of the nation, and yet, although Manila is a city of gleaming skyscrapers and superhighways, it is also a complex network of peasant villages. The Southeast Asian city is not the analogue of its Western counterpart. It is not only made up of people who are rich and poor, people who are born there and born elsewhere, people who are educated and illiterate—that mixture could be found in every city in the world—it is also a place that has within it the full spectrum of life-styles from traditional to modern.

At one extreme, there are the world-class hotels, many built in the mid-1970s by President Marcos to help make Manila a world-class city capable of holding major international conferences. These ultramodern palaces charge a daily rate that is in excess of the annual income of some Filipinos in the provinces. In this same category are the Cultural Center complex and museums built on the shore of Manila Bay. A few miles inland is the extraordinary new city of Makati, with its vast shopping centers, high-rise office buildings, and luxurious homes. This new city within a city, developed by the Zobel de Ayala family, is one of the most forceful examples of private entrepreneurship and architecture in the world. It is affluent. It is, in the main, very handsome. It is reminiscent of Beverly Hills, of Houston.

At the other extreme, are the miles of slums, warrens of tin huts, and planking over open sewers that are the lot for most Filipinos in Manila. Driving from the Cultural Center out to Makati, one must pass tens of thousands of squatters, many of whom have either no employment or such a meager income that subsistence is problematic and services are marginal. For these people, the cockfight (*sabong*) is one of the very few outlets for escape from life's misery.

Despite this brutal existence for the tens of thousands of squatters and the hundreds of thousands of urban poor, Manila is still a more affluent place than the *bundok*. According to some estimates, Manila and its environs have 48 percent of the gross national product (GNP) of the country and two-thirds of the cars and trucks. Virtually all the insurance, banking, communications, advertising, and cultural activities of the country are in Manila. The population of the city has just about doubled since 1970, and the new inhabitants have moved there in large measure because they are convinced that they and their families will have a better opportunity and a greater chance of success in Manila. Despite the enormous infusion of World Bank and Asian Development Bank funds, however, the struggle to maintain public services has failed.

The Cultural Center of Manila. (Courtesy of the Philippine Ministry of Tourism)

The water supply system, for example, is woefully inadequate for the population's needs. Built by the Americans in the colonial era, it was designed for a city of well under a million people. However, when experts examined the potential of Laguna de Bay, the great freshwater lake only eight miles from the city, they discovered that close to 2 million people live on the lake shore, that they generate nearly 700 tons of garbage daily, that 120 industrial plants nearby are discharging toxic chemical wastes into the lake, and that virtually none of those plants has adequate waste treatment facilities. The squatters in the most notorious slum (the area of the city called Tondo), the poor who live in the suburb of Pasay, and people in other areas of the city lack all essential services; they drink water either from a government-supplied tap in the marketplace or from fouled streams or the river. In few cities of the world is the gap between the rich and the poor so great. From the residential areas of Makati, Forbes Park, and the other subdivisions, a stream of air-conditioned Mercedes Benzes moves through the poverty-stricken zones as if through a separate world. Most of the elegant residential neighborhoods have high walls, barbed wire, and armed guards to protect them. During the Vietnam War, when President Lyndon Johnson and the U.S. allies met at the 1966 Manila Conference, the Philippine government spent substantial sums of money erecting white picket fences

The new city of Makati. (Courtesy of the Philippine Ministry of Tourism)

along the motorcade route so that the visiting dignitaries and television camera crews would not see the appalling slums they were driving through. During the pope's visit in 1981, the same thing happened again.

Urbanization is stretching around the shoreline of Manila Bay and into the interior, and rice fields and swampland are being converted into squatter settlements and urban compounds. Manila itself is relatively small, but metropolitan Manila, the greater zone, is enormous, with four cities and thirteen towns. It has been estimated that the population of this larger zone is close to 10 million people, and that the city is growing at a rate of 5.6 percent per year. In 1903, the city of Manila had 220,000 inhabitants, and the suburbs 17,000, for a total of 237,000. That figure represented just over 3 percent of the total population of the country. In 1939, the city of Manila had 633,000 inhabitants, and the suburbs held 225,000 more Filipinos, for an approximate total of 858,000, or 5.3 percent of the total population. In 1948, the city of Manila had a population of 984,000, and the suburbs an additional 383,000, for an approximate total of 1,377,000 Filipinos, 7.1 percent of the national total. By 1958, the city of Manila had 1,243,000 inhabitants, and the suburbs 780,000, approximately 8.5 percent of the nation's population. The social, economic, and political definition of the city has been substantially expanded.

The life-style of people living in Manila is far more sophisticated; the suicide and crime rates are much greater. Manila is a depersonalized, monetary society in which traditional verities are blurred by anomie. It dwarfs its rival cities—Cebu, Iloilo, Davao, and a few others. Woefully underfinanced, underserviced, and underplanned, Manila is pulsating, clogged, dirty, and alive. The juxtaposition of its pathetic shacks of tin and cardboard without water or sanitation and its elegant suburbs with private guards and fancy clubs is a visible example of the confusion that underlies so much of Third World "development."

And yet, it is essential not to dismiss this urban phenomenon as the corruption of a simpler, better, traditional world. Manila is a melting pot, blending the geographic, linguistic, and racial divisions of the Philippine people. It is an archetypal example of a plural society. The Spanish originally created distinct cities within a city so that the Spaniards themselves lived within the walls while the Chinese, mestizos, and *indios* each had their own quarter and, more important, their own governing council (*gremio*). But as Manila grew in the twentieth century, wealth, rather than race, established neighborhood character, and the city offers people of all backgrounds the vehicle, educational resources, and job opportunities for upward mobility.

In the late nineteenth century, the newly emergent mestizo families moved to Manila so their children could be educated. Without the sharing of educational and living experiences in Manila, there could not have been the consensus of values and interlocking of marriage ties required to build a national leadership cadre. By World War II, four out of five people in Manila could read and write; in distant Sulu, fewer than one in five could do so. Today it is claimed that approximately 95 percent of the residents of Manila are literate in some language, although that figure is suspect, and the press, radio, television, and the movie industry are all important means by which Manila dominates the culture and news of the nation.

Manila has also had a strong influence on the root and character of the twentieth-century national language, Pilipino. Manuel Quezon, lamenting that he needed an interpreter when he traveled through the islands, wrote, "I am all right when I go to the Tagalog provinces, because I can speak to the people there in the vernacular, in Tagalog. But if I go to Ilocos Sur, I am already a stranger in my own country, I, the President of the Philippines!" The Visayan languages of the central islands have the largest numbers of speakers, but Manila's power as the cultural and political center of the country has made Tagalog the dominant language, even though, in theory, elements of all the languages of the country were to be fused.

3

A Singular and a Plural Folk

One of the central dreams of all modern nation-states is the emergence of an integrated homogeneous society in which the citizenry shares a sense of common identity and an allegiance. The U.S. formulation of that aspiration is *e pluribus unum.* Nations exist through the delicate balance of the coercive power of the center and the willing compliance of the citizenry. If individuals or groups of individuals choose not to pledge their allegiance to the flag and to the nation for which it stands, that nation is unstable and must rely on the military or on the police power of the government for survival. Lincoln warned that "a house divided against itself cannot stand," and virtually every modern nation has experienced some form of civil war as the new patterns of allegiance and the priority of nationalist values have collided with older patterns. This reformulation of values, by which allegiance to the nation-state becomes paramount, is one of the central issues of twentieth-century history.

Virtually every subjugated colony has sought to define itself by waging an external struggle of liberation against the former imperial overlord and an internal struggle of reformulation of values against traditional, pre-nationalist value systems. Ethnicity, religious difference, linguistic identity, geographical and historical experiences, different life experience, familial or clan obligation, kinship patterns—all of these represent priorities that are potentially antithetical to the nationalist dream. People will not think of themselves as Filipinos or Indonesians or Americans if they posit their religious, linguistic, geographical, or tribal values as being more central to their lives than their nationalist identity. Modern nationalism demands that the nation must be the prime allegiance, the cause to which its citizens devote their loyalty and offer their lives.

THE PLURAL SOCIETY

The Philippines, like virtually every other former colony in Asia and Africa, has been struggling to build its modern nation-state on a "plural society," a term coined many years ago by J. S. Furnivall to describe the lack of social consensus in a place like the Philippines. The nationalist dream of a single folk sharing a common set of priorities must be juxtaposed against the reality of the centrifugal, noncohesive facts of life. National integration is incomplete in the Philippines, although, compared with many other places in Africa and Asia, the Filipinos do have a sense of common identity, a feeling of bonding that has grown over the decades and centuries, and an awareness of a shared national experience and common past.

Internalizing the symbols of the modern nation-state is the gradual, subtle process of national identity. The years 1896–1901, the time of the struggle against Spain and the Philippine-American war, were critical in raising the consciousness of the people and in instilling a sense of common cause and a shared heritage. The years 1941–1945 tested the emerging sense of national identity through the terrible crucible of war. The Filipinos felt collectively that their national integrity was threatened by the Japanese attack and that that attack was an assault on their peoplehood, their leaders, their way of life, their nation. They fought the Japanese fiercely, and their nationalism came of age. The Bataan death march and the years of occupation forced Philippine society to define itself. Except, ironically, for a key segment of the national leadership, which chose to collaborate in sharp variance with the decision of the masses, the Philippine nation spoke with a common voice and a unified aim. The traumatic period between the brutal murder of Benigno Aquino in August 1983 and the peaceful overthrow of the Marcos dictatorship by "people power" in February 1986 marks another era of national consensus.

But such coalescing experiences do not in themselves create a sustaining sense of union. In a speech given in September 1975, President Ferdinand Marcos bluntly stated that the Philippines was "a nation divided against itself—divided between urban and rural, rich and poor, majorities and minorities, privileged and underprivileged." Marcos went on to comment that martial law may "have liquidated an oligarchy only to set up a new oligarchy . . . , [establishing] massive opportunities for graft, corruption, and misuse of influence—opportunities which are now being exploited within the government service."

Philippine society divides between a tiny, almost all-powerful, elite and the great mass, which consists both of a rural peasantry and of urban poor. A middle class is growing, but the oligarchy to which

Marcos referred with such scorn is the paramount social institution. As Marcos observed, it has not been benign. This oligarchy has shaped much of Philippine history and has altered the value system of the country. Its attitudes and mores are often at sharp variance with those of the rest of the people, and, as will be seen, it is the most plural of all the cultural communities.

LOWLANDERS AND UPLANDERS

The Filipinos are a blend of ethnic groups and different races. Among the earliest settlers were the Negritos, a group of aboriginal people. They were followed by the Malays, who developed what is now called the lowland peasant culture. Most mountain peoples are migrant, slash-and-burn farmers; lowland Filipinos are usually sedentary rice farmers, sharecroppers, fishermen, and the like. The lowlanders make up the cultural and numerical core of the nation. They are the peasants (*tao*) who have been romanticized by the many folk dances of the Bayanihan. As Lincoln once said, "God must have loved the common man, he made so many of them." Filipino lowland peasants share many traits and a seemingly common lifestyle from one part of the archipelago to the other. As a class, however, they are fragmented by geography and by language. There are seventy languages spoken, although nine of them—Tagalog, Cebuano, Ilocano, Hiligaynon, Bicol, Waray, Pampango, Pangasinan, and Maranao—are used by about 90 percent of the people.

The variation among upland peoples is equally broad. There is a wide variety of tribal groups whose oral traditions, dress, and art are a delight to linguists and anthropologists. Long ignored by virtually all lowlanders, these upland peoples were proselytized by Protestant missionaries and photographed by *National Geographic* photographers. For most Filipinos, the uplanders were exotic, primitive, and very fierce. Acceptance of diversity has replaced acculturation as the prevailing attitude, and the upland tribes have gained a greater sense of pride and self. An emphasis on tourism and the celebration of diversity in cuisine, dress, and folk art have further solidified this new interest and tolerance.

Most uplanders practice slash-and-burn cultivation (swidden), living in the interior mountains and farming a plot of land no more than a year or two before moving on. Modern anthropological research has clearly demonstrated that they maintain a sophisticated, if oral, tradition. The key to slash-and-burn cultivation is to avoid destroying too much of the jungle cover while burning a field and to use the fertilizer generated to increase the yield. Slash-and-burn cultivation can be utilized only in those areas where there is very thin population pressure and where the land cannot stand constant cultivation. Rainfall and the risk of

Village cooperation; the Bayanihan spirit. (Courtesy of the Philippine Ministry of Tourism)

erosion are the limiting factors, and these migrant families understand the laws of letting a field lie fallow until a new ground cover can restore it and preserve the soil beneath it. Modern civilization and the pressure to increase land cultivation have driven the swidden migrant farmers further into the hills and increasingly forced many of them to abandon this most ancient Southeast Asian form of cultivation.

MIGRANTS

The Philippines, increasingly, is not a sedentary society. Over the past century people have migrated within the archipelago or abroad to improve their lives and to participate in the new opportunities of urban life. Economic gain, population pressure, the pursuit of education, and the dream of success prompted Filipinos to leave their barrios, their families, their linguistic or geographic homes. The society has been partially homogenized by these migrations, but place of birth, dialect, and family background are still potent, divisive elements. Manila has myriad villages hidden within its seemingly similar streets and avenues.

Filipinos who have migrated to Manila resemble the immigrants to the United States because, in Oscar Handlin's words, the immigrants "lived in crisis because they were uprooted." Handlin, attempting to illuminate American history, focused on the transplantation process, the way old roots were sundered before new ones were established. He observed that "the shock, and the effects of the shock, persisted for many years; and their influence reached down to many generations which themselves never paid the cost of the crossing." The migration from the countryside to Manila has not had the same traumatic impact as the Atlantic or Pacific crossing, but it has been a psychological journey of profound importance for individuals and an economic, social, and political reality for the society.

Not all migration in the Philippines has been from country to city, however. A second, equally important migration has been out to the rural frontiers of the archipelago. One of the brightest historians of the Philippines, John A. Larkin, has linked this migration to the frontier with the gradual "attachment of the Philippine economy to the world marketplace." Larkin argues that the modern Philippine experience has been shaped by the movement of remarkably large numbers of Filipinos from one place to another as they either followed new economic opportunities or escaped the grinding poverty caused by rice tenancy and a decreasing standard of living. The reality of an export economy and an external marketplace has driven some Filipinos toward the city and others toward new land, new islands, and new crops. The development of the frontier and the emergence of an export economy together present a more complicated and integrated pattern of change than one in which the city is seen as the center of modernity and the countryside as the center of tradition.

Larkin maintains that "using notions of the tie to world commerce and the advancing frontier, we may ascertain certain continuities in Philippine society which transcend regional variations. Some experiences Filipinos from North to South have shared." This thesis transcends the traditional periodization of Philippine history—the Spanish era, the American period, the Japanese interregnum—by offering a framework for viewing the entire society over the past 150 years. Changing land settlement; the development of the transportation infrastructure; the emergence of export industries that employ Filipinos; the dependence on world market forces, over which no one in the society has control; the relative importance or unimportance of literacy, technology, and sophisticated work forces—all of these factors flow from the meaning of industrialization and economic development. Urbanization, integration into a world economy, and the existence of available land and an advancing frontier also put in vivid relief the sociopolitical tensions and economic unrest that have undercut national consensus.

Another group of migrants are the landless rural poor who work to harvest commercial crops, sugar in particular. These rural workers may also farm as tenants or work for members of a landowning peasant family for part of a year, or they may come down from the mountains. But many of them move in large labor gangs to places where work is available for them. They have traditionally been among the lowest paid and the most unprotected members of the Philippine work force, and in the twentieth century, they have often left the Philippines to work as "stoop laborers" in the sugar fields of Hawaii and in the agricultural lands of California. Because of the fluidity of this group and because many are either underemployed or unemployed, it is difficult to know exactly how many there are.

Only abroad, where distance and an alien culture blur such differences, do local factors recede. There are about 1.2 million Filipinos in the United States, making them the second-largest community of Asian-Americans. Hundreds of thousands have worked on contract labor in the Middle East, remitting home a major annual source of hard currency of $1 billion or more a year. By 1986 the workers' remittances equalled 18 percent of the merchandise exports. Many of these migrants perform menial labor as domestics or on job gangs, but many more are trained professionals, nurses, accountants, and physical therapists who seek career opportunities not easily found at home.

THE CHINESE

Although the Chinese have always been a relatively small group, they have collectively held great economic power. Because of this influence, they are both a distinct stratum in the occupational order and also, of course, an ethnic community. Chinese traders visited the Philippines centuries before either Islam or Christianity reached the archipelago, and since its establishment in 1571, the Chinese have played a central role in the urban life of the primary city of Manila. They were the artisans who built the churches, carved the statues, and constructed the houses. They rapidly became central to the rice milling and marketing activities of the islands, establishing elaborate trading networks across the countryside and providing the early Spanish settlers with the key items for subsequent export to Acapulco on the famed Manila galleon. The galleon trade carried Chinese goods from Manila to the New World, and those items were exchanged for silver bullion from Mexico and Peru. From the beginning, Manila was a way station for the trade that exchanged Chinese finished goods for specie. Hundreds of millions of silver dollars flowed from the New World to China via this route.

The Chinese who took up residence in Manila or the countryside were feared and needed. Periodically, they were massacred or expelled, and they lived with both overt and covert discrimination. Most Chinese were confined to a ghetto called the *parian,* and they were known as sangleys—perhaps from the Chinese phrase *xang-lai,* which means "we want to trade."

The Spanish settlers had neither the manpower nor the inclination to provide the commercial and middle-class services required by the colony, and the Chinese, who were skilled in crafts and sophisticated in urban living, soon became indispensable. Many centuries later, the king of Siam would refer to the overseas Chinese as the "Jews of the East"; there are clear parallels, including their marginal but successful economic position, their socioreligious differences, and their persecuted condition.

By the nineteenth century, the Chinese were seizing the opportunities of a new economic order and a weakened Spanish imperial structure. After the termination of the galleon trade, the Spanish desperately needed to generate new sources of revenue to finance the colony. They liberalized the immigration rules, allowed the Chinese to live outside the *parian,* and emancipated this economic community from prior commercial restrictions. The Chinese did the rest. They developed a symbiotic relationship with Western traders, supplying raw materials and distributing imported goods. Operating through the *cabecilla* system of a central agent and rural factors—many of whom were related by kinship ties—the Chinese acted as a bridge between the native economy and the modern export sector. The opening of China as a result of the Opium War of 1839–1842, the rapid growth of the crown colony of Hong Kong, and the unrest generated by a massive civil war (the Taiping Rebellion of 1850–1864) were powerful inducements for Chinese to leave China, but the opportunities in the Philippines also drew Chinese like a magnet. Virtually all of the Chinese in the Philippines at the end of the Spanish era were men, since Chinese tradition encouraged the man to venture forth as a soldier of fortune, remitting to his parents and often his wife and family whatever he made. The flow of funds from the Philippines to China has been a major grievance of the Filipinos from the Spanish era until the present.

The emancipation of the Chinese and their movement out of Manila into the countryside had consequences that still exist today. During a ninety-year period prior to the liberalization of commerce, the Spanish had permitted the local Spanish governors to monopolize trade, even though the imperial Law of the Indies technically prohibited this. The provincial governor was allowed to pay a fine in advance (*indulto de comercio*) in order to make his fortune. This privilege was so badly abused and became so dysfunctional economically, as an expanding export market required a rationalization of the flow of trade, that the Spanish had to abolish the system, which permitted the Chinese eventually to dominate retail trade. Their near monopoly of internal trade meant that an ethnically distinct and alien group, speaking a foreign language and with alien habits and traditions, assumed a position in the society that made the Chinese collectively both vulnerable and powerful.

During the twentieth century, the Chinese community continued to expand, exacerbating the plural, centrifugal forces operating within the society. The official census of 1903 listed the Chinese population as 41,035, although private estimates tripled that number. William Howard Taft, the first governor-general and the architect of U.S. colonial policy in the Philippines, was eager to limit Chinese immigration in order to prevent the Filipino from being relegated "to the position which the Malay occupies in . . . Singapore and the Straits Settlements." However, illegal immigration made a sham of that policy. The Chinese never seemed to die. An illegal entrant would buy a dead man's name and papers and live happily ever after. According to the 1939 census, there were 117,487 Chinese in the Philippines, although, again, everyone at the time understood that this figure represented only the small tip of the iceberg. Today, there are approximately 800,000 Chinese scattered across the archipelago, but that number is as suspect as previous estimates have been for the last 250 years.

The central question has been the degree to which the Chinese have chosen to identify themselves with the Philippines and the countervailing trend by the native society of welcoming the Chinese into the community. As a result of the emergence of Chinese nationalism in the early twentieth century and the struggle between the Communists and the Nationalists on the mainland, the overseas Chinese have participated in the politics of a "middle kingdom." This diasporan sense of nationalism, including economic contributions and political agitation, has kept a segment of the Chinese community from becoming emotionally involved with the Philippines. Chinese schools have increased over the twentieth century, and many Chinese men have married Chinese women who were either already in the Philippines or who have been imported. Newspapers, schools, dress codes, and life-styles all play an important role in differentiating the Chinese from the Filipino community in which they live. Many overseas Chinese are insecure about their Chinese identity, fearing a loss of tradition and a separation from the mainstream. In such a climate, it is not surprising that many of the Chinese view the Philippine culture around them with condescension and often enrage the Filipinos with whom they come in contact.

THE MESTIZOS

The most important single social group within the Philippine social fabric is the racially mixed community of the mestizos. This term, which means of mixed blood, carries little of the pejorative connotations of the terms *Eurasian* or *half-caste.* As in Brazil and a few other nations, the mestizo community in the Philippines created the modern country.

To understand the origins of this community, it is necessary to recall that the Spanish Empire was global, stretching from Europe halfway around the world through Latin America to the Philippines. Since Spain saw itself as the temporal arm of the Roman Catholic church and since innumerable peoples were subsumed under Spanish dominion, conversion to Roman Catholicism was the key to inclusion in the Spanish socio-economic structure. With the exception of blacks—in medieval theology deemed the children of Satan and therefore incapable of conversion—all in the Spanish empire could receive the sacrament and could be saved. The Philippines became a fertile ground for Spanish missionary activity and as a result now has the largest Roman Catholic society in Asia and is one of the largest Catholic countries in the world.

Some members of the Chinese community in the Philippines saw advantages in becoming Roman Catholic. Restriction to the *parian,* limitations on trade, and other exclusionary practices were partially mitigated by conversion, and many of the Chinese traders and merchants who wished to make their fortune in the Philippines chose to be baptized and frequently chose to marry a local woman. Although many of these Chinese may have left a wife behind in China and may eventually have planned to return to China to die, apostatizing when they returned, becoming Roman Catholic was a part of living and working in the Philippines.

The offspring, reared by their *india* (native) mothers within the sacraments of the church and within Philippine cultural traditions, eventually became the core of the elite. They were conversant with both societies, able to move within the Chinese community through association with their fathers and able to move across the Philippine landscape through association with their mothers' extended kinship networks. A subculture arose that was neither *indio* nor Chinese, and these mestizos lived in their own section of Manila, Binondo. By the mid-nineteenth century, these mestizos probably numbered approximately a quarter of a million people out of a total population of 4 million. The Chinese mestizos, like the ethnically pure Chinese themselves, were concentrated in Manila and some lesser cities, and they engaged in the main channels of trade and commerce. Unlike the comparable mixed-Chinese communities of Malaysia and Java, for example, they were not a special subgroup of Chinese. They were a special kind of native.

There were other types of mestizos as well. Because of the diversity of the Spanish Empire, all sorts of interracial permutations and combinations occurred. Because the Philippines was so far away from Spain;

because it was, in fact, a colony of the vice regal outpost of Mexico, linking itself to the New World rather than to Spain directly; and because few Spaniards chose to bring their wives with them, hoping instead to make their fortunes quickly and to return to Mexico or Spain, there were virtually no Iberian women in the archipelago until the nineteenth century. Many Spaniards and Latin Americans, ethnically Caucasian, took up with concubines while living in the Philippines. Some of the foreigners, especially those on the lower levels of the bureaucracy and the military, chose to stay after their tour of duty had ended, marrying into the local gentry and inheriting a level of wealth through their wives' families that they had not known in Spain, Peru, or Mexico. The native woman who married such a Caucasian gained status and raised her family's economic potential through this non-Malay connection. By the mid-nineteenth century, there were approximately 20,000 Spanish mestizos, many of the second or third generation, living in the archipelago. There were also probably about 10,000 ethnically pure Chinese and 5,000 ethnically pure Caucasians there at that time.

The success of the Chinese mestizo, in contrast to the more socially exclusive Spanish mestizo, depended usually on the brain power and economic acumen of the individual mestizo. Ironically, growing pressure from the pure Chinese migrating into the Philippines during the nineteenth century forced the Chinese mestizo community into new pursuits, new abodes, and new identities. During the long period of Chinese exclusion, which had been mandated by the Spanish, the mestizo community had prospered. The arrival of new Chinese—with their access to credit and their willingness to accept narrow profit margins by living frugally—placed sharp pressures on the mestizo community. Mestizo families, operating within a native context, felt a strong obligation to participate in the customs of the Philippine society—including fiestas (large parties at each of the joyous sacraments of birth, confirmation, and marriage) and financial obligations to members of the extended family who might not be as fortunate economically. In any extended economic conflict or price war, the ethnic Chinese almost always beat the mestizo, even though the mestizo had much stronger ties to the society and a historical record in the community.

Lacking easy credit and unable to compete with the highly disciplined Chinese, the mestizos, or at least a large number of them, shrewdly shifted their economic base into land and into the newly emerging export crops—migrating to the island of Negros in the nineteenth century, for example, to lead in the development of the new sugar industry. Mestizos became important in developing indigo for export, and they moved into rice production, leaving the urban areas and moving out onto the central plain of Luzon or to other equally fertile areas. They acquired land via two distinct methods. They became lessees (*inquilinos*) of the friars, developing the virgin land owned by the Roman Catholic orders and then subletting tracts to native farmers for a percentage of the crop yield. This system, known as *kasamahan,* became widespread, especially in the areas around Manila.

The second method of acquiring land was through moneylending. Spanish law limited an *indio*'s debt to twenty-five pesos. To circumvent that statute, a mestizo would buy an *indio*'s land and grant him the option of repurchasing it later. Known as the *pactos de retro,* this ploy usually meant that the moneylender gained ownership. In either case, native farmers became tenants of the mestizos, and the process became so prevalent that Father Zuñiga warned in the nineteenth century that "if no remedy is found, within a short time, the lords of the entire archipelago will be the Chinese mestizos."

THE NEW FILIPINOS

Despite their successful economic response, the upsurge of Chinese immigration threatened the Chinese mestizos in a far more profound way. The newly arriving Chinese brought with them a sense of cultural identity and saw the acculturated Chinese mestizos as apostates, as bastard Chinese. The cultural identity of the mestizos was challenged as they became increasingly aware that they were true members of neither the *indio* nor the Chinese community. Increasingly powerful but adrift, they linked with the Spanish mestizos, who were also being challenged because after the Latin American revolutions broke the Spanish Empire, many of the settlers from the New World, Caucasian Creoles born in Mexico or Peru, became suspect in the eyes of the Iberian Spanish. The Spanish Empire had lost its universality.

The mid-nineteenth century, therefore, was not only a time of rapid economic development, it was also a period of substantial social change. The reformulation of identity created by these upheavals in the social fabric of the society made this a watershed period. Both uprooted social groups, in all of the ethnic gradations that can come from a mestizo community built over many generations, sought and found a new identity by using and reinterpreting the term *Filipino.* In the earlier centuries of Spanish rule, a Filipino had been a type of Creole, a Caucasian born in that particular piece of the Spanish Empire, the Philippines. The new meaning of the term was a nationalist one, and a Filipino became someone who was born in and identified with the interests of the archipelago, whatever his or her race, creed, or national origin might be.

The emergence of this group with its new sense of national identity had profound consequences on the subsequent political history of the islands, especially in the development of an articulated, anticolonial, and nationalist movement. In the sociocultural sphere, its meaning has been equally profound, since the identity of the society was defined by a community that in other countries might be dismissed as marginal. Pure-blooded Malays (*indios*) who had the wealth, connections, or family history to qualify joined the new mestizo social orbit, rejecting the Spanish term *indio* as a pejorative. It has only been in the past decade or so that groups in the society, especially within the student university community, have returned to using the term *indio,* seeking to infuse it again with legitimacy and meaning. The name of the coffee shop Los Indios Bravos in Manila marks the still hesitant return to this name. One did not have to be mestizo to become a modern Filipino, but the mestizo determined the values of the modern Filipino.

Social status was not determined by ethnic purity, family tree, or caste. It is not surprising, therefore, that the mestizos considered wealth and consumption to be the only available means by which a social hierarchy could be established. It did not matter who your parents or grandparents were if you had the funds to join, to intermarry, and to claim position. Land ownership was the tangible symbol of success, and the acquisition of land became one of the central pursuits, especially during the Spanish era when political and government opportunities were severely restricted. This heritage of a preoccupation with material measures for social standing meant the mestizo and Philippine society rapidly adopted the Horatio Alger mythology during the American era, and they continue to promote its current Philippine variant. If a person is rich enough, he can buy or build a house in Forbes Park, the most exclusive of the many posh suburbs around Manila. Except in extraordinary circumstances, that wealth will also permit an individual to purchase a membership in the polo club or the yacht club and to gain status in the many other ways by which wealth today is measured and marked.

THE *ILUSTRADO* ELITE

The nineteenth century was the period in which the current Philippine elite was formed. There has been a local hierarchy dating back to the pre-Spanish era, and the local headmen of the small communities that dotted the Philippine landscape had formed a class known as the *datu.* These hereditary chiefs were retained in office by the Spanish who renamed them *cabezas de barangay* (village headmen). The Spanish co-opted the headmen's allegiance by increasing their privileges and by guaranteeing their tenure. The *cabezas* were drawn from a pool of important families known as the elders or *principalia.* In time, hereditary power was broadened to include individuals from many of these key families, and the Spanish system bent its bureaucratic rules to accommodate to the Malay custom of seeking consensus from elders.

The Spanish were thinly stretched across the Philippines, and they relied to an extraordinary degree on the indirect rule of these local headmen, which was monitored by the exceptional temporal powers held by the local priests, who were almost exclusively Caucasian. This indirect system of colonial rule reached up to the provincial level as well where the petty governor (*gobernadorcillo*) was the senior native official serving as the fulcrum between the Spanish above him and the natives below. Each *gobernadorcillo* governed a pueblo of approximately 500 tribute-tax payers. The hierarchical system of traditional power permitted the *principalia,* the hereditary elite, to convert its power into economic landholding. Known as *caciques,* these landlords grew rich over the years. In the nineteenth century, the mestizos often married into a *cacique* family, domesticating and entrenching the mestizo community and injecting new blood, ideas, and values into the traditional, isolated, local gentry. The reliance on "natives" to perform government functions led to a more unified authority structure across the land and ultimately to a greater sense of shared institutions and values. The quality of the Spanish policy of indirect rule varied over the centuries, but it set a process in motion that has been vital in defining Philippine nationalism.

This process was neither as universal nor as simplistic as described here. The reality of social change rarely can be reduced so neatly to paper. What is certain, however, is that this explosively dynamic group within the Philippines not only sought to find a nationalist identity for itself but also sought greater influence and authority through the educational opportunities that the mestizos could now afford, either in the Philippines or abroad. Jose Rizal, the greatest nationalist leader and hero of the Philippines, was a fifth-generation Chinese mestizo. He was also a medical doctor, a skilled linguist speaking five or six languages, and a man of culture and letters. His education is a paradigm of the intellectual pursuit of this new class on behalf of its children. Known as the *ilustrados* (enlightened ones) these children grew into maturity with a high level of education and a nationalist self-awareness. Among the first modern Asians, they were sophisticated in a way that is very understandable even today.

Their knowledge, gained in Manila and abroad, made them aware of the world beyond, including Spain's weakness and the rising might of industrialization. By coming together in Manila, they developed a network of contacts that formed a bridge across the geographic, linguistic, and regional differences that divided the archipelago. By living abroad together in places like Barcelona and Madrid, they discovered how much they had in common with each other in contradistinction to the alien ways of Europeans, Chinese in Hong Kong, or Japanese in Tokyo. Their travels made them acutely aware of the history of Spain and of that of the Latin American republics that had broken from Spain, and many of them knew a great deal about their Cuban counterparts in the years leading up to the Cuban revolution of 1895. They were optimists, believers in their own capacity to improve their society, and increasingly hostile to the repressive and suffocating inequalities of colonial rule.

Self-appointed arbiters of the nation's values, they saw the Philippine future in self-serving, conservative ways. Strong believers in private property and staunch defenders of the economic opportunities that they and their parents had already created, they embraced nationalism in order to increase their share of the pie. Thus, Philippine political history assumed an evolutionary quality as a new, ambitious group sought to improve its lot and to justify its existence as the leadership for the entire Philippine people. Moderates like Jose Rizal turned away from more radical and nonoligarchic activists who, by the 1890s, were advocating radical violence to achieve total independence. Ironically, it was Rival's martyrdom, clumsily ordered by an incompetent Spanish bureaucracy, that so enraged this *ilustrado* elite that its members repudiated the last links to Spain and supported independence.

THE FUNCTION OF EDUCATION

The U.S. victory in the archipelago fulfilled *ilustrado* dreams to a degree that even startled them. In exchange for the allegiance of these leading Filipinos, the Americans yielded to the *ilustrados'* control of the society and of the panoply of institutions within it. The early American administrators were delighted to discover the sophistication and educational level of these men, and the Filipinos, in turn, were amazed to see the degree to which the United States was committed to educational achievement as a measure of potential socioeconomic success. The American emphasis on professionalization prompted the U.S. government to establish what was called the *pensionado* movement, in which hundreds and later thousands of Filipinos were sent to the United States for training and then installed in both the public and private sectors to manage the society. To this day, foreign study is one of the critical avenues for upward social mobility.

The U.S. emphasis on mass education has been deeply internalized into Philippine social life, and having a diploma is essential for a good job in the Philippines today. In 1900–1901, there were 150,000 students in elementary schools. By 1920–1921, that number had risen to just under a million, and by 1941, there were over 2 million students being educated on all levels. By 1961, there were 4,369,000 students in government-supported schools and an additional million in private schools of all levels and types. The estimated 1990 student population was over 14 million in kindergarten through high school and an additional 1.8 million in colleges and universities. Many of the institutions of higher learning are diploma mills, run for profit, but many more are either church-sponsored or government-supported institutions of quality. Today, the society is having difficulty absorbing the number of graduates it is producing. The problems of white-collar unemployment and underemployment are among the most intractable in the Philippines.

The Americans saw education as a means of democratizing the Philippine society. Believing that the greatest risk of social unrest lay in a "vast mass of ignorant people easily and blindly led by the comparatively few" *ilustrados,* the Americans held control over the Ministry of Education long after other key agencies of the Philippine government had been transferred to Philippine control. Between 1901 and 1902, more than a thousand U.S. teachers were recruited to teach in the Philippines—a precursor of the Peace Corps. Known as the "Thomasites," from the name of the ship that first brought them to Manila, these teachers sought to modernize the society, to instill a love of democracy in their students, and to establish what the Americans articulated as a "showcase for democracy." It was at this time that English became a national medium of communication and instruction; it remains today one of the important ways in which Filipinos from different communities can communicate with each other. Since there was no communal language and Tagalog was a minority language spoken only in parts of Luzon, and since less than 5 percent of the Filipinos could speak Spanish, English was made the language of instruction so the Filipinos could be "citizens of the world" and all, rather than only the wealthy few, would have the opportunity to participate in the new Philippines. As David Barrows, the architect of this educational policy, put it, "The knowledge of English . . . will contribute materially to the emancipation of the dependent classes . . . which is necessary to the maintenance of a liberal government."

The reality has been far less clear than the optimistic, progressive U.S. colonial administrators had hoped. Although mass education has given all citizens a chance to learn and to grow and the educational policy has opened the electoral process substantially, the franchise was linked to literacy, and the *ilustrados* gained distance during the decades of U.S. colonial rule and postcolonial national independence. The Philippines has, in effect, an aristocracy based on economic and educational criteria—a privileged upper class and a gap between the entitled few and the masses that is comparable to that in eighteenth-century France.

If, as it has been claimed, the modern nation exists to serve the dreams and aspirations of the people, then has the Philippine nationalist dream been perverted by this oligarchic control? The modern nation-state trying to achieve a secular utopia of material comfort promises to deliver a better quality of life, a higher standard of living, and greater opportunities for children than parents. Legitimacy in the modern nation is not a mandate from heaven but a mandate from the people. Even in the most authoritarian, openly dictatorial societies, ideological lip service is paid to "guided democracy" or "new democracy," not because there is a real interest in having Western-style democratic institutions but because in Asia, those terms mean that everyone has an opportunity to enter the secular, materialist Eden of our day. The colonialists and imperialists were expelled because they were identified as aliens who were taking more than their fair share. In the postindependence reality, the dream is that all citizens have access to the cookie jar. That dream of the commonweal suffuses modern nationalism and supplies much of the cohesion that helps to hold a nation like the Philippines together. The centrifugal forces—of ethnicity, of religion, of geography—are counterbalanced by the centripetal aspirations of the people organized collectively for the common good.

The discrepancies and contradictions of the plural society of the colonial era not only have survived through the postindependence period but are still growing. As education and the mass media work on people's values, nationalism—that binding belief in the centrality of the Philippine people—brings people together in a sense of unity. But inequalities of wealth and questions of access exacerbate traditional divisions, distorting the vision of national harmony. This tension is at the core of twentieth-century Philippine society. The abstract dream of a single folk is a powerful one that bumps continually into the plural realities.

4

The Search for a Usable Past

"For no nation is worth anything unless it has learned how to suffer and how to die." With these words, Manuel Quezon announced that the "zero hour had arrived" in December 1941. He summoned his people to fight "for human liberty and justice, for those principles of individual freedom which we all cherish and without which life would not be worth living." The appeal to Philippine nationalism had been issued before; it had been raised by Andres Bonifacio when he destroyed his Spanish *cedula* and proclaimed national independence at Pugadlawin in 1896. It had been echoed again and again by Emilio Aguinaldo, Apolinario Mabini, and the other leaders of the independence movement. It was raised by Benigno Aquino and his widow, Corazon, in the 1980s.

The brutal exigencies of a fight for national independence do force an articulation of values that otherwise might remain inchoate. The struggle is a catalyst that requires decisions of life or death, sacrifice or self-interest, allegiance or treason. It is an acid test for nationalism. The glory and the agony are both manifest, not only for the generation enduring the conflict but for subsequent generations as well. Nations that survive this ordeal believe that they have lived through their finest hour. Every nation subsequently turns to its hallowed past to find cohesion and to help articulate national identity. The leaders in a struggle for independence, the defenders of a nation's integrity, and the spokesmen for a nation's glory are all given special niches in the pantheon of martyrs and heroes.

There is little recorded history predating the arrival of the foreigners. Unlike Indonesia, Thailand, or Vietnam, in which great cultures and societies flourished prior to the arrival of the Westerners, the Philippines lacked an indigenous history when Islamic influence was first felt in the fourteenth century. When Magellan sailed to Cebu in 1521, there was still only a local form of political structure and economic development;

Three versions of historical truth, Mactan Island. *This page,* the nineteenth-century Spanish version. *Opposite, top,* the 1941 United States version; *bottom,* the 1951 Philippine version. (Courtesy of the author)

FERDINAND MAGELLAN'S DEATH.
ON THIS SPOT FERDINAND MAGELLAN DIED
ON APRIL 27, 1521, WOUNDED IN AN EN-
COUNTER WITH THE SOLDIERS OF LAPU-
LAPU, CHIEF OF MACTAN ISLAND. ONE OF
MAGELLAN'S SHIPS, THE VICTORIA, UNDER
THE COMMAND OF JUAN SEBASTIAN
ELCANO, SAILED FROM CEBU ON MAY 1, 1521,
AND ANCHORED AT SAN LUCAR DE
BARRAMEDA ON SEPTEMBER 6, 1522, THUS
COMPLETING THE FIRST CIRCUMNAVIGATION
OF THE EARTH.
1941

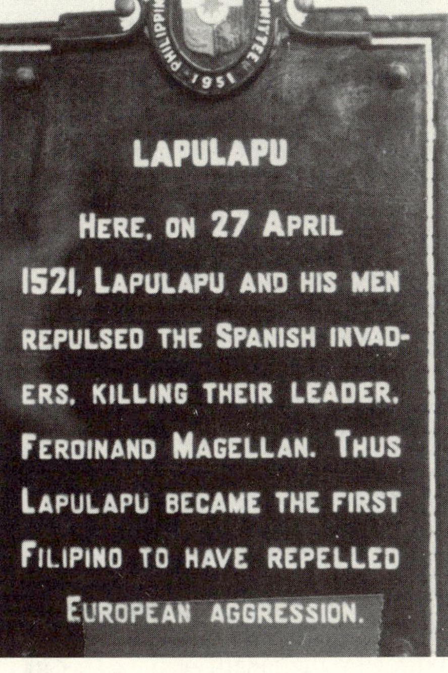

there was no central government, no sense of insular identity, and no notion of a historical past. Islam spread from village to village, but it did not have enough time to alter the way people lived or organized their social groupings. There is no evocative era prior to the Spanish period to which the Filipinos can now turn with pride. Philippine history, at least what has survived in a written form, began with the foreigners—the Chinese, the Muslim Malays, the Arab traders, and the Spaniards. The foreign-dominated quality of Philippine history is compounded by the insidious consequences of Spanish and American colonial rule, which, among other things, have negated Philippine pride.

THE SPANISH ERA

This external focus has distorted Philippine history, stressing the role of the alien and denying the reality of the native. Outsiders have tended to see the islands as a cipher, an open opportunity for advancement, and a way station to further and more challenging areas of Asia. The early Spanish goals in expanding across the Pacific were to find fabled new wealth in the Spice Islands and to gain a forward launching station in the effort to convert China to Christianity. The Philippines had no spices worth exporting; the conversion of China to Christianity was beyond possibility. Only reluctantly, therefore, did the Spanish look at what they actually had. Only slowly did they abandon their view of the Philippines as a conduit to greater things. The Philippines had been conquered in order to serve as a springboard. When those dreams came crashing down, Spanish interest in the archipelago withered. By the end of the sixteenth century, Spain was overextended, the Armada had been destroyed, Holland was in active rebellion, and this distant chain of islands became the last ripple of the original expansionist splash, faint and all but unnoticed except by the friar priests and a small coterie of government officials and entrepreneurs.

Because of the distance from Spain and an ancient agreement with Portugal that the Spanish route to the Philippines would be via the Americas rather than the Cape of Good Hope, the Philippines was, in many ways, a subcolony of the Spanish Empire in Mexico. Philippine trade went primarily to Acapulco, and in turn, many Mexican Creoles or Latin American mestizos went out to the Philippines to find their fortune. These emigres from Peru, Mexico, and Central American filled key professional roles, especially as junior officers and senior noncommissioned officers in the army, navy, and civil bureaucracy. Lacking political contact, educational attainment, and Iberian contacts, they were effectively barred from the top positons. However, what they may have lacked in status was compensated for by the length of their stay in the archipelago. Some chose to stay after the completion of their period of service; unlike their few Iberian superiors, they put down roots through marriage and landholding. When these Creoles married Caucasian women, their offspring were the so-called Filipinos. Most of the mestizos or Creoles who had emigrated from the New World married local women. Although the actual numbers were minute, their relative power was substantial.

Another of the reasons for the Spanish conquest of the Philippines was its role as a natural entrepôt for a China trade. The lure of the vast China market and the ease with which goods could be transported in Chinese junks made Manila a way station between China and the New World. Indeed, so much Chinese silk was transshipped in the early years that the silk merchants in Spain forced the Madrid government to impose strict limits on the value and volume of the galleon trade, known in Mexico as the *nao de China.* The galleon trade, which lasted for about 250 years, was carefully controlled so that it yielded enough to keep the colony functional, but not so much that it competed with Spanish exports. The galleon was divided into shares (*boletas*) of a fixed size, and the Spanish community of Manila survived on the income. The church supplied most of the capital to buy the Chinese goods, outfit the galleon, and tide the community over; it received 30 to 50 percent interest when the galleon returned. When a galleon was lost or captured, the colony was immediately in risk of bankruptcy.

The impact of this galleon trade on Philippine development was stultifying. Since the colony was totally dependent on it and since the galleon siphoned off almost all available capital, there was little interest in developing the country internally or ability to do so. By the mid-eighteenth century, the rigid mercantilist restrictions of this quasi monopoly were inhibiting the development of natural trade patterns with other Southeast Asian states, although there was a clandestine trade in bullion and Southeast Asian produce. The ease with which the colony could survive created a kind of torpor and, for better or for worse, kept the foreigners—except for the priests—isolated and uninvolved. The various restrictions also encouraged endemic corruption, since the regulations were honored more in the breach than in the observance. The frequency of proscriptions against violating the rules indicates the universality of the abuse, and respect for law was severely tarnished by these witting violations.

The governor and captain-general of the Philippines was theoretically one of the most powerful rulers in Southeast Asia. From his fort in the walled city of Manila, he was commander in chief, the king's own representative, and vice-patron of the Roman Catholic church. Since virtually all connection between the Philippines and Spain was via

Mexico, the governor was insulated by time and space. Because instructions and replacements had to await the galleon's semiannual departure from Mexico, it could take months before an order from the Spanish court reached Manila. If the governor chose to request clarification, he could stall his instructions for a year or more. However, despite the pomp and his tripartite control over the civil, military, and ecclesiastic bureaucracies, the governor's position was a fraction of what it seemed.

First, the governor's tenure was insecure and dependent entirely on the whim of the monarch. Since it was a patronage position for the king, he appointed his friends and supporters rather than men dedicated to the job. It was clearly understood, if rarely articulated, that the governor was to profit personally, provided he did not plunder too grossly. The whole system was predicated on a presumption of graft; before an incoming governor would permit the outgoing governor to return home, he subjected the outgoing governor to an official investigation or *residencia.* Bribery was endemic. Each outgoing official knew that he would have to use a certain percentage of his profit to bribe his way home.

Second, the administrative structure of the colony was such that the governor was forced to compete with his principal assistants in the Royal Council (Audiencia). The bureaucracy was usually nonresponsive and often openly hostile. Since petty officials also came to the archipelago to make their fortune, few devoted much attention to the directives from Manila. The provincial governors, usually called *alcaldes mayores,* established nearly autonomous fiefdoms, which were frequently in remote areas.

Third, the major Spanish preoccupation was the galleon trade. Manila was a parasite; it drew what it needed from the interior but was fundamentally uninterested in indigenous development. The only viable link between the small foreign community in Manila and the mass of the peasants was the church. Thus, finally, the governor was dependent upon the friars. Although he was the vice-patron of the church and had clear ecclesiastical authority granted by Rome, he could not command the friars' allegiance automatically. He was in the anomalous position, therefore, of being totally dependent on the clerics to rule the archipelago. The scope of the governor's power seemed far more impressive in Madrid than in Manila; since each governor usually saw his tenure as brief, his goal as staying alive in the tropics and returning home rich, and his legacy as perpetuating the system, he rarely tried to reform the colony.

Operating under this alien colonial structure, the lowland peasants continued to live their lives in what seems at first glance to be a static, traditional way. The annual cycle of nature and the cycle of life appeared to flow without the discontinuities of new ideas, institutions, or values.

Beneath the overlay, however, substantial change was occurring as Western, Christian values spread across the archipelago, as more and more people became devout Catholics, and as an initially alien world view was integrated and domesticated in the Malay, peasant context. Tracing the changes on the substrata levels of the society is very subtle, but the reality of the process was clear and constant.

New crops and commodities and the continuing struggle with the Muslims were elements of constant change. A sudden, powerful agent was the British occupation of Manila in 1762. This attack, which occurred because Spain had allied itself with France against England, found the colony ignorant of the alliance and unprepared to defend itself. Although Manila quickly fell, a member of the Audiencia, Don Simon de Anda, escaped to the interior, repudiated the surrender, and organized a highly effective resistance, which circumscribed British power to the Manila Bay area. The British returned the whole archipelago to Spanish control as part of a general peace two years later, but powerful social forces had been unleashed in the interim. The Chinese, smarting under a Spanish expulsion order and misjudging English intentions, openly supported England, with the result that they incurred increased Spanish hostility. The collapse of the central Spanish authority also prompted a spate of *indio* uprisings of varying intensity in many provinces throughout the island.

When the Spanish regained control of Manila, the government was bankrupt. The British had captured the outbound galleon *Santisima Trinidad* in 1762 and had seized about 3 million pesos. The inbound galleon *Filipino* had financed Anda's war resistance, but thereafter this vital lifeline had been cut. The British had sacked Manila, seized the ships in the harbor, and departed with whatever bullion they could find. Moreover, by 1764, the seemingly endless supply of bullion from the Spanish Empire had been depleted so that rehabilitation could not easily be financed by the mother country. The entrance of other European traders into the China market forced the Spanish to pay more for Chinese goods than they had in the past. Merely resurrecting the galleon trade no longer seemed to be a panacea; to restore authority, the Spanish needed a means of making the archipelago self-supporting.

The postwar governors, especially Jose de Basco y Vargas (1778–1787), attempted to apply new ideas to reform the system. The most famous of a whole series of reform plans was written by Francisco Leandro de Viana in 1765. It advocated opening a direct link with Spain via the Cape of Good Hope; the establishment of a trading company with permission to develop a trade from Cadiz to Manila to Canton; the encouragement of Spanish immigration; the creation of planations; the reform of the army, bureaucracy, and tax structure; and many other similar provisions. Such ideas were profoundly disturbing to the conservative elements in the colony, both ecclesiastical and temporal. As Governor Basco noted in 1780, "The first task must be to level the massive mountain of prejudice that stands in the way of the enlightened purposes of the central government."

The Philippines was a backward part of the empire, and Spain was a conservative, backward corner of Europe—for example, the Enlightenment reached Spain much later than elsewhere in Western Europe. By the time the Bourbon monarchs attempted to generate new life through the empire, Europe was consumed with a series of wars that were global in character and disrupted mercantilism, colonial trade, and the very foundations of the ancien régime. The Seven Years' War, the American Revolution, the French Revolution, and Napoleon's effort to conquer Europe created a half century of turmoil and war that changed both Europe and its colonial appendages. The shock tremors rippled out, eventually sweeping across Latin America and reaching the Philippines. The national revolutions in Latin America ended Spanish dominion; they had a direct and, ultimately, an overwhelming effect on the Philippines.

THE NINETEENTH CENTURY

The collapse of Spanish rule in Latin America ended the galleon trade. By 1825, the total import and export from the archipelago to the New World was a mere 1.6 percent of the 1810 level. The end of the galleon trade also ended an annual administrative subsidy. Perhaps some 400 million silver pesos had flowed from the mines of Potosí to Manila during the galleon trade's long life, and the termination of the flow not only caused economic dislocation but also made the Philippines directly dependent on Spain. The galleon trade had been a constant channel of communication and personnel and had kept the Spanish Empire catholic racially as well as Catholic religiously.

The loss of the empire in Latin America was a trauma from which the Iberian-born Spaniards (*peninsulares*) in the Philippines never fully recovered. Since they also were helpless to control the economic changes of the nineteenth century, they became increasingly defensive. The specter of rebellion seemingly paralyzed them, rendering them unable to undertake the reforms the colony needed. Suspicious of everything, they alienated the native-born Filipinos, who were, of course, also Caucasian. Social legislation was passed to mark by dress and privilege the different classes within society.

After Spain was expelled from Latin America, many Iberian-born Spaniards fled to Manila. These Iberians looked upon all Creoles as suspect, and as empire loyalists, they considered it their duty to protect the archipelago for Spain. However, since the Philippine bureaucracy was traditionally staffed by Creoles and mestizos, the tension rapidly polarized the tiny upper echelons of society. The *peninsulares*, including the friars, not only distrusted the Creoles and mestizos born in Latin America but also those born in the islands. Pushed from power, the locally born Filipinos began to see the country as rightfully theirs and the *peninsulares* as alien rulers.

Technological changes, the new need to sell and export products, ninteenth-century free trade, and the flow of capital from Hong Kong and elsewhere further threatened Spanish control, permitted vast new economic opportunities, changed the way many people made their livelihood, created urban areas, and unleashed the development of the mestizo community. By 1879, the Philippines had been dubbed "an Anglo-Chinese colony flying the Spanish flag." It developed an agricultural export economy, although with a different character from that of Java as most cultivation took place on small holdings. The key to development came with the arrival of the non-Spanish merchants. These entrepreneurs were often affiliated with the great banking and trading companies of the United States, Europe, and China. Functioning initially as commission merchants who would advance the money for a future crop of sugar, copra, coffee, or hemp, they evolved into sophisticated merchant-banking and insurance concerns with agents, usually mestizos, throughout the archipelago.

It was not only the mestizos who were chafing at the limited opportunities and reacting to a rapidly changing world. Throughout the peasant communities, there was an increasing expression of discontent. The history of the peasantry offers a different but no less important view. Popular movements, usually framed in religious rather than in secular modes, are not "aberrations," to use Reynaldo Ileto's phrase, "but occasions in which hidden or unarticulated features of society reveal themselves." Ileto argues that "the mass experience of Holy Week fundamentally shaped the style of peasant brotherhoods and uprising." In particular, the *pasyon* offered a language and a metaphor for expressing the suffering and hope within peasant society. Christ's passion was and still is an intensely personal and understandable experience for the Filipino, and the string of peasant leaders who led movements in the nineteenth century all assumed both political and religious significance. Such men were latter-day echoes of Christ in both symbol and power. The rhetoric of these movements was distant from that of the elite; it was often not even seen in political terms, but it was a key to and an indigenous expression of the society under stress.

Spanish control rested on repression and pursued a policy that, as Sinibaldo de Mas put it, was "suspicious and unenlightened but still useful for preserving the colony." The Spanish hoped to hide endemic domestic instability in Spain and political, economic, and military weaknesses in the Philippines by bravura. Between 1835 and 1898, there were fifty governors-general. Secular nationalist sentiment, which has been inchoate, found focus through hostility to the Spanish. As the *ilustrados* found their identity and voice, they blamed the friars for the evils of the Spanish system because the friars were the most visible, most conservative, most able, and most permanent segment of the Spanish community. As such, they represented a major stumbling block for the aspirations of the Filipino *ilustrados.* During the last quarter of the nineteenth century, the congruence of wealth, awareness, education, and discontent among the Filipinos led them into direct confict with Spanish authority.

ILUSTRADO NATIONALISM

The articulation of Philippine nationalism occurred not in the Philippines, where censorship was rigidly imposed after a brief mutiny at the Cavite arsenal around the bay from Manila in 1872, but in Spain itself. The Spanish arrested or exiled many *ilustrados* and, executed three native priests. The exodus to escape repression also permitted the younger *ilustrados* to improve their education abroad. This Filipino diasporan group organized what became known as the Propaganda movement; meliorist and evolutionary in approach, it advocated equality for Filipinos, representation in the parliament, freedom of speech and assembly, nonrepressive taxation, and staffing of the clergy with natives. The movement embraced an element of cultural nationalism, including an emphasis on Tagalog literature and the arts, pre-Spanish Philippine history, and a self-conscious effort to identify the national character. The movement was permeated with a strong element of youthful moralism and romanticism, and unenlightened Filipino institutions like the *cacique* system were censured as well as Spanish repression.

Jose Rizal, the most famous *ilustrado,* was a relatively wealthy fifth-generation Chinese mestizo. He wrote about himself that "had it not been for 1872, Rizal would now be a Jesuit, and instead of writing the *Noli me Tangere* [his first and most famous novel], would have written the opposite." Another *ilustrado,* Marcelo H. Del Pilar, the son of a *gobernadorcillo* in the central Luzon province of Bulacan, witnessed his oldest brother's exile to Guam because his brother, a diocesan priest, was considered too liberal.

The Spanish leadership, fearful and condescending toward the *ilustrados,* saw them as the enemies of Madrid and Rome. The rector of Santo Tomas University in Manila attacked Rizal's novel as "heretical, impious and scandalous in the religious order and anti-patriotic, subversive of public order, offensive" in the temporal sphere. Friar landholdings, in particular, became a bitter issue, especially those of the Dominican estate of Calamba. In 1887 Rizal and his family joined in a group petition requesting fair legal contracts or the sale of land to the tenants. The controversy became a test case for all parties. Because of the dispute over rental payments, the Dominicans instituted proceedings, and the issue went to court. After four years of litigation, the tenants lost decisively. Rizal returned to Spain, in part to continue the legal struggle. But Governor-General Valeriano Weyler, aware of the political character of the issue, sided with the Dominicans and forcibly resettled members of the Rizal family. The governor sent in troops, suspended the court hearings, gave 400 tenants twenty-four hours to leave, and burned everything. In 1892, when Rizal again returned to the archipelago, jittery Spanish officials arrested Rizal and deported him to Mindanao.

THE DECADE OF STRUGGLE

Simultaneously, Andres Bonifacio, a non-*ilustrado* who worked in an office in the Manila port area, founded the Katipunan, a Tagalog abbreviation for the Highest and Most Respectable Association of the Sons of the People. The Katipunan was secretive and neo-Masonic; it was also linked directly to the socioreligious tradition of popular movements. The language of the Katipunan was suffused with the images of the *pasyon,* and the quality of the secret brotherhood was totally familiar to the Filipino masses. Bonifacio's retreat to the caves of Mount Tapusi during Holy Week, caves claimed to be those of the Tagalog folk hero Bernardo Carpio was a symbolic act of vital importance. To the Katipunan, independence and redemption were one. The dream of *kalayaan* (independence) was beyond secular politics and reached into a higher realm, that of redemption.

Bonifacio, aware of the power of the *ilustrados,* sought to attract them into the Katipunan. His more openly revolutionary goals and peasant language, however, frightened away many *ilustrados,* including Apolinario Mabini, Antonio Luna, Rafael Palma, and, most important, Jose Rizal himself. Bonifacio eventually despaired of winning their support; instead, he plotted to implicate them through forgery in the hope that Spanish repression would achieve his goals for him. The Spanish police moved to arrest the Katipunan leadership after a friar,

Mariano Gil, learned of the conspiracy and informed the Spanish authorities. On August 26, 1896, Bonifacio and his supporters fled to the Manila suburb of Pugadlawin, where he issued a call to open rebellion, often misnamed the "cry of Balintawak." Bonifacio's rebellion spread throughout the Manila area, but his effort to win over the Manila *ilustrados* failed. Although the Spanish arrested and tortured many of these men, they did not then rally actively to Bonifacio's side as he had hoped.

Spanish clumsiness achieved what Bonifacio could not accomplish by cajolery or forgery. Spanish officialdom, well aware that the *ilustrados* had developed a Westernized, nationalist consciousness, put Rizal on trial as "the principal organizer and the very soul of the Philippine insurrection." Rizal had rejected appeals by Bonifacio to lend support because Rizal considered the Katipunan's plan to be "disastrous." The Spanish failed to see their opportunity to isolate Bonifacio from a group instinctively hostile to him. Instead, they did the one thing that would unite the *ilustrados* with Bonifacio—they executed Rizal publicly. Many years earlier, Rizal had written that "the day the Spanish inflict martyrdom . . . farewell, pro-friar government, and perhaps, farewell, Spanish government." Rizal's martyrdom created an alliance, albeit a fragile one, since hatred of the Spanish now transcended all other considerations.

Increases in population, dissemination of the ideas of the Propaganda movement, rising rice prices, a business recession that lingered after 1893, a plague of locusts, an increasingly unfair tax burden, the Cuban revolution, and the growing incapacity of the Spanish bureaucracy all helped the revolutionaries. Bonifacio and the Katipunan were no match for Spanish troops. Indeed, it was only in Cavite, where the friars held 50 percent of the rice land, that a young *gobernadorcillo* of Chinese mestizo stock, Emilio Aguinaldo, was able to win a significant battle against Spanish troops. Aguinaldo's victory at the Imus River gave the Filipino revolutionaries a psychological and military boost and made Aguinaldo a local hero. He moved in time to challenge Bonifacio for leadership and launched a campaign that led to Bonifacio's overthrow and subsequent execution. This divisive power grab, coupled with an increasing Spanish military presence, forced the revolutionaries to retreat far into the mountains of Bulacan where Aguinaldo set up a temporary headquarters in a small barrio called Biyak-na-bato.

Fortunately for Aguinaldo and the Filipinos, the Spanish were also in trouble. The Spanish governor, Primo de Rivera, was well aware that he lacked the power to crush a national liberation movement while Spain was also fighting in Cuba, and he moved to gain time and to restore peace. Operating through a well-known *ilustrado,* Pedro Paterno, de Rivera contacted Aguinaldo to discuss terms. Aguinaldo's initial conditions were the expulsion of the friars, representation in the Cortes (Spanish parliament), equality in judicial proceedings, Filipino participation in government, adjustment of property taxes, parish assignments for Filipinos, and a bill of rights. The terms that Aguinaldo accepted, however, included none of those provisions. Instead, Aguinaldo took amnesty, a chance to go without harm into enforced exile, and 800,000 pesos to be paid in three installments. Although he subsequently claimed that de Rivera had promised much more, the only things written into the three-stage agreement concerned amnesty and money (only a portion of which was actually paid); they had got Aguinaldo to end his resistance and leave the country. Aguinaldo, preoccupied with his own strategic weakness, failed to realize how weak the Spanish were. Although he, if not his supporters, intended to use the initial payment of 400,000 pesos to buy arms in Hong Kong, the Spanish had good reason to order a Te Deum sung in Manila Cathedral.

Aguinaldo's reputation and the independence struggle were revived by the serendipitous intervention of U.S. power after the battleship *Maine* was sunk at Havana, and the situation was now dramatically altered. Although President McKinley, by his own admission, did not know within 2,000 miles where the archipelago was, he and his advisers quickly saw the imperial possibilities of annexing the Philippines. Whether it was the "voice of God" intoning Manifest Destiny or, in Richard Hofstadter's phrase, "the carnal larynx of Theodore Roosevelt," the Americans were tempted by the "white man's burden." Thus, during the awkward period between Admiral Dewey's victory of the Spanish fleet at Manila in May 1898 and the U.S. Senate's decision to ratify the peace treaty with Spain, there was a growing escalation of American demands for the archipelago. Although Rudyard Kipling urged the United States to take up the "white man's burden," Finley Peter Dunne's caustic character, Mr. Dooley, less reverently noted that "tis not more thin two months since ye larned whether they were islands or canned goods." After testing the mood of the country, McKinley eventually announced that he had no choice but "to educate the Filipinos, and uplift and civilize and Christianize them, and by God's grace do the very best we could by them." Maintaining that "the march of events rules and overrules" his actions, he systematically strengthened Dewey's flotilla until the Americans had more than 10,000 troops around Manila Bay.

The Americans returned Aguinaldo to the islands, allowed him to reorganize what evolved into a government in the central Luzon provincial city of Malolos, and entered into a tacit collaboration with him against the remaining Spanish garrisons. They were also clearly developing a policy "of benevolent assimilation, substituting the mild sway of justice for arbitrary rule," which was not only incompatible with the equally escalating demands of the Malolos government but was also guaranteed to destroy those Filipino aspirations.

Aguinaldo did not perceive this inexorable conflict at first, in part because the U.S. policy was not fully articulated, in part because the Americans on the scene dissembled, and in part because of a lack of political sophistication. The real intentions of the United States became painfully clear, however, after Aguinaldo was duped into yielding his military position around the city of Manila; after a sham battle against the Spanish in Manila in which the Americans denied the Filipinos any role; after the diplomatic efforts of the Filipino emissary, Felipe Agoncillo, were ignored in Paris and Washington; and after the Americans had built up a major expeditionary force in the islands. The armed struggle that began on Feburary 4, 1899, probably inadvertently, was rapidly escalated, primarily by the Americans, into a major conflict, one that proved far more costly and prolonged than the U.S. military had expected. As the U.S. commander, Arthur MacArthur, noted in 1900, "This unique system of war depends upon almost complete unity of action of the entire native population." The valor of Tirad Pass, the sacrifice of thousands of unremembered *tao* (lowland peasants), and the commitment of tens of thousands of citizens to a cause of national independence made this struggle one of the first modern wars of national liberation.

And yet the struggle was quixotic. Had Philippine nationalism been comparably mobilized against the Spanish just a few years earlier, it would have triumphed resplendently. Pitted against the overwhelming firepower of the Americans and against the Republican determination to civilize with a Krag rifle if necessary, the nationalism movement failed. Defeat is not necessarily dishonorable, but the ultimate success of the Americans in coopting and altering the independence movement has tarnished the historical memory of the struggle.

The Filipino side lost its cohesion militarily after the Americans captured the city of Malolos, and more important, it lost its political cohesion after the anti-imperialist forces were defeated by the Republicans in the 1900 U.S. presidential election. Increasing numbers of important Filipino leaders began slipping away from the independence movement, both because it was losing and because opportunity clearly existed in the new apparatus established in Manila by the Americans. The attrition at the top took place during a period of maximum sacrifice by the masses, and a sense of scuttling and a feeling of abandonment resulted.

ILUSTRADO-AMERICAN COLLABORATION

Over the years, some people have scorned the *ilustrados*, using the pejorative term *Americanistas* to describe them and seeing these men as merely self-seeking oligarchs who scrambled for U.S. patronage. However, many of the *ilustrados* went back to Manila and collaborated because the Americans did offer to fulfill the *ilustrado* demands. Even as late as the Biyak-na-bato pact in 1897, Aguinaldo was not demanding independence. Rizal and the other propagandists had sought autonomy, and the Filipino military under Aguinaldo would have accepted some form of limited sovereignty in which the United States assumed obligations of external defense in exchange for internal concessions.

The U.S. policy of attraction was successful because it promised a government that would be structured to "satisfy the views and aspirations of educated Filipinos." The Schurman and the Taft Commissions enunciated a conciliatory framework that met the catalog of nineteenth-century demands, promising a self-liquidating colonialism in which Philippine nationalism could evolve peacefully. Taft reversed Karl von Clausewitz's maxim by making politics an extension of war by other means. As early as 1900, Taft had permitted the establishment of the Federalista party, actively promoting T. H. Pardo de Tavera as its leader. It is significant that the Federalistas, misunderstanding McKinley's vague promise of "benevolent assimilation," moved initially for statehood, a mere variant on the nineteenth-century goal of autonomy under Spain. This move was a fundamental error, not only because it misread U.S. intentions but also because it was an attempt to articulate a position that had been overtaken by events. After Malolos, no Filipino leader could accept anything less than eventual total independence. A contemporary, Rafael Palma, noted that "Tavera had all the qualifications for perfect leadership. . . . His one defect was that his superior talent and education had withdrawn him from the masses so that he did not understand their ideas and aspirations."

New parties rapidly developed, and soon the only question dividing the political elite was the timing of independence. The struggle shifted into the political arena. As one of U.S. official noted, the policy of attraction had "charmed the rifle out of the hands of the insurgent and made the one-time rebel chief the pacific president of a municipality or the staid governor of a province." Boasting that the policy had "accomplished all and more than was expected of it," he observed that it "made feasible the establishment of civil government while every barrio and municipality was still smoking hot with insurrection and rebellion."

The collapse of the fragile coalition of social groups that had been erected after Rizal was martyred had important consequences. In the face of Spanish repression, disparate groups found consensus, and the interlocking network of kinship patterns within the *ilustrado* community permitted the independence movement to spread laterally across the archipelago. For a brief time, the provincial *gobernadorcillo* leadership symbolized by Aguinaldo and the national *ilustrado* leadership symbolized by Paterno and Mabini came together. The resultant alliance unleashed the potential power of modern nationalism. When the U.S. policy of the carrot and the stick succeeded on both fronts, however, the coalition collapsed in acrimony. The *ilustrados* rejected Aguinaldo's claim to leadership because they had already arrogated to themselves the right to define Filipino values and goals. Some years earlier, Rizal had written that "a numerous educated class, both in the archipelago and outside it, must now be reckoned with. . . . This educated elite grows steadily. It is in continuous contact with the rest of the population. And if it is no more today than the brains of the nation, it will become in a few years its whole nervous system. Then we shall see what it will do." The raw power of revolutionary nationalism was both appealing and frightening to the group that had the most to lose. Rizal had explored this tension in his novel *Noli me Tangere* in which an *ilustrado,* Ibarra, and an uneducated, charismatic *tao,* Elias, have a complex symbiotic relationship. Rizal dreamed that a fusion was possible—a brief reality at Malolos—but Elias sadly acknowledged that he was not eloquent enough to convince Ibarra about the rightness of his political views. Elias felt that because of his lack of schooling, Ibarra would always "doubt my right to say anything, and whatever I say will always be suspect."

The complexity of the social evolution that occurred concomitantly with the political fight for independence transcends any simple categorization of elite and masses, but in the five years between 1896 and 1901, the Philippine elite triumphed in its conservative goals. The Americans, predisposed to favor those Filipinos who most nearly resembled the progressivism of Taft, Elihu Root, and Theodore Roosevelt, took sides and determined the outcome. U.S. representatives quickly saw that "these picked Filipinos will be of infinite value to the United States. . . . As leaders of the people they must be the chief agents in securing their people's loyal obedience to which, therefore, the dictates of policy, as well as plain common sense and justice, require us to secure their cordial attachment." The Americans, in their effort to justify imperialism as altruism and to blunt revolution by evolutionary nationalism, naturally allied with the *ilustrados,* giving them access to power and wealth in exchange for collaboration. The *ilustrados,* in turn, quickly saw the advantages of such an arrangement. Neither side ever regretted this decision to collaborate.

Even without U.S. support, however, the *ilustrados* would have won control and bent the revolution to accommodate their own view of it. The congruence of money, training, and experience gave them a degree of leverage that assured their leadership. The *ilustrado* unwillingness to join the Katipunan had aborted Bonifacio's dreams. The critical difference between Aguinaldo's efforts before Biyak-na-bato and those after he returned in 1898 was that he won widespread *ilustrado* support in the latter period. Aguinaldo paid a very high price for that support, however; he lost control of the government he nominally headed. Mabini effectively became the brains of the cabinet as soon as he joined Aguinaldo's staff. Aguinaldo, a member of the interlocked provincial gentry, drew his political strength from his proximity to his native area of Cavite. Like the shorn Samson, he lost his power in the national arena of Malolos. Moreover, with the establishment of a constitutional convention and the development of a parliamentary branch of government, the landowning *ilustrado* community established legislative hegemony over the executive branch. Any radical goals disappeared as private property was guaranteed and the suffrage was limited to men of high character, social position, and honorable conduct. Eighty of the 136 delegates were trained professionals (45 were lawyers). The government inaugurated on January 21, 1899, was dominated by conservative *ilustrados*.

Some years earlier, Rizal, in a "Manifesto to Certain Filipinos," had rejected the idea of achieving independence by revolution. Rizal believed that "reforms, if they are to bear fruit, must come from above, for reforms that come from below are upheavals both violent and transitory." He condemned the Katipunan for its "ridiculous and barbarous uprising." Whatever the validity of Rizal's views on change, his belief in an evolutionary, elitist government won out. "Filipinos of education, intelligence, and property" gained power and held it as the Americans systematically withdrew from control, operating on the premise that "no American should be appointed to any office in the Philippines for which a reasonably qualified Filipino could be found." Rizal's ideological descendants gained the social, economic, and political positions that the Spanish had denied to Rizal and to his peers.

Mabini, one of the few *ilustrado* dissenters, stressed frequently that the Philippines required a "simultaneous external and internal revolution." He was authoritarian, romantic, and nationalistic, and he saw social regeneration as the vital component required for the Philippines. By 1908, Taft, in his own way, was also having doubts about the success of the U.S. policy of collaborating with the elite and fretted that the policy was "merely to await the organization of a Philippine oligarchy or aristocracy competent to administer and turn the Islands over to it." American progressives were sure that education, if properly given and extended to all, would eventually break "the feudal relation of dependence which so many of the common people now feel toward their wealthy or educated leaders," but, by accepting the elitist social structure and land tenure pattern, they acknowledged that they would not tinker with what they had found. One of the assumptions of the U.S. administrators was that the new government should "conform to the customs, habits, and even prejudices" found in the Philippines. By allowing the *ilustrados* to define the nation's norms and needs, the United States greatly accelerated the creation of a preponderant oligarchy.

As early as 1907, T. H. Pardo de Tavera, himself a pillar of the establishment, noted that if the Filipinos had complete control of government, the "government would not be democratic but autocratic, and the people would be oppressed by those who would be in power." Over the years, increasing numbers of critics both within the elite (Juan Sumulong and Claro Recto) and in opposition (Pedro Abad Santos and the Lava brothers) came to excoriate the Americans and to lament the elite domination. If, as these men charged, the years between 1896 and 1901 represent the triumph of a repressive elite at the expense of the nation, then clearly much of the historical luster of those war years is gone. The validity of this assertion need not be proved in order for its consequences to be felt historically. The Philippines suffered grievously during those years. Thousands of combatants and tens of thousands of noncombatants died. Famine and disease took a savage toll on the archipelago.

The Filipino elite was consistent. The *ilustrados* sincerely believed that what was good for them individually and as a class was also good for the country. Arrogating power to themselves, they forced the American reformers to accept them and their world view. When the Americans declared that they would respect even their "prejudices," the commitment to accommodation was clear. Norman Owen, a distinguished historian, has noted, "If the *ilustrados* had not existed, however, it would have been necessary for the Americans to invent them." The policy of attraction and accommodation has been called "compadre colonialism," and it describes the mutuality of advantages found in the collaboration.

Ironically, however, the very success of the arrangement limited the capacity of the United States to effect genuine democracy or social change. Whatever the motives that led the Americans to annex the islands, however, "unjust the attempt to impose on an alien culture their own institutions and values," to quote Owen, it would have been logically consistent for the United States to retain the ability to carry through its dream of making the Philippines a "showcase of democracy." The Americans surrendered to the *ilustrados* the means to achieve that goal. "The result was an odd mixture of theory and expediency, a perpetual compromise, a modern variant of indirect rule."

HISTORICAL AMBIGUITIES

Hyperbole abounds in the historical literature about the Philippines. Mabini is always the "sublime paralytic"; Bonifacio, "the great plebeian."

There is a constant effort to cloak the men and events with an aura of grandeur. For example, one historian has noted that "whatever mistakes Aguinaldo had committed, it seems certain that his place in the Philippine history is secure." This curious and slightly apologetic statement continues, "The Philippine Republic which he shaped and led gave the Philippines its most glorious and significant epoch." Is this statement really true? Or do the Filipinos wish it to be true? And if it is true, then why was Aguinaldo virtually ignored for the next fifty years of his life? How was it possible for the great leader to be relegated to the role of living dead? Why was he left sitting in isolated retirement, summoned from obscurity periodically on ceremonial occasions but basically treated more as an abstraction than as a man?

The ambiguous way in which Aguinaldo was treated encapsulates the historical dilemma of that whole era. Nationalist movements crave a man on a white horse, a military leader who can be revered as a George Washington or a Simón Bolivar. Aguinaldo almost met this need, but his record raised just enough questions to cloud his status and to leave the Filipinos ambivalent. Like so much in Philippine life, the anomaly is elusive. Aguinaldo was, in a very real sense, the embodiment of the struggle, a figure of great power and attraction for his era; and yet, his feet were made of clay, not only because of some very questionable political decisions (such as the pact of Biyak-na-bato and his initial decision to declare a dictatorial government immediately after his return with Dewey), but also because of his ruthless efforts to destroy his rivals. Both Andres Bonifacio and Antonio Luna met violent ends because of their power struggles with Aguinaldo. Although his complicity in their executions has been hotly contested—he himself did much to obfuscate the situation in his self-serving memoirs—it seems fairly clear that he could have prevented the murder of either man if he had really wanted to do so. More important, both executions deeply demoralized the revolutionary forces, weakening them at times of maximum stress.

After Aguinaldo's one key victory over the Spanish troops at Cavite, he was acknowledged to be the Philippines' most effective general. Bonifacio made a strategic error in shifting his base of operations to Cavite, Aguinaldo's stronghold, but Bonifacio's paramount status would have been threatened in any case. The complex details of the struggle between these two men are not important here. It is sufficient to note that after Bonifacio was deposed, in part by a subterfuge, he petulantly refused to accept his demotion. After much impassioned rhetoric on both sides, he was arrested, tried, and convicted of treason and sedition. The charges and trial were farcical. Despite the alleged claims of military necessity by Aguinaldo's supporters, Bonifacio was not guilty of treason to Philippine nationalism—he had merely lost control of the Katipunan, which, significantly, was reformulated into a revolutionary government.

Bonifacio, sentenced to death, had his sentence commuted by Aguinaldo. The commutation order was never delivered, however, and Bonifacio was shot. Aguinaldo emerged as undisputed leader, but the further he went from Cavite, the weaker was his influence. Not surprisingly, Bonifacio's supporters never rallied to Aguinaldo. By the time of the pact of Biyak-na-bato, Aguinaldo felt that his position was so weak domestically that he decided to settle with the Spanish.

The violent confrontation with Antonio Luna had striking parallels with the earlier Bonifacio fight. During the fighting with the Americans, Luna emerged as the most talented general. As an *ilustrado* with wide contacts and a secure social position, he posed a threat to Aguinaldo that could not be ignored. Luna, then secretary of war, was implacably against any compromise, and he attempted to block the growing drift toward collaboration with the Americans. He also "aspired a great deal," in Mabini's words, "convinced perhaps that he was better educated than Puno (Aguinaldo)." In confused circumstances, Luna went to Cabanatuan believing that he would have a conference with Aguinaldo. Aguinaldo was not there, but a detachment of Cavite soldiers gunned Luna down. Aguinaldo claimed innocent surprise and ordered an official investigation. Mabini, however, believed that Aguinaldo had killed Luna and excoriated Aguinaldo for his "immeasurable ambition of power." Mabini was convinced after the fighting ended that "with Luna, its firmest support, the revolution fell, and the ignominy of the fall, weighing entirely upon Aguinaldo, caused his moral death, a thousand times more bitter than the physical one." The savagery of this attack from one who had been Aguinaldo's alter ego suggests the degree of disillusionment felt among the revolutionaries because of the internecine struggle. Such rifts clearly made the U.S. policy of attraction much more likely to succeed.

The Philippine revolution ended with a whimper. After Aguinaldo had surrendered, the guerrilla movement fragmented into small bands and eventually trailed off into what the Americans called dacoity. The ongoing peasant-led resistance that continued clearly embodied the more traditional expression of the Filipino hope for freedom. Such peasant resistance was easy to discount in Manila, but it was a fascinating expression of native resistance and faith in a redemption through resistance. The strength of the Philippine nationalism on both the elite and the peasant levels was a factor in shaping the U.S. policy of self-liquidating colonialism, in which the "little brown brother" was permitted to achieve independence when he grew up, a maturation process that took forty-five years. People at the top of the autonomous social pyramid increased their political, economic, and social power at the expense of other groups in the society. The great heroes of the revolution all had flaws that rendered them ill-suited to the role of supermen required by nationalist mythology. And yet the years of struggle achieved a great deal. The peoples of the Philippines did come together during those five years in a most fundamental way. Philippine nationalism came of age; the parochial ties were loosened. There were watershed years for the nation.

The 1896–1901 era was in one sense a violent discontinuity, but in another sense, it must be seen as part of the ongoing process of national unification and socioeconomic development that had begun earlier in the nineteenth century and continuing today. The reality of such changes was not diminished during the interwar years (1901–1941) by the triumph of the conservative evolutionaries over the more radical revolutionaries and peasant activists. Even the *ilustrado* elite did not remain unaltered despite its clear domination during those forty years. The oligarchy expanded rapidly by absorbing the newly rich and recently educated as the nation's need for more technocrats, bureaucrats, and functionaries escalated. Filipinization and economic growth diffused the tight control of an interlocked and interrelated class, substituting instead a host of subelites that shared a common outlook but interacted in a far less concentrated way.

THE AMERICAN INTERREGNUM

Within every segment of the population during the decades before and after the United States assumed control of the Philippines, there was a restructuring of priorities, a reformulation of authority, and a reaction to acculturation and change. English became a medium of communication, binding together the disparate linguistic, geographic, and religious constituencies in a way that Spanish never did. Mass education not only increased functional literacy from about 20 percent in 1901 to about 50 percent in 1941, but it also altered the character of the electorate, which rapidly expanded. To the U.S. colonial administrators, education was a prerequisite for democracy and a tool to limit oligarchic domination. If the electorate never repudiated the oligarchic leadership at the polls, it did force the elite to go to the people and to justify its actions. Media penetration (especially radio), road contruction, interisland shipping, and urbanization—greater Manila almost quadrupled during this period—all combined to accelerate national integration. The protracted political battle to win independence from the United States helped to articulate the Filipino identity. The decision to develop Pilipino as the national language (the Institute of National Language was established in 1936) was a manifestation of this growing awareness of a national self.

From 1907 on, the key political issue in both the United States and the Philippines concerned the timing of independence. The Nacionalistas, aware of the political value of immediate independence, advocated that policy continually. The opposition, led by Juan Sumulong, came out for a more gradual independence. Like Taft, Sumulong believed that premature independence would establish an oligarchy rather than a democracy. His voice went unheeded, however, as nationalism made independence the all-embracing goal. This fact became especially clear after Woodrow Wilson's victory in 1912, since the Democratic party had advocated rapid independence since 1900. Under the influence of William Jennings Bryan, Moorfield Storey, and Felix Frankfurter, Wilson appointed Francis B. Harrison as governor-general and instructed him to increase the tempo of decolonialization. Harrison established a Filipino majority on the governing commission and increased the number of Filipinos in the bureaucracy from 71 percent to 96 percent. In Washington, the Democrats passed the Jones Act in 1916, and it promised independence "as soon as a stable government can be established." The Clarke amendment, defining the time limit as four years, was passed in the Senate and barely defeated by the Republicans in the House. Since independence seemed imminent, especially after Wilson's articulation of worldwide self-determiniation, Harrison abdicated his supervisory functions and permitted the Filipinos to modify U.S. institutions to satisfy autonomous inclinations. For example, the principle of separation of power and checks and balances was altered by the creation of a Council of State, which "brought about the closest relationship between the Legislature and the Secretaries."

Harrison actively supported the Philippine Independence Mission, which went to the United States in 1919, but the 1920 U.S. election returns delayed independence for a quarter of a century. The new Harding administration, unhappy about what it saw as the lax quality of the Harrison era, dispatched Leonard Wood and William C. Forbes to investigate conditions in the Philippines. That mission concluded that "it would be a betrayal of the Philippine people . . . , and a discreditable neglect" of national duty to withdraw "without giving the Filipinos the best chance possible to have an orderly and permanently stable government." Recommending that the governor-general's office be strengthened, the Wood-Forbes mission postponed the seeming immediacy of independence. Harrison, bitterly against this delay, noted that no government would ever meet the ideal standards set by the mission.

President Harding's appointment of Leonard Wood as governor-general guaranteed a confrontation between Filipino leadership and the U.S. administration. As an authoritarian, Wood served as a magnet for Filipino hostility. Manual Quezon shrewdly saw great personal opportunity in this situation and used Wood to establish himself as the most important Filipino leader. Accusing his colleague Sergio Osmeña of dictatorial and autocratic tendencies, Quezon split the Nacionalista party. He then magnified the tensions with Wood and summoned the political leadership to form a united front. Osmeña, caught by Quezon's charismatic rhetoric and appeal for a transcending nationalism, found himself forced to accept second place, whereas he had previously been number one in the party. Having established his own position, Quezon then whipped the opposition parties into forming a coalition in which the Nacionalistas manipulated opposition to Wood. By the time of Wood's death in 1927, Quezon had projected himself as the embodiment of the Philippine nation.

Quezon and the Nacionalistas dominated Philippine nationalism up to World War II. Opposition critics like Sumulong were relegated to a peripheral position as the Manila-based oligarchy arrogated to itself the right to articulate national aspirations. The one major challenge to Quezon's position came during the depression period from 1930 to 1933 when a concatenation of factors—including the 1930 and 1932 Democratic victories in the United States, the rise of Japanese militarism, growing opposition from U.S. labor and farm groups to retention of the Philippines, and racial hostility toward Filipino immigrants—combined to make the U.S. Congress again receptive to Philippine independence. The Hare-Hawes-Cutting independence bill was passed by the U.S. Congress after Osmeña and Manuel Roxas had lobbied for it. It was vetoed by Hoover, passed over his veto, and then blocked in the Philippines by Quezon who was afraid that Osmeña might regain his earlier position as the architect of independence.

During the bitter "pro-anti" fight in the Philippines, the Nacionalista party again split. Quezon, the master politician, used his patronage and leverage to block the Hare-Hawes-Cutting bill and then negotiated (as he knew he could) a slightly more favorable bill from Franklin D. Roosevelt. This measure, known as the Tydings-McDuffie Act, established a commonwealth for ten years with total independence to follow. Osmeña, much to Sumulong's disgust, decided not to established himself as an opposition leader and ran as Quezon's vice-presidential candidate in 1935. Sumulong noted that "any reunion of the followers of Quezon and Osmeña—call it fusion, coalition, cooperation, or conjunction—would mean the restoration, inexcusable from all angles, of the feared and detested oligarchy. Such a reunion would undo a transcendental political reform, providentially or accidentally effected through our own dissensions over the Hare-Hawes-Cutting Law." This oligarchy was in firm control, therefore, when the Philippines were sucked into the holocaust of World War II.

5

The Religious Impulse: Global and Local Traditions

The Filipino has an abiding faith in the omnipresence of the supernatural, and for the mass of society, the religious experience is a central part of the passage through life. The *pasyon* is relived with an awesome intensity. For Christian Filipinos, the death and resurrection of Jesus is not an event that happened millenia ago but a living reality. Flagellation and even crucifixion are physical acts of remembrance each year, and the epic is at the core of folk literature and tradition, another expression of personalism.

A similar religious impulse is shared by the millions of Filipino Muslims. Folk religions, innumerable cults, and superstition—often linked directly to ancient animism—suffuse the daily routine, and the global traditions of Christianity and Islam intermingle with the local traditions of peasant belief. Most Filipinos, even the most sophisticated in Manila, live their lives with a comfortable, if eclectic, blend of the two.

Roman Catholicism and Islam have been adopted, therefore, passionately but selectively. The grafting of these foreign faiths onto earlier traditions changed both the scions and the stock. Filipino Catholics personalized God and domesticated their creed. The connection between man and God was understood in the classic terms of the peasant family. God was the wise father, the Virgin was adored as the devoted mother, and Christ was identified as the Filipinos' savior. This framework established a cosmic *compadrazgo,* and the debt of gratitude (*utang na loob*) to Christ for his sacrifice transcended any possible repayment. Christ performed a set of favors (*puhunan*) that forever demanded that every good Christian acknowledge this transcendental burden through faith, sympathy (*damay*), and charity. To the devout Filipino, Christ died to save him; there could be no limit to an individual's thanks-giving.

The lofty grandeur of God and the enormity of Christ's sacrifice, however, so humbled the individual Filipino that he felt unable to articulate or to deal with the gap between his own sense of inadequacy and the Godhead. Filipino society has searched for human and celestial intermediaries, turning to apostles, saints, martyrs, and others who served as role models for the individual, including some native leaders who were infused with grace. The piety and the devotion of the saints gave the individual a chance to find a broker for his or her prayers, and the extraordinary Filipinos, though often persecuted as heretics by the authorities, were often clear Christ models for the Filipino peasants.

Of all of these intermediaries, Peter, the rock of the church, became one of the most important, for the church, with its imposing physical structure and its ritual, supplied the center of gravity for the individual's life. The local priest became the vital authority figure. Ritual and observance lent beauty to the peasant's life; the communion supplied awe. The priest was the arbiter of all values and the interpreter of law. Combining local custom, biblical teaching, and his Spanish-Roman statutes, the local cleric historically was the teacher of truth, the font of wisdom. The priest derived tremendous authority from the distant ecclesiastical and temporal powers in Madrid and Rome.

THE SPANISH CHURCH

Spain colonized the Philippines in part as an act of devotion. The proselytizing zeal to make the archipelago a "showcase of the faith" made ecclesiastical concerns central to colonial policy. To Philip II and his successors, glory in this life and in the next was to be found through mission work. Both priests and bureaucrats were dedicated jointly to the service of God and king, and the result was an interpenetration of functions.

At the Synod of Manila in the 1580s, the several orders of friars—Augustinians, Dominicans, Franciscans, Jesuits, and others—agreed to divide the Philippines into spheres of influence and to proselytize in the vernacular rather than in Spanish. Except for the urban areas, where a patois called *chabacano* was spoken, most natives never learned much Spanish, and they gained education and religion through the friars in their own Philippine language. In sharp contradistinction to most of Latin America, therefore, only a minute percentage of the Philippine population was able to speak Spanish in 1898, the end of the Spanish era. The long period of friar control had created common religious and ethical precepts, a common faith, but not a common language or sense of single community. Since only the friars were willing to devote their lives to working in the Philippines, and since most other Spaniards hoped to leave the Philippines as soon as their term of office was up or they had made sufficient money, the friars became the translators of government decisions made in Spain or Manila. The church became figuratively and literally the great structure on the Philippine landscape. So long as the interests of Rome and Madrid were united, the problems were manageable. As the temporal interests of Spain diverged from the temporal and ecclesiastical interests of Rome, however, the stresses and strains rapidly increased.

The interrelationship between church and crown was very complex. Based on a series of papal bulls, the Spanish monarchs were given extraordinary rights such as *real patronato* (the right to approve or disapprove of religious personnel) in recognition of Spanish missionary zeal on behalf of Rome. In return, the Spanish crown provided free transportation for priests, paid each priest's annual salary, and guaranteed to support the church. The crown also had the right to intervene in matters of ecclesiastical jurisdiction through another concession, the *recurso de fuerza.*

The friars, also known as *regulares* from the Latin word for vows, received from Pope Adrian VI the right to administer the sacraments and to hold parishes free from any supervision by the diocesan hierarchy. In theory, the friars were supposed to move on to new missionary stations after converting the natives. In fact, because the Philippines was the furthest major colonial outpost of Spanish Catholicism, they stayed. The Council of Trent had attempted to curb worldwide the independence of the friars by ruling that any local bishop had the right of episcopal visitation in any parish. The friars held all power, however, since only the friars could recruit clergy willing to live their lives in the Philippines. After 200 years of struggling, only 142 parishes out of the 569 in the Philippines were staffed by secular clerics who reported to the diocesan bishops. Whenever the archbishop of Manila attempted to impose his will on the friars, they formed a cartel and threatened resignation en masse. They always won.

During the second half of the eighteenth century, however, the Bourbon monarchy in Spain, with its anticlerical colonial administration, attempted to weaken the power of the friars. These reformers saw the friars as the implacable enemies of the Enlightenment. In one famous memorial to the king, it was argued that the friars "should not meddle in worldly affairs" and that they "ought to sell their estates even though they are just owners, since such business is inconsistent with their ministry." The Bourbons thought that educating and ordaining native clerics was the obvious solution through which a manpower pool of trained priests could replace the friars in their several parishes. In 1767, the Jesuits were expelled from the entire Spanish Empire, and under a comparable threat, the Dominicans in Manila reluctantly accepted visitation by the king's confidant, the archbishop of Manila.

The Spanish joke of the time was that there were no longer any men to row the ferryboats across the Pasig River in Manila because the archbishop had ordained them all. Unfortunately, the rapid effort to educate and ordain mestizos and *indios* proved to be too hasty, and the conservative elements in the Philippines rejoiced when some of the new diocesan priests proved inadequate to the responsibilities given them. Increasingly, racism became an important force, especially after the loss of the other Spanish colonies in the New World in the early nineteenth century. Nineteenth-century Spanish literature is filled with condescension to *indio* priests and fear that such people would spearhead an independence movement away from Spain. Francisco Cañamaque noted that the native priest was "a caricature of the priest, a caricature of the Spaniard, a caricature of the *mestizo,* a caricature of everybody. He is a patchwork of many things, and is nothing. I put it badly; he is something after all; more than something . . . he is an enemy of Spain."

This combination of racism and anxiety eventually became a self-fulfilling prophecy. The uprising of Apolinario de la Cruz in 1841 began because Cruz, a devout and charismatic Catholic, was denied entrance into a monastic order. Rejected, Cruz undertook a pilgrimage (*lakaran*) and gained leadership over a native religious brotherhood, the Cofradia de San Jose, which spread rapidly in the provinces around Manila. Cruz's piety and authority were misunderstood and threatening to the Spanish, and eventually Cruz and his followers found themselves under attack. When the government used force to suppress the movement, Cruz initially was able to defeat Spanish troops and killed the governor of Tayabas on the eastern coast of Luzon (now known as Quezon Province). The Spanish subsequently defeated the Cofradia, killed Cruz, and hung his body in pieces throughout the Cofradia region. In response, the church permitted seven key parishes in Cavite to be transferred back from native, diocesan to friar control in 1849. In 1859, the Jesuits were permitted to return to their eighteenth-century mission stations, and the displaced Recollects, another friar order, were given the remaining diocesan parishes in Cavite. By 1871, just prior to the outbreak of the Cavite uprising, only 181 of the 792 parishes were staffed by mestizos or *indios.* The global faith could not tolerate the plurality implicit in the local traditions.

The French consul in the Philippines, Fabre, had noted, "This whole affair in which the Spanish government, in effect, told the Creoles 'you are our enemies,' has added hatred to the jealousy that already existed between Spaniards and Creoles." Fabre, commenting on the unbelievable lack of prudence shown by the Spanish, noted that the Iberian Spanish, "encouraged this hatred and jealousy by arrogantly assuming an attitude of supreme contempt toward the colonial born."

Religion was thus the battleground on which the Creoles, mestizos, *indios,* and newly emergent Filipino *ilustrados* defined their differences from the Iberian Spanish, developed their sense of national self-awareness, and developed their sense of class difference between those who were Westernized and those in the local tradition. Friarocracy became the most hated symbol of colonial rule.

During this period, Spain itself vacillated between periods of strong Catholic revival and eras of staunch anti-Catholic, Masonic government. Far from being a universal church, Roman Catholicism was stamped with a "made in Spain" label. One pro-Catholic governor-general declared that he would govern with a cross in one hand and a sword in the other. It was not surprising, therefore, that the pretext of the Cavite arsenal mutiny on January 20, 1872, led to the arrest, trial, and execution of the leading advocates of Filipino clerical equality, including Father Jose Burgos, Father Jacinto Jamora, and Father Mariano Gomez.

Although the Roman Catholic church was not a monolithic structure, its nineteenth-century image was Caucasian, racist, enormously wealthy, and very conservative. The church (and its several orders) had underwritten the galleon trade during the 250 years it had survived, the church had acquired or had been given vast tracts of land, especially in the region immediately around Manila, and it had become—and still remains—one of the great banking institutions of the Philippines. Through *obras pias* (charitable foundation), the church loaned money with land as the collateral. Over the centuries, these foundations emerged into banks, which were still under the ownership of religious institutions. The very dominance of this institutional structure, the interlocking way it stretched across the society, and the passionately felt religious impulse that sustained the Filipinos and brought them to their church created an institutional outer shell out of the religious impulse that undergirds the structure. Philippine nationalism, the Philippine identity, the Filipinos' value system, and the economic and social fabric of the society are all linked directly to the Roman Catholic experience.

IGLESIA FILIPINA INDEPENDIENTE

One of the most interesting offshoots of the Roman church—and one between the global and the local institutionally—is the Iglesia Filipina Independiente founded by Gregorio Aglipay. The anticlerical movement that so altered Jose Rizal and his associates—leading them ultimately to a modern, secular nationalism—also created a movement to Filipinize the Roman Catholic church. The earlier eighteenth-century effort to train native clerics had sparked the issues of nationalism and racism, but the struggle to gain control of the parishes did not end with the execution of the three Filipino priests in 1872. Aglipay was a young Filipino priest who was appointed chaplain-general of the revolutionary forces by Aguinaldo and excommunicated by the Spanish hierarchy. Although he initially did not want to break with Rome, the intransigence of the Vatican and the seeming alliance between Madrid and Rome drove Aglipay and many others toward a Philippine national church. Like the schism involving the Church of England, Aglipay broke from Rome to guarantee that Filipinos would have national control of their own religious institutions. By 1902, Aglipay had become archbishop of the Philippine Independent Church. Shaped by the important lay leader Isabelo de los Reyes, Aglipayanism filled the religious vacuum created by the Spanish defeat and the overwhelming Filipino desire to expel the friars. Most of the Filipino priests took over the parishes formerly held by the friars and joined the new movement.

Within a few years, the Aglipayan movement claimed 1.5 million adherents, or about 25 percent of the Christian population. Under different circumstances, the movement might well have developed like the Church of England, but it suffered two sharp setbacks during William Howard Taft's years as governor-general. Taft prohibited "the forcible dispossession of a priest of the Roman Catholic Church," and in 1906, the conservative, U.S. mestizo Philippine Supreme Court ruled in the Barlin-Ramirez case that all the Roman Catholic properties taken by the Aglipayan church had to be returned to the Vatican. The Aglipayan loss of control over the physical fabric of the church gave an opportunity to the Vatican that was not lost.

Taft had noted that "the adherents of Aglipay came largely from the poorer classes throughout the islands," although current scholarship suggests regionalism and ethnicity were more important than class. Some of these peasants followed the Aglipayan priests into makeshift chapels, but many continued to worship where they always had prayed, at the imposing, baroque structures that dominated the town plazas. By 1918, therefore, Aglipayanism had fallen to about 13 percent of the population. The movement survives today, increasingly assisted by the Episcopal church of the United States, but the Iglesia Filipina Independiente has never quite succeeded in becoming the vehicle for the unique religious expression of the Filipinos.

THE ROMAN CHURCH DURING THE AMERICAN INTERREGNUM

The opportunity to embody Filipino religious aspirations was in part denied to the Aglipayan movement because control of the Roman Catholic church passed rapidly from Spanish to American hands and then to Filipino ones. The Roman Catholic church made major adjustments, bending to survive under American advice and Filipino pressure. In the twentieth-century, the Vatican Americanized and Filipinized the church hierarchy and accepted the reality of the separation of church and state in the archipelago. It agreed to limit the activities of the priests to ecclesiastical and charitable work, and most significant, it accepted William Howard Taft's offer to buy the former friar estates. Taft, who wanted to "buy these large haciendas of the friars and sell them out in small holdings to the present tenants," liberated the church from the severe liability of being a hated landlord.

During the Spanish era, the interconnection of tenancy and absentee ownership, the sharecropping system known as *kasamahan,* created widespread peasant penury. Some of the wealth used by the *ilustrados* to gain their education was made because they and their fathers were the intermediaries, the estate managers who operated the system on behalf of the friars. During the Malolos era, there had been a clear effort on the part of this *ilustrado* elite to increase its power and to impose its values in the vacuum created by the revolution, especially since the Katipunan had such strong elements of religious revivalism and peasant faith. Taft's land policy, based on the somewhat naive dream of an American homesteading frontier, offered the *ilustrados* great opportunities for wealth and for socioeconomic hegemony in the new structure. Instead of the land reform scheme Taft wanted, most of the friar lands eventually were bought by large landlords, leaving the peasants still trapped as sharecroppers on someone else's land.

Although the Roman Catholic church continued to own vast properties, especially after the conservative Filipino courts—on which both American and Filipino jurists sat—upheld the right of the church's ownership, it was freed of the liability of being the major landlord of the society. During the twentieth century, virtually all traces of the Spanish church disappeared. American priests, primarily Irish-American, went out to the archipelago, and the Philippine Catholic church came under the supervision of the great East Coast archdioceses of the United States. Open educational opportunity encouraged devout and talented Filipinos to enter the clergy. The trend toward Filipinization that took place throughout the American era meant that, by 1941, the Roman Catholic church had been partially Filipinized and given an autonomous place in the ethnically diverse and evolving Roman Catholic world that has developed in the post-World War II era.

THE LOCAL TRADITION

The solidity of the church and the dominance of its institutions in the life and culture of the people do not mean that folk Catholicism

The Church of St. Agustin, Intramuros, Manila. (Courtesy of the Philippine Ministry of Tourism)

and traditional eclecticism have vanished. One of the measures of a global religious tradition is its capacity to acculturate, and Catholicism absorbed much from and tolerated even more in the traditional codes and mores of the people. Over the centuries, Catholicism permitted both the initially alien faith and the domestic environment to fuse so that many traditions and customs have a global exterior and a local interior.

The Catholic "miracle" is very close to the "magic" of the *baylan* (the spirit medium), and to most peasants, the "miracle" was just a new name for a familiar phenomenon. The way the ancient blood compact was reinterpreted as the *compadre/comadre,* God-parenthood associated with baptism has already been described. Artistic and iconographic images often verge on idol worship, and the concept of the meaning of life and the belief in a life after death are at times at variance with canonic law as it is interpreted in the Vatican.

Outside the canonic and institutional structures, local tradition survives in a range of millennial movements that have sprung up out of the needs of the society. Many of these movements have been economic in nature but have cloaked their rebellion and resistance in the apocalyptic dream. Since the priest was the authority figure and since redemption also offered the dream of independence through the *pasyon,* the spiritual and material worlds fused. Millennial movements have existed virtually everywhere in the archipelago. Some of the movements are well known, as, for example, the one led by Papa Isio, but others have existed without leaving any trace other than a folk tradition or a vague reference or memory.

One of the better known and more interesting of these movements was the Guardia de Honor. This movement became important during the late nineteenth and early twentieth centuries and is illustrative of the way in which religion, social discontent, and political action can merge. It was founded originally by the Dominicans in the region around Pangasinan in central Luzon. Initially a cofraternity devoted to the Virgin Mary, the friars used it as a paramilitary force to counterbalance the Filipino revolutionaries. The Guardia de Honor evolved into a messianic sect shrouded in mystery, and it was equally misjudged by the *ilustrados,* the Spanish, and the Americans. A barrio known as Cabaruan attracted thousands of peasants, and the leader, known simply at Baltazar, ruled the town as a theocracy. He claimed to be God Almighty, and his aides were worshiped as Jesus Christ, the Holy Ghost, the Twelve Apostles, and the Virgin Mary. The peasants who came to await salvation brought with them their rice and dedicated it to the communal granaries. Landlords and apostates were sinners, but the economic component of the movement was subordinated to its religious dimension.

At its peak, the town of Cabaruan had 25,000 Filipinos living in it, but in 1901, the Americans shattered the movement, arresting the leadership on the charge of provincial banditry and murder and dispersing the community. The movement seemingly subsided from view, but thirty years later, it reappeared in a modified form known as the Colorum. The town of Tayug in central Luzon, where the Colorum rebellion occurred, was twenty miles from Cabaruan. As Reynaldo Ileto has noted, "The continuity in form between the Cofradia of 1841, the Katipunan revolt of 1896, the Santa Iglesia, and other movements we have examined can be traced to the persistence of the *pasyon* in shaping the perceptions of particularly the poor and uneducated segments of the populace."

This example and many others that could be offered suggest that there is a substructure, not visible to outsiders or even to "informed" Filipinos, lying beneath the surface of the peasant experience. Millennial movements emerge during times of economic hardship, and they tend to gain ground in times of social change and societal disruption, when traditional values and verities seem threatened by new ideas, institutions, or people. The pattern of response has varied in different parts of the country, however. Alfred McCoy has argued correctly that in the Tagalog regions, the *pasyon* created a local tradition with a clear vision of utopia. "It was the Kingdom of Christ come to central Luzon," McCoy argues, but "in contrast, peasant religion in the western Visayas remained based on a fundamentally ancient, pre-Hispanic conceptual system."

During the twentieth century, many of the millennial movements have combined Christian symbolism and nationalism. Urbanization, mass media, universal education, new transportation networks, television, relatives living in urban areas, and many other elements have combined to disrupt the peasant's world and to leave him anxious and uncertain, even when economic conditions are good. If conditions are bad, as they often have been, either because of natural disasters or the grinding alienation of land through tenancy and sharecropping, malaise increases rapidly.

At times, the millennial movements have taken on a seemingly antireligious character. Masonry was perhaps the most significant expression of an antireligious, utopian dream, although current scholarship suggests that within the masonic institutional structure, there was a movement based on the Filipino's belief in the *pasyon*. In the secular movements of the more recent past, including a right-wing Sakdalista peasant rebellion in the 1930s, the left-wing Hukbalahap movement of the 1940s, and the New People's Army of the 1980s, there have been echoes of the local religious tradition. Gregorio (Gringo) Honasan, a swashbuckling colonel who led a series of coups d'état against President Aquino, has become a charismatic cult figure, someone clearly in the millennial tradition. His hold on his fellow officers and especially on the enlisted men comes out of this environment.

Rizal has become a figure, like the saints of old, who can serve as an intermediary for the peasantry. By his status as the father of his country, the man most responsible for *kalayaan* (independence), he has also become a figure of magic property. The memories of Rizal and of Christ have been fused. In 1967, a group of Rizalistas, Lapiang Malaya—led by an eighty-six-year-old Bikolano, Valentin de los Santos, who was a spirit medium (*baylan*)—attempted to destroy the modern, secular Philippine government by attacking the city of Manila. They believed they were immune to death as they marched down Taft Avenue in Manila because of their amulets (*anting anting*) and the intensity of their faith. They provoked the military and police into violent reaction. Thirty-three died. Their symbolic attack on urbanization, Westernization, and modernization demonstrates the pressure under which they lived. Today, the newspapers periodically report on sects such as the Salvatoris who have claimed that their amulets can repel bullets. A UPI dispatch of 1980 noted that there were many hundreds of these Salvatoris on Negros, the large sugar island, and that probably a hundred people in all had been killed. Newspaper stories of this sort tend to portray these movements as a kind of low-grade static in the process of development. To dismiss the religious fervor of the Salvatoris as a violent and irrelevant, if quaint, peasant tradition is to misread the language by which the peasants have attempted to express their dream for a better life.

Ferdinand Marcos publicized his *anting anting*, a sliver of wood that Gregorio Aglipay inserted into Marcos's back just before the Bataan campaign in 1942. He claimed it gave him supernatural powers; if nothing else, it confirmed him as someone graced in the peasants' spiritual tradition.

The martyrdom of Benigno Aquino has also become fused with this folk tradition, elevating Aquino into the pantheon of national heroes and, Filipinos believe, to heaven, where he has joined Rizal in Christ's court. His widow was immediately identified with the grieving Mary Magdalene. Corazon Aquino's transcendent grace and exceptional piety (she is a devout woman and committed Marist) have given her political power a religious underpinning. Far more potent than any *anting anting*, her serene and accepting faith in the face of evil, as represented by the Marcoses, lifted her above normal politics in the eyes of most Filipinos. As already noted, the Tagalog word for political independence, *kalayaan*, also means religious redemption. For most Filipinos, Corazon Aquino has embodied both nuances of this word, and her sustaining popularity has only slowly been diminished by the failures and disappointments of her government. To many Filipinos she is both the government and somehow above it; she is the living example of what the Filipinos see as the best in themselves. And yet her limitations; her acceptance of family, class, and social stratification; and her passivity in the face of open threats to her values and her person clearly remind Filipinos of what has kept them from achieving the economic and political progress they see in the Asia around them.

ISLAM

Islam, as one of the global religions of the world, would normally be categorized as being within the great religious tradition. And yet, Islam in the Philippines has not generated the same cultural and institutional sophistication found elsewhere in the Muslim world. That lack of development can be partially explained by the minority position that Islam has held for virtually its entire lifespan in the archipelago. It can also be partially explained by the isolation in which Philippine Muslims have lived. Islam is the faith of a relatively poor, traditionally fragmented, and persecuted minority, itself divided ethnolinguistically. Philippine Muslims are fiercely proud and very devout, but they also are highly eclectic and, as in the case of Philippine Christians, are believers who have merged classic orthodoxy with local beliefs and traditional customs.

The global struggle between Christianity and Islam erupted shortly after the Prophet's death. That battle, which began as an expanding Catholicism collided with an expanding Islam, was fought all across the frontiers of Europe and North Africa. The Crusades, the struggle in Spain, the struggle over Turkey and the eastern Mediterranean all shaped both the Christian and the Islamic experiences. Islam spread not only toward Europe but across Asia as well, and the sultanates established in Sulu and on Mindanao represent the farthest expansion of an Islamic network that was partly religious, partly economic, and partly political. Islam was introduced into the archipelago a century before Christianity. The expansion of Christianity, especially as proselytized by Philip II of Spain, was equally motivated by a religious faith, and the Philippines became the furthest outpost of militant Christianity. For 400 years, the struggle between Christianity and Islam has been waged in the southern Philippines, and for 400 years that battle has been basically a standoff—neither faith has had the political or the military muscle to overwhelm the other.

The Spaniards laid claim to Mindanao and Sulu, even though they lacked sufficient military force to impose their will. The Muslim community waged a jihad, or religious war, fighting a running guerrilla struggle that was usually very similar to the contemporary nationalist

A Muslim mosque. (Courtesy of the Philippine Ministry of Tourism)

wars of liberation. Muslims took an oath (*parang sabil*) on the Koran that they would pursue the holy war by killing Spanish Christians. This extended struggle touched the raw nerves of both Catholics and Muslims and carried forward an implacable hostility from the Middle Ages until today.

During the late nineteenth century, other European powers coveted bases in Muslim areas for trading and military beachheads, so the Spanish felt the strategic need to assert their sovereignty and to erode the traditional autonomous influence of the local sultans. The development of Spanish technology, the motorization and mechanization of the armed forces, and the development of the telegraph and, ultimately, the telephone all penetrated the Muslim zone. As early as 1847, the Spanish permitted a Basque soldier of fortune, Oyanguren, to mount a private expedition against the Muslims in the Gulf of Davao. This last of the conquistadores brought the city of Davao under Spanish control, and the return of the Jesuits to their missionary stations on Mindanao in 1859 further increased the pressure on the Muslims. The Muslims of Mindanao were driven into the interior, and the seafaring sultans, especially those of Sulu, were labeled pirates.

The United States "pacified" and "integrated" the Muslim areas under the centralized control of Manila. The Americans triumphed in what they called "the Moro region" because of superior technology, an efficient army and navy, and new economic incentives. In August 1899,

U.S. General John Bates negotiated an agreement with the sultan of Sulu, promising stipends, religious liberty, and protection in return for allegiance and an end to the slave trade and "piracy." This "Bates treaty" with the Sulu sultan seemed too lenient to puritans like Leonard Wood, who became commander of the Moro area, and the Americans later repudiated the treaty unilaterally. Wood saw the Moro leadership as "corrupt, licentious, and cruel . . . nothing more or less than an important collection of pirates and highwaymen." This increasingly hard line exploded into a series of battles, including a struggle in 1906 during which 600 Muslims died. The imposition of U.S. hegemony, never challenged the legitimacy of the sultan as the "titular spiritual head of the Mohammedan Church in the Sulu archipelago."

The U.S. colonial administrators saw the massive and virtually unpopulated island of Mindanao as the Philippine frontier. Drawing on the geopolitical experience of the United States, they saw resettlement from the more densely populated northern islands as the pivotal means by which the Philippines could increase production, ease land pressure, eliminate tenancy, and reform the society. Offering the carrot of religious protection and respect for Muslim traditions and wielding the stick of U.S. military might, they subjugated the five major Muslim groups—the Maguindanaos, the Maranaos, the Yakans, the Samals, and the Sulus. Through legislation, based on U.S. models, they created a homesteading and land policy that was designed to encourage especially the landless peasants of the north to migrate to Mindanao. Since apparently there was an excess of land and since many of the Muslims were hill people practicing slash-and-burn agriculture, this land policy went forward for decades without being aggressively challenged by the Muslims. The establishment of the great Del Monte pineapple plantations in northern Mindanao and the economic investment sparked by prewar Japan in Davao accelerated the changes that occurred on Mindanao. This vast island was integrated into the economic system of the archipelago and was brought forward fairly rapidly.

Culturally and religiously, however, the policy was explosive, because it underestimated the continuing level of hostility between Muslim and Christian and because it failed to realize how the demography of Mindanao was shifting away from Muslim dominance. The policy of resettlement was accelerated after World War II when Ramon Magsaysay, in his effort to blunt the Huk rebellion on Luzon, encouraged tens of thousands of Philippine peasants to migrate from their Christian lowland homes to new farms and homesteads on Mindanao. There are now more Christians than Muslims on Mindanao, and the economic and social control of the island is in the hands of the Christians. The Muslims, an embattled minority, feel that they have lost control of their homeland

and, like the American Indians and many other ethnic groups, feel that they have been savagely treated by both the colonial imperialists and the postindependence national governments.

The Muslim revival generated by Arab nationalism, by the creation of the independent nations of Pakistan and Indonesia, by oil (much of it held by Muslim nations), and by the dynamics of nationalism in the Philippines itself have become important in contemporary Philippine life. With the support of Libya and a number of other radical Muslim states, and with Muslim Malaysia and Saudi Arabia, Muslim nationalists inside the Philippines organized a guerrilla war based partially on Vietnamese models and partially on ancient Catholic-Muslim hostility. This rebellion, or war of national liberation, depending on one's perspective, has gone through violent and passive phases, as will be described in subsequent chapters. Explosive or quiescent, it has been one of the most intractable problems facing the archipelago, a struggle that tears at the fabric of the nation.

RELIGION TODAY

When the Spanish colonized the Philippines, they were ideologically incapable of separating their religious from their temporal motives. The congruence of interest between Spain and Rome was complete. Even though the church and its interests grew apart from the interests of Spain as the centuries wore on, religion stamped every institution and aspect of Philippine society, as it continued to do during the American era even though the religious tradition articulated then was primarily the secular one of American nationalism. The United States took the Philippines in "a fit of absence of mind" during an imperialist binge. It kept the Philippines because it felt it had to justify its initial decision through altruism. The American dream of establishing a new Jerusalem prompted Americans to proselytize the world. Manifest Destiny prompted President McKinley to talk of uplifting, civilizing, and Christianizing the Philippines. The American dream, drawn by Norman Rockwell and restated by the slogans of each president, is a secularized form of religious conviction. The U.S. effort to rework the Philippine society into an American image conjures up hubris as well as the loftiest idealism. Although the profit motive was far from absent, the United States, like Spain, proclaimed economic gain in the Philippines as a subservient objective. The Americans wanted to make the Philippines a "showcase for democracy." The idealistic fervor demonstrated at the turn of the twentieth century by the so-called Thomasites—young Americans who went out by the hundreds to teach English, science, and secular education to the Filipinos—and redemonstrated by the thousands more Peace Corps

Imelda Marcos's private chapel. (Courtesy of the Museo ng Malacañang Foundation)

volunteers who have been going since 1961, marks those young men and women as missionaries in the same tradition as the Franciscans and Jesuits. The message was different, but the goal of converting the Filipinos to their way was constant. Philippine wags speak of the archipelago as having been 300 years in the convent and 50 years in Hollywood.

Religion, both from the global traditions and the local, has suffused Philippine life and culture. Roman Catholicism has asserted its historical dominance in numbers of parishioners. Today, approximately 85 percent of the population is Catholic, 5 percent is Aglipayan, 5 percent is Muslim, and the rest is scattered among the Protestant sects, a number of which have grown rapidly in the past decades. Iglesia ni Kristo is by far the largest and fastest-growing sect. The Roman Catholic church continues to reach into every nook of the country, and the clergy, now almost exclusively Filipino, is one of the most potent forces for change.

It is a historical irony that after national independence became the diocesan hierarchy the conservative voice of tradition, whereas a new breed of friars, Jesuits in the lead, embraced a radical, more militant commitment to social action. Many native Filipino bishops voted at Vatican councils as if they were members of the nineteenth-century

Spanish clergy. Especially on issues of abortion, birth control, and liturgy, they have resisted change. The Jesuits and other members of religious orders openly supported land reform and unionization, worked for squatters' rights, and became advocates for social change.

Rufino Cardinal Santos, the first Filipino cardinal, was elevated in 1960. A staunchly conservative prelate, he joined fellow bishops from Chile and Nicaragua in accepting the world as it was, with all its socioeconomic dichotomies. He knew more about interest rates in Germany than hunger in Bohol. Jaime Cardinal Sin, appointed archbishop in 1974 and elevated to cardinal in 1976, has had to deal with the explosive social changes created by Ferdinand Marcos's declaration of martial law and with the expanded mission of the church voted at the Second Vatican Council in 1965. A Chinese mestizo, his evolution as a political and social activist has been a paradigm for the church's transformation.

During the years of repression under martial law, Sin and thousands of priests, nuns, and seminarians were morally outraged by the Marcos regime's abuse of the rights of Filipinos both famous and insignificant. These human rights violations politicized the church. Cardinal Sin wrote in the early 1980s that "when people lose faith in their leaders, fear the military, and do not trust the courts, the only person left for them to go to with their grievances is the parish priest, . . . and he cannot just file away their complaints like everyone else and pretend they do not exist. He has to act to do something or he too will lose all hope."

In the years prior to the assassination of Benigno Aquino, the church was sharply divided over the appropriate response to the army's "salvaging," or abusing, of the villagers. Throughout the countryside Basic Christian Communities became popular, as local priests and lay leaders attempted to reorganize society along more equitable means. Liberation theology, as developed and practiced in Mexico and Central America, gave moral and religious justification for sociopolitical action.

As early as the 1960s, Father Luis Jalandoni, the son of a wealthy Negros family, became a Communist because he could not accept the socioeconomic inequalities he saw around him. Captured by Marcos soon after martial law was declared, he became a symbol of a militant wing of clerics who increasingly rejected the hierarchy as indistinguishable from the rest of the oligarchy. The Christians for National Liberation, founded by Father Edward De la Torre, was a small, militant group of priests and nuns who openly preached revolution. Cardinal Sin and, to a lesser degree, Cardinal Vidal, attempted to adjudicate this growing schism within the church, seeking to avoid the polarization between those who subscribed to liberation theology and those who rejected it. In the middle were clerics like Bishop Francisco Claver and Bishop Julio

Jaime Cardinal Sin. (Courtesy of Jaime Zobel de Ayala)

Xavier Labayen, a Carmelite, who argued at the bishops conferences and in the Association of Major Religious Superiors for a more open antigovernment position.

In March 1981, Pope John Paul II visited the Philippines, the second time a pontiff had made a pastoral pilgrimage to this Catholic outpost in Asia. The visit was both religiously and politically charged. President and Imelda Marcos attempted to make the visit a public relations bonanza for themselves. Everywhere the pope went, Imelda Marcos flew ahead in her own jet so that she was constantly at the foot of the stairs as the pope deplaned. The reception in Malacañan Palace was so lavish as to be acutely embarrassing to the pope and to Cardinal Sin. At the great open-air mass celebrated in Manila, President Marcos sat on a special platform just below the pontiff, with Imelda Marcos on another platform directly below her husband's. The Marcos family insisted that it be the first to receive communion.

John Paul II, a veteran of the struggle in Poland, upheld conservative church dogma, telling 5,000 clergy in Manila that "you are not social or political leaders or officials of a temporal power." But if the pontiff refused to authorize greater political activity of the church, he did speak out often and pointedly about the greed, degradation, and social injustice of the Marcos government. Global politics and instant communications affect the church as much as they do other institutions. Events in Poland, where the church was the center of opposition prior to 1989, and in Latin America, where local priests organized social action through liberation theology, have influenced—and, in turn, have been influenced by—the church's activism in the Philippines.

Benigno Aquino's murder (see Chapter 7) radicalized Cardinal Sin and, with him, nearly the entire Roman Catholic church of the Philippines. It became clear to the tens of thousands of priests, nuns, seminarians, and lay leaders that Marcos had lost all moral force and that the political struggle could be seen in terms of good and evil sides. Cardinal Sin's position evolved from one of "critical collaboration" at the outset of martial law to unequivocal hostility. In the waning years of the Marcos era, the church became the center of anti-Marcos activity. Radio Veritas, run by a U.S. Jesuit, Father James Reuter, broadcast news that the Marcos-controlled press censored everywhere else. Week after week pastoral letters were read from every pulpit in the country, especially during the months from the announcement of the snap election by Marcos in late 1985 until Marcos fled the country in February 1986. Marcos did not feel strong enough to confront the church directly.

Cardinal Sin became one of the key actors in the drama. It was he who imposed a compromise on Corazon Aquino and Salvador Laurel by which the opposition agreed to field a single slate against Marcos.

Prayers overwhelming bullets. (Courtesy of Tom Gralish and *The Philadelphia Inquirer*)

The cardinal insisted that Aquino be the presidential candidate and that Laurel accept a vice-presidential slot. Sin and others in the hierarchy actively supported political action by priests and nuns who organized at the local level to prevent a fraudulent election. Bishop Fortich of Negros, co-chairman of the National Movement for Free Elections (NAMFREL), moved out on election day, the cross held high, to rally the people against the evil of electoral fraud. In the days that followed the election, Radio Veritas broadcast the "quick count," revealing the fraud. Finally, in the confused last days of the regime when Defense Secretary Juan Ponce Enrile and General Fidel Ramos broke from Marcos, started an insurrection, and appealed to the cardinal for help, he actively intervened by going on Radio Veritas and calling on a multitude of people to go into the potential battle zone and physically block the

Marcos forces, then approaching the military camps from which the two insurgents had raised the rebellion. That throng stopped the attack, and the pictures of nuns and seminarians praying before tanks were transmitted around the world. Active nonviolence (*lakas-awa*) proved that people power can work and that moral force can triumph over military might.

One needs to go back to a pre-Renaissance world to find examples of a reigning cardinal openly intervening in a temporal succession dispute. Cardinal Sin's role in the struggle between Aquino and Marcos shaped, if not changed, the outcome: Aquino became president because the cardinal used the power of the church. In effect, Cardinal Sin and his associates expanded the meaning of liberation theology to include clerical intervention on behalf of democratic and peaceful change around the world. Having intervened so extensively, Cardinal Sin found it impossible to avoid being again sucked into the vortex of later power struggles. During the December 1989 coup attempt against President Aquino, Cardinal Sin tried to rally public support for her with only modest success. Unlike four years earlier, the people were passive, unresponsive to clerical exhortation.

After Marcos fled, Pope John Paul II issued a strongly worded warning to the bishops of the Philippines urging them to avoid political involvement and to confine their work to the "disinterested service of the common good." The activist posture of the Philippine church offered a new model for prelates in Korea, Nicaragua, and even Poland. Whatever the impact these events in the Philippines may have elsewhere in the world, the power of the church has been reconfirmed.

6

Collaboration and Restoration

THE TRAUMA OF WORLD WAR II

At the beginning of December 1941, the Philippines was a relatively prosperous colony controlled by an entrenched, sophisticated elite. These commonwealth leaders, comfortable in New York and San Francisco, empowered and self-assured in Manila, believed that evolutionary nationalism would lead to stability for the country and prosperity for them. They shared economic dominance with a small group of white-suited Americans and Europeans who enjoyed Packard automobiles, polo clubs, and multitudes of servants. Although there were tensions below the surface—including the lack of an industrial policy capable of producing prosperity in a postindependent era, a land ownership pattern that gave overwhelming control of wealth to a tiny fraction of the society, and an uncertain sense of cultural identity—this was an era of complacency. Only the threat of war between the United States and Japan challenged contentment.

Early in the morning of December 8, 1941, Douglas MacArthur was awakened in his penthouse suite at the Manila Hotel with a phone call informing him that the United States had been attacked at Pearl Harbor. Despite the decoding snafu that led to the Pearl Harbor bombing prior to the formal declaration of war, the Japanese plan was highly legalistic, seeking to avoid any violation of international law. The air attack on the U.S. forces in the Philippines was delayed intentionally. MacArthur had hours of warning. He ordered the bomber force at Clark Air Base into the air, but the planes returned to Clark rather than striking at Taiwan because they were not deemed powerful enough to penetrate Japanese air defenses. Thus it happened that the planes were lined up in neat rows without protective earthwork embankments and the pilots were in the mess eating lunch when the Japanese planes attacked the

B-17s, destroying the United States' small strategic bomber force. That swift defeat was a harbinger of the ultimate debacle at Bataan and Corregidor.

Filipinos from Aparri on the northern tip of Luzon to Sulu in the far south fought, suffered, and died, not only during those first months of war, but also during the dark era of occupation that followed. By the end of December 1941, Douglas MacArthur evacuated Manila, declaring it an open city and shifting his operation to the heavily fortified tunnels on the isle of Corregidor, there to await the arrival of a U.S. relief fleet that was already rusting on the bottom of Pearl Harbor. Just prior to the surrender of Fil-American forces, MacArthur, Quezon, and Sergio Osmeña were evacuated—MacArthur to plan reconquest from Australia, Quezon and Osmeña to establish a government-in-exile in the United States.

On January 2, 1942, the Japanese army occupied Manila. In short order, it persuaded most of the prewar Manila politicians to collaborate. With the notable exceptions of Chief Justice Jose Abad Santos, the opposition leader Juan Sumulong, and a few others, the elite acceded to the Japanese demand that Jorge Vargas, Quezon's former executive secretary, establish a Philippine executive commission. Although few of these prewar politicians were pro-Japanese, most were pragmatists used to serving colonial masters. They saw this summons to continuing service as an obligation that would mitigate the suffering of the masses in whose name they justified their roles in society.

Those masses, however, saw the Japanese as brutal conquerors rather than liberating fellow Asians. The guerrilla movement, which sprung up almost immediately across the entire country, was one of the largest of any in an occupied country during World War II. The guerrillas had the open sympathy and support of virtually the entire population, and the Japanese proved incapable of stifling them despite savage repression.

Filipinos resisted because they felt they had come of age as a nation. They had been attacked, their values had been threatened, and their impending independence was jeopardized. It was their war. The few genuinely pro-Japanese Filipinos (the Ganaps), were regarded as loathsome traitors. Despite the Japanese claims that they were there to emancipate the Filipinos, drive out the wicked white rulers, and establish a true bond with the Filipinos, their brutal beating and abduction of ordinary people, their seizing of property and lifestock, and their cruelty toward Filipinos and Americans alike during the Bataan death march doomed their chances.

Not all guerrillas were motivated by lofty ideals. Individuals joined guerrilla movements for complex reasons, including severe economic dislocation, starvation, and misery, as well as greed, excitement, and political opportunity. Old grudges and wanton violence could be hidden under a patriotic mantle, and prewar factionalism played a key role in determining who became a guerrilla and who a collaborator. Nevertheless, the will to fight the Japanese was genuine; sacrifice sprang from a sense of standing on that front line of democracy. The promise of redemption, issued incessantly by Douglas MacArthur, was fulfilled as he waded ashore at Leyte Island, telling Filipinos that "the guidance of divine God points the way." He urged them to strike "for future generations of your sons and daughters" and "in the name of your sacred dead." MacArthur melodramatically exhorted the Filipinos to "follow in His Name to the Holy Grail of righteous victory." They did with heroism.

The price of victory was brutally high. In 1945 many were homeless and most were starving. Medical and sanitation facilities were destroyed, transportation paralyzed, industrial output at a standstill. Manila bore the brunt of this destruction. Because the modern sector of the economy was almost exclusively within this urban environment, precious resources of facilities and skilled personnel were lost. Although by 1946 the population increased about 3 million from 1937, the combined index of physical production stood at 38.7 percent of the 1937 level. Port facilities were twisted steel and concrete, the newspaper presses smashed. The universities, banks, hospitals, libraries, factories, government offices, and hotels were in shambles. Soon after the Japanese surrender, MacArthur could fly off in his C-47, *The Spirit of Bataan*, to new challenges in Japan. The Filipinos were left limping through the rubble, their cities and their government alike in shambles.

The war did break the hermetically sealed isolation created by colonialism, giving the Filipinos a new sense of place in Asia. The wartime Japanese use of Tagalog and their glorification of indigenous institutions and culture generated a new pride. In 1935 Pio Duran, an apologist for the Japanese, had been dismissed as a right-wing extremist for advocating the idea that the Philippines was "inexorably linked" to Asia. But this message became key to the thinking of Claro Recto, Ferdinand Marcos, Carlos P. Romulo, and Benigno Aquino as they incorporated pan-Asianism in their nation's postwar world view. In an article in *Foreign Affairs* in 1968, for example, Benigno Aquino wrote that "they were an Asian people not Asian in the eyes of their fellow Asians, not Western in the eyes of the West. . . . Bold efforts [were essential] to break away from the fetters of the past."

The occupation also exacerbated a deep ambivalence within Philippine society. By challenging some of the essential assumptions under which the Philippine nation had been functioning, the Japanese occupation painfully exposed contradictions that only a short time earlier had lain hidden. General Homma Masaharu, the commanding officer who defeated MacArthur and accepted the surrender of U.S. troops under Lieutenant General Jonathan Wainwright, told the Filipinos that "as the leopard cannot change its spots, you cannot alter the fact that you are Orientals." Demanding a rational approach toward the Philippine "place in the universal order of things," he ridiculed the Filipinos' "inferiority complex" and told them to assert themselves. Similarly, General Wachi Takaji noted that "regardless of whether you like it or not, you are Filipinos and belong to the Oriental race. No matter how hard you try, you cannot become white people." During the 1930s, Pio Duran had called the commonwealth leadership "apostates of Orientalism who have aligned themselves with the governing West in an effort to emasculate a portion of the Oriental race." A value system established over 350 years of colonialism was thus challenged, and the Filipinos have been seeking to resolve this ambivalence ever since.

Wartime realities heightened social, political, and economic tensions between tenants and landlords, patrons and clients, exiles and captives, city dwellers and rural *tao*, guerrillas and collaborators. The Hukbalahap, which emerged as a guerrilla resistance movement in central Luzon, was equally a peasant movement to redress ancient grievances against the landlords. Not all guerrillas were radicals, nor all conservatives collaborators. Not all peasants were Huks and not all landlords were absentee owners. But the disruption of war and occupation gave the Huks a special opportunity to challenge the economic balance of power, and this struggle helped to define the early years of independence.

The war also fragmented the preponderant Nacionalista party, shattering its monopoly of authority created by Manuel Quezon prior to the war. After Quezon's death in exile in 1944, Sergio Osmeña, the new president, returned to the archipelago burdened by the United States' insistence that he prosecute his peers (and two of his sons) as collaborators. But Washington's perspective on collaboration was challenged vigorously by those who lived through it in Manila. Osmeña's position was awkward. He was forced to be chief inquisitor rather than forgiving leader.

Osmeña had to make hard decisions, on the legitimacy of a recall of the 1941 legislature, the fitness of cabinet appointments, the need for a people's court to try collaboration cases, the priorities for postwar planning and economic rehabilitation, and factional issues that dated back a decade or more. Before leaving for Japan, Douglas MacArthur had personally asserted that Manuel Roxas, his prewar friend and Quezon's heir presumptive, was free of wartime guilt, even though Roxas had been involved (albeit reluctantly) with the collaborationist government run by the wartime president, Jose Laurel. By that single act of military fiat, MacArthur established Roxas as Osmeña's rival for the post of president in the upcoming 1946 elections. Osmeña had lost touch with his own political network of supporters, his own clients. He was returning without staff, money, or room for maneuvering to govern a bankrupt, devastated, and divided nation. Moreover, he was put into the difficult and compromising position of doing the bidding of the U.S. colonial masters, of collaborating with Washington rather than Manila.

The April 1946 election was bitterly fought. Roxas, having formed a rival political party, the Liberal party, won with a modest majority. Osmeña, unable to gain backing from his former supporters, was forced to accept into his coalition, among others, the political arm of the Hukbalahap, the Democratic Alliance. It was widely understood that MacArthur, then in Japan, wanted Roxas, whereas Secretary of the Interior Harold Ickes, in Washington, wanted Osmeña. After Roosevelt's death, Truman's lack of firsthand knowledge and his growing preoccupation with the Communist threat in Asia meant that U.S. policy was changing rapidly. However understandable Osmeña's defeat might be to a political scientist, the election carried another message: The emoluments of office triumph over the liabilities of public trust. Politicians and bureaucrats, whether they were collaborators or guerrilla leaders, often seemed to be corrupt, self-seeking opportunists. The postwar political scene demeaned wartime sacrifice; the unseemly scramble by the politicians appeared vulgar. The prompt decision of the recalled Congress to vote itself three years back pay made cynics of many. Factionalism, traditional political struggle, a return to the old order of political alliances from the 1930s indicated that historical continuity was a powerful force, as it has continued to be until today.

One of the most complicated aspects of this restoration of the status quo ante was the issue of collaboration with the Japanese. How could a nation unquestionably believe that through resistance it had achieved national dignity, when its own elite was accused of treason? How could the suffering of Filipinos during the war serve as a model for future generations, if those charged with the defense of national ideals not only seemingly violated those ideals but retained power after the war? The wartime experience made it seem that to obey authority was to abandon the good fight and to resist government was heroic. Nations that have been put in this terrible situation have discovered that they cannot turn on or shut off respect for the law as if it flowed from a spigot. Was it a crime to shoot a Japanese sentry while he stood on guard? If it was not a crime, then why would it be a crime to shoot a rival or a Communist or a landlord? The war permitted violence to be institutionalized, and the use of weapons for whatever reason became justified as patriotic. The readiness to resort to force has been a pervasive and disturbing feature of postindependence Philippine society.

In wartime and shortly thereafter, the elite had argued that it was motivated "only in the interest of the people, to save them from the brutalities of the Japanese army of occupation." The elite maintained that these wartime public officers "should not be classified as collaborationists in any sense . . . but should be credited with the highest sense of patriotism comparable to that of those who, in one way or another, participated in the underground resistance movement." Was it possible to entertain different conceptions of how best to serve one's country? Was there even "heroism in collaboration"? In Jose Laurel's words, "Everyone was a collaborationist; no one was a traitor."

The wartime governor of Leyte Island, Bernardo Torres, argued, "I am a Filipino agent working to the best of my ability to serve my unfortunate country at an unfortunate time in her history." He asked rhetorically, "Who will say I am a traitor to my country because I happened to have been called to make government—peace, order, security—function in our province? I was not privileged to fight in the battlefield and to make a military choice. I was fated by circumstances to be the governor of our province before and during this war." Torres's argument glossed over the fear of immediate reprisal, subtle duress, ambition, group self-interest, and personal gain, but motivation is never simple.

During the war, the guerrilla leader Tomas Confesor commented that "this struggle is a total war . . . in which the question at stake with respect to the Philippines is . . . what system of social organization and code of morals should govern our existence." Confesor had maintained that national ideals had to take precedence over pragmatic considerations of tranquility and short-term peace, for what was at stake was "something more precious than life itself: the principles of democracy and justice, the honor and destiny of our people." The martyrdom of Jose Abad Santos, the prewar chief justice of the Supreme Court who was executed by the Japanese a few months after they conquered the archipelago, showed a road not taken and suggested a definition of sacrifice that has left an ambivalent legacy. For although Abad Santos is memorialized by the many elementary schools named for him, he is virtually never recalled in the pantheon of Filipino martyrs and heroes.

Power, it seemed, begot more power, even as legal and ethical restraints were challenged. Laurel maintained during the war that "public office is a public trust. The beneficiaries of an established government are the people and the people only. . . . The holding of a public office is not an occasion for personal aggrandizement, but an opportunity for public service." It is still a dubious claim almost half a century later.

In 1945 Francisco Delgado, one of Osmeña's strongest supporters, asked whether a man "can speak and act against his nation, and, later on, again be accepted as a worthy son of that nation." With everyone claiming to be equally patriotic, whether they had fought as a guerrilla or had collaborated, how were the norms to be determined? Is it enough to claim to have the nation's interests at heart, or must there be some consensus to finding the boundaries of proper behavior? Is swearing allegiance equal to that allegiance? Since words became corrupted, it became difficult even to phrase the question clearly. During the war, the Japanese and the Japanese-sponsored Filipino governments almost invariably spoke of maintaining peace and order as the code words for curtailing the guerrillas. The symbols of flag and anthem were manipulated. Laurel was named president of the Republic of the Philippines, and even if the outer trappings of independence do not equate with independence itself, Laurel's portrait now hangs in the presidential palace, Malacañan, along with the other pre- and postwar presidents. The label attached to the portrait reads simply, "President Jose B. Laurel." The guerrillas and the collaborators both claiming to possess the regalia of nationalism, the symbols themselves became tainted.

Laurel had recognized that "it is not easy for a self-respecting man to change convictions overnight even after objective realities have rendered such convictions irrelevant." But by his reasoning, such changes were required. If national allegiance is a lodestar for modern man, must its verities remain fixed despite the countervailing pressures? Antonio Quirino, a judge on the postwar People's Court, noted that "the phrase 'for the good of the people' means and should mean the ultimate good; not merely the temporary relief from want and harm." Quirino argued that "the country must be preserved; the government must have unstinted loyalty, [and] national dignity and honor must be maintained at any cost."

The long quest for an elite-defined independence had "come to occupy the most sanctified status of a political faith," as an astute Japanese wartime observer noted. "The real substantive question is whether independence would lead to nationhood; independence per se is not important." Laurel argued after the war that the Japanese "offer of independence could not have been rejected for historical reasons and as a matter of national dignity." By stressing how "succeeding generations have worked and labored for independence," he maintained that his generation could not afford to appear in the history of the country as the one that, "offered to become free, rejected the priceless boon and preferred something else." But the reality juxtaposed against this claim was that the Japanese understood that their control extended "to all aspects of Philippine life, thereby rendering Philippine 'independence' a sheer sham—only name without substance."

The war years also led to disillusionment with the United States. Dissatisfaction began as early as 1942, when Quezon had bitterly complained to Charles Willoughby, MacArthur's chief of staff, that "America writhes in anguish at the fate of a distant cousin, Europe, while a daughter, the Philippines, is being raped in the back room." Most Filipinos felt that the United States owed them generous postwar support, not merely because they had been good allies but especially because they had fulfilled handsomely the obligations of reciprocity, of *utang na loob*, that cemented the "special relationship." But the Filipinos were stunned to discover that the United States was insensitive to their plight. The relative meagerness of postwar economic aid, especially in comparison with the far more substantial support given to Germany and Japan, and the crude way in which the United States tied its aid to postwar concessions soured many Filipinos. They expected gratitude; instead, the United States proved to be niggardly, calculating, and neocolonial.

MacArthur's mystique and rhetoric had raised hopes that were dashed by what followed. Even worse than the haggling over war-damage claims, the dispute over parity, exchange rates injurious to the Filipinos, and strong-armed techniques to get economic and military concessions was the low priority that Washington gave to things Filipino. Laurel had said the war served as a catalyst, "speeding up transformations in social and political life which under peace-time conditions may require years or even generations to carry out." After the war the Americans forgot about the Filipinos and their sacrifice, leaving many Filipinos feeling angry and rejected. Kinship obligations do not cease merely because younger brothers turn twenty-one. How, Filipinos wondered, could the United States ignore its own family in such a way? This question, which has bothered Filipinos for decades, surfaced again during the last months of Ferdinand Marcos's reign. How could the United States have closed its eyes to the years of gross corruption under Marcos? How could it have failed to insist that Marcos repatriate his stolen wealth as a precondition of remaining in exile in the United States? How could President Reagan have dithered about embracing the ideals articulated by Corazon Aquino?

The years 1941–1945, therefore, were traumatic in ways far more lasting than the physical death and destruction, dreadful though those were. If the society's wounds in a metaphorical sense simply damaged the flesh and bone of the nation, then eventually, after the pain, the healing process would begin and scar tissue would form. If, on the other hand, as with the wounds caused by atomic weapons, a cancer develops, then the society may have to deal with metastasis as the disease spreads throughout the body politic.

The historical biopsy showed evidence of cancer. Filipinos have seen public service used as a means for private gain. To be sure, the obligations of real and fictive kinship, the awareness of reciprocity in relationships, and the high social value placed on wealth as an arbiter of status have all contributed to the prevalence of nepotism and other "anomalies." The collapse of law and order, the taint of collaboration, the confusion of allegiance, the starvation and deprivation, and the chance for quick profit—in wartime buy-and-sell-rackets, in U.S. rehabilitation, in Japanese reparations, in import quotas, currency restrictions, in land-grab schemes—all played a role in shaping an independent Philippines. The Philippines entered an era of independence a very different place from the self-satisfied colony that entered World War II.

THE OLD ORDER

On July 4, 1946—a date subsequently abandoned by the Filipinos as national independence day—Manuel Roxas became the first president of an independent republic of the Philippines. Over the next twenty-five years, the Philippines rebuilt itself, entered into a period of fairly rapid economic growth and even more rapid population expansion, and learned to live with the jumble of tensions, contradictions, anomalies, and values that defined the nation and have shaped its personality. This era has often been vilified, or at least discounted as the old order, worn like a comfortable, if torn, old slipper. These were years in which few challenged the priorities of the society, however incongruous they might seem. Those that did try to change the existing order were either defeated or incorporated. Some prophesied the inevitable collapse of the system through demographic pressure, social tension, or political breakdown. Others saw in the old order a conservative process that made the Philippines far more stable, in retrospect, than most people gave it credit for during the several administrations by which these years are counted.

If this era began with the end of colonialism on July 4, 1946, it ended abruptly with the declaration of martial law by Ferdinand E. Marcos on September 22, 1972. During those twenty-six years, Philippine society domesticated the U.S.-imposed institutions of government and social structure. This period looked back to the factional, regional politics of the commonwealth and before, solidified the power of the prewar elite, and confirmed the priorities of ownership of private property, Horatio Alger's dream of upward mobility, and the role of the church as the protector and arbiter of social values.

To describe the old order as conservative does not mean that it was necessarily regressive, although Marcos and others, including the Communists, claimed that it was. The process of rebuilding the economy, especially the modern sector in Manila; the expansion of infrastructure and industrial development as the nation began to manufacture and even to export products previously imported from the United States; and the development of educational and social services, which permitted a new vehicle for access to millions of aspiring Filipinos, all profoundly changed both the culture and the society. Gone were the white-suited colonial bureaucrats, replaced by a somewhat raucous, increasingly self-assured cadre of Filipinos who aspired to European perfumes, Rolex watches, and international travel. Rich landlords, proud of their new power, sent their children to the United States and redecorated their main *salas* (living rooms) with gleaming, stainless steel refrigerators from the United States. If one had money, one had status; how one got that money, how the rules were bent or observed, was not very important. And the gap between rich and poor, those few with opportunity and the great mass trapped in poverty, widened rapidly and cruelly.

"Anomalies" abounded. The rapid increase in the size of the bureaucracy gave enormous opportunity for politicians and bureaucrats to staff the new jobs with kin. Price controls, import/export licenses, U.S. foreign aid and Japanese restitution funds, a black market, a pent-up demand for luxury and consumer items, contract kickbacks, traditional greasing and imaginative creative entrepreneurial schemes that some called corrupt and others accepted as normal—all were hallmarks of a rough-and-tumble, expanding capitalist environment. The urban centers pulled ahead of the rural environment, and Manila, in particular, was an irrestible lure to those in the provinces who had money and those who did not. While foreign observers tended to focus on what they defined as "corrupt" practices, the economy was expanding and the nation was finding its own voice and character.

The prewar oligarchy split into two major parties, the Liberals and the Nacionalistas, and dominated the political landscape. Traditional factionalism and the hierarchical obligations of Philippine political life created alliances and coalitions that were constantly changing. People alternated between parties with a mercurial flexibility that amazed outsiders: As in a kaleidoscope, every rotation of some piece of political environment changed the patterns throughout. Oligarchic control, however, did not mean that upward mobility was blocked. Someone with either money or leverage, could join the elite, in effect, by expanding it, by buying into the clubs, neighborhoods, and businesses that conferred elite status. There were a series of regularly scheduled elections in which people out of power could and did win office. Authority was transferred peacefully from administration to administration. And if votes were bought, if cemetery residents appeared on registration lists, if political violence occurred, there were checks and balances through an independent judiciary, a free (perhaps licentious) press, and an electorate able to vote the rascals out.

From 1946 to 1953 there were three overriding issues: rebuilding the economy, working out the relationship with the United States, and addressing the Hukbalahap challenge to oligarchic control. These issues came together in complicated ways. Rehabilitation required U.S. financial support and, later on, Japanese restitution. The United States was prepared to give aid—although far less than the Filipinos believed they deserved—but only after the Filipinos had agreed to a number of conditions that, in hindsight, are properly called neocolonial. It insisted, for example, that the peso be tied to the U.S. dollar at an artificial exchange rate, which seriously inhibited Philippine economic development by linking the archipelago to the United States and by overvaluing the peso. U.S. corporations and individuals were to be given special access to economic development and the same legal protection that struggling new Filipino corporations had in the development of natural resources. In effect, the United States demanded and got sustaining opportunities for domination of the Philippine economy, including insurance, banking, construction, and plantation export and import. The imposition of these conditions rankled Filipino intellectuals and business people and led to a long process of renegotiation as the Philippine government sought to establish full control over its own economy.

The United States had also insisted upon retaining the giant military installations at Subic Bay and Clark Air Base, taking out ninety-nine-year leases and treating these and numerous smaller military installations as if they were still part of the United States. Such satrapies of *pax Americana* excluded even token concessions toward Philippine nationalism and sovereignty. If there was a crime on the base or off, the soldier or sailor in question was to be tried before a U.S. military tribunal rather than before a Philippine court. The question of compensation was equally vexatious. The Filipinos, almost from the beginning, argued for rent. The United States denied that any military assistance tied to the bases should be considered rent, regarding the bases as a part of a global strategy of containment of communism and as the shield protecting the new nation.

From the late 1940s, Philippine nationalist leaders, most prominently Senator Claro M. Recto, railed against the bases. Recto argued for an assertion of Philippine sovereignty, maintaining that far from serving as a shield for Philippine defense—as the United States claimed—the bases were likely to invite attack, as they did in 1941. These bases became the second-largest employer in the Philippines, hiring tens of thousands of Filipinos and housing many thousands of U.S. service people and their dependents. Surrounding each of these bases was a vast sprawl of people and businesses that lived off the wealth the bases spawned. The cities of Olongapo and Angeles were "sin cities," sustaining bars and brothels, massage parlors and casinos. The dollars transferred into the local economy kept tens of thousands of people alive and, ironically, helped underwrite the Hukbalahap uprising as the Huks skimmed this wealth Mafia-style. Thus, the U.S. military establishment, committed to help defeat the Huks, financed them directly.

As communism triumphed in China and Vietnam during the late 1940s, the U.S. government became increasingly afraid that communism could spread to the Philippines as well. Cold war ideology cemented the U.S. commitment to those very oligarchs who either owned the great estates of Tarlac and Pampanga or represented the people who did. U.S. policy planners addressed socioeconomic issues with military solutions and saw the uprising more as part of a global conspiracy of communism than an indigenous reaction to tenancy, landlessness, demographic explosion, and poverty. Although some Americans argued for an essential commitment to land reform, most were unprepared to push the Filipino elite toward significant redistribution of wealth.

Governmental corruption, low morale and inadequate training of the Philippine army, rampant inflation, and economic exhaustion prevented the Manila government from defeating the Huks militarily. Prior to his death from a heart attack (which, ironically, he suffered while at Clark Air Base in 1948), Manuel Roxas, and his vice-presidential successor, Elpidio Quirino, lacked the capacity to break the agrarian uprising of central Luzon led by the charismatic, if unsophisticated, Luis Taruc. In a pattern that would be repeated in Vietnam and later with the New People's Army in the Philippines, the United States supplied sufficient weaponry to outfit the enemy as well as the ally.

In 1949 Jose Laurel challenged Quirino in a venal presidential election in which Quirino used U.S. relief aid to buy votes. Quirino won, defeating Laurel only by circumventing the democratic process. Laurel's supporters urged him to contest this fraud, but a combination of patriotism and awareness that the United States would not support him because of his wartime record prompted Laurel to accept his loss without bloodshed. By 1950 the country was going through an economic, moral, political, and military crisis, even though Taruc had not managed to expand his influence across the countryside beyond central Luzon. In October of that year, the Central Bank had to borrow from abroad to meet the government payroll.

The rise of Ramon Magsaysay altered the history of the Philippines. Born in a bamboo hut, son of a teacher who became a blacksmith, Magsaysay was no scion of an elite family. During World War II, he had been a guerrilla leader; after the war he had become Quirino's secretary of defense at the insistence of the United States. Closely allied to the Americans, especially to a controversial CIA officer, Edward Lansdale, Magsaysay achieved three major successes in his years as secretary of defense. First, he infused a corrupt, demoralized military with a new sense of purpose and esprit de corps. Second, with the help of the CIA, Magsaysay's intelligence network enabled him to arrest en masse the Politburo of the Communist party and seize documents that listed sympathizers. Although the Politburo and Taruc were distinct elements of the left-wing challenge, this intelligence coup did much to fragment support by urban sympathizers, especially in the city of Manila. Finally, Magsaysay used the army to guarantee that the 1951 congressional elections would be relatively honest. This military intervention to control ballot-box tampering and fraud restored a degree of confidence in the electoral process.

Magsaysay was an open, direct, engaging Filipino. His modest origins, delight in people, accessibility, genuine successes, and support of the United States made him a clear winner in the 1953 presidential election. He gathered together a brain trust of exceptional young Filipinos (and U.S. advisers) to help him govern. The society prospered, in part because of Japanese reparations and in part because of U.S. expenditures during the Korean War. Magsaysay broke the threat of the Huk rebellion by using heavy military pressure against those who continued to fight, at the same time offering amnesty to those who surrendered. He resettled the landless of central Luzon who were willing to move to Mindanao and other parts of the archipelago. Magsaysay understood, as perhaps no Filipino politician has before or since, the legitimate grievances of the peasantry. His resettlement scheme brought thousands of homesteaders to Mindanao, permanently altering the balance of Muslims to Christians on that enormous island. Resettlement postponed but did not alleviate the ongoing crisis of land ownership, because demographic pressure and inequity in wealth eventually reignited these problems twenty years later. It would, however, offer an opportunity to make structural changes in the years to come, an opportunity not necessarily taken.

In 1957 Ramon Magsaysay died when his plane crashed into a mountain. Hope died with him. His immediate successors lacked the vision and political power to maintain his momentum. Carlos Garcia, an old-line politician from Bohol in the southern Visayas, was a journeyman. He was elected president in his own right later in 1957 and was succeeded in 1961 by Diosdado Macapagal. Unlike Magsaysay, neither Garcia nor Macapagal had the capacity to transcend the limitations of their class and time. During these years, there was prosperity and economic growth, but there was also a growing sense of frustration with the lawlessness, the propensity to violence, and the seeming drift of society. Magsaysay's death created a leadership vacuum, a hiatus waiting to be filled. On April 5, 1963, a young, ambitious senator from the northern part of Luzon challenged the hierarchy of the Senate and in particular the wily old patriarch Eulogio (Amang) Rodriguez, winning the Senate presidency for himself. Ferdinand Marcos had positioned himself to fill the political void.

7

The Marcos Era

THE MAN HIMSELF

Ferdinand Marcos, brilliant, charismatic, wily, was a confidence man, a human being who believed his own falsehoods. Marcos lied to himself, his cronies, and his nation audaciously. He was able to dominate his people for two decades, first as a symbol of hope and progress, later as an omnipotent dictator, and finally as a worldwide symbol of corruption and decay. He and his flamboyant wife, Imelda, created a "conjugal dictatorship," and, for a while, became in themselves national symbols like the flag, the anthem, and Malacañan.

Ferdinand Edralin Marcos was born September 11, 1917, in the town of Sarrat in Ilocos, the poor and rugged northern area of Luzon. He was part of the provincial, Chinese mestizo elite. His mother was a grade-school teacher who also worked in her parents' store. Her ancestors were *cabezas de Barangay* under the Spanish. Marcos's grandfather, Fructuoso Edralin, owned about 200 acres (80 hectares) of irrigated rice land and coffee plantation and an additional 120 acres (50 hectares) outside of Sarrat. During the early part of the American interregnum, Edralin expanded his property to include 250 acres (100 hectares) of virgin forest. He sold the lumber to Chinese mills linked to his wife's family, the Quetulios, wealthy Chinese mestizo merchants in Ilocos Sur. Both Marcos's mother, Josefa, and his father, Mariano, were educated in Laoag, where they had been taught by Thomasites, young, idealistic schoolteachers who had come from the United States to spread the English language, American values, and modern educational techniques to "the little brown brothers." Mariano Marcos's grandfather was an illegitimate son of a Spanish provincial judge. The family was thus both Chinese and Spanish mestizo. Ferdinand Marcos's paternal grandfather, Fabian, served as mayor of a provincial town, Batac. This genealogy is a paradigm of the dominance by mestizos described in Chapter 3.

As with most things connected to Ferdinand Marcos, however, there is unsubstantiated rumor suggesting that his mother actually became pregnant by Ferdinand Chua, the son of one of the major Chinese families in Ilocos. The story, chronicled by a hostile biographer, Sterling Seagrave, claims that the Chua family blocked the marriage, encouraging instead an arranged marriage between Josefa Edralin and Mariano Marcos, who was seven years her junior. In exchange for this, the Chua are claimed to have assisted Mariano Marcos's career dramatically, and Ferdinand Chua, known later in life as Fernando, became young Ferdinand's godfather. The Chua family, according to Seagrave, encouraged and perhaps paid the Marcos family to move to Manila, where Mariano graduated from the University of the Philippines in 1924, running for Congress that same year. Josefa became a schoolteacher in Manila and the family thus developed ties to the city as well as to the provinces. In 1930 young Ferdinand enrolled in the University of the Philippines high school and, later, the University of the Philippines.

Mariano Marcos for years sought reelection to Congress. In 1935 he aligned himself with Bishop Aglipay, who ran for president against Manuel Quezon. Quezon won by a landslide, even in Ilocos, and Marcos's opponent, Julio Nalundasan, won easily. Mariano Marcos was ridiculed by Nalundasan's supporters. Shortly after the election, someone assassinated Nalundasan. One of Mariano Marcos's supporters was accused, but the case was dismissed for lack of evidence.

Three years thereafter, Ferdinand Marcos, along with his uncles and, later, his father were arrested for Nalundasan's murder. Ferdinand, then in his last year of law school, petitioned the Philippine Supreme Court for release on bail, which was granted, permitting him to complete his education and get his degree. The case received national attention. At the end of 1939, Ferdinand Marcos, found guilty beyond any reasonable doubt, was sentenced to a minimum of ten years in prison. There, he wrote his own appeal brief, took the bar exam, and graduated top in the nation. Late in 1940, in a well-publicized Supreme Court hearing presided over by Jose Laurel, Marcos defended himself vigorously. Laurel, too, had lived through a comparable case early in his career; he had been convicted of murder only to have it overturned as legitimate self-defense. Now writing for the court, Laurel ruled that the evidence offered at the original Marcos trial was insufficient and contradictory. Marcos was freed and cemented a special relationship with Laurel when Laurel swore him in as an attorney a few days later.

Much of Marcos's later political success was based on his claims that he was a war hero, a guerrilla leader, and one of the most highly decorated combat veterans of World War II. These boasts, like many others, were made often and proudly without the slightest suggestion of doubt. Domestic and foreign audiences, including presidents of the United States, accepted the claims on face value. They have since been recognized as highly suspect. Marcos was called into active service as an ROTC reserve officer, he was at Bataan, and he did have some sustaining involvement with several guerrilla organizations. But it is also possible that at some point he was involved with Laurel during the period Laurel was recovering from the assassination attempt by guerrillas in 1943.

Did Marcos himself discern truth from fiction, from the puffery Filipinos call *palabas*? Could he genuinely separate reality from what he wished reality to have been? All great confidence men must themselves believe what they say in order to be believed by others. The Marcos mythology—at one point it neared hagiology—suffused his life with those attributes required to lay claim to the regalia of leadership. Every story, every tale, even his *anting anting*, added an element of legitimization. The path down the yellow brick road toward the presidency was clear. The marriage to a beauty queen from the Visayas, Imelda Romualdez, strengthened his appeal and gave him a formidable partner, one who, in her youth, appeared to embody all of the Filipina charms—beauty, talent, and ambition. Marcos was elected to Congress from Ilocos Norte in 1949. After three terms he ran for the Senate and won, winning its presidency in 1963. In 1965 the charismatic Marcos, campaigning against Diosdado Macapagal and the old order, summoned the nation to a new era. His people granted him everything he wanted and more.

THE CONSTITUTIONAL PRESIDENCY

By his first inauguration, there was a malaise in the Philippines. Was the nation adjusting adequately enough to meet the changing realities of independence? Political power was in the hands of an oligarchy. The population was growing rapidly. Economic activity was not keeping pace. Unemployment and underemployment were rampant. Manila was growing without proper planning or infrastructure development. Corruption seemed universal. There was a segment, embarrassingly large to Filipino nationalists, that openly yearned for a somewhat romanticized, tidier past when the American colonial administration seemed to function more effectively. There were labor unions, students, and peasants who said that society was corrupt. They yearned instead for radical change, the redistribution of wealth, and a Marxist solution. U.S. intervention on an ever-increasing basis in Vietnam was assisting the local economy in the archipelago, but it raised serious political and social questions.

And so, after his decisive victory over Macapagal—Marcos had changed parties in order to position himself to run for president—Marcos addressed his nation: "The Filipino, it seems, has lost his soul, his dignity, and his courage. Our people have come to a point of despair.

Ferdinand and Imelda Marcos, circa early 1970s. (Courtesy of the Office of the President)

We have ceased to value order." Marcos, a master player in the old order, went on to note that the "government is gripping the iron hand of venality, its treasury is barren, its resources are wasted, its civil service is slothful and indifferent, its armed forces demoralized, and its councils sterile." Presenting himself as the saviour from the anomalies and corruption of the past, Marcos called upon the Filipino people: "Not one hero alone do I ask from you, but many—nay, all." Some years later, in words virtually identical to Marcos's, Benigno Aquino wrote in *Foreign Affairs*:

> Here is a land in which a few are spectacularly rich while the masses remain abjectly poor. Here is a land where freedom and its blessings are a reality for the minority and an illusion for the many. Here is a land consecrated to democracy but run by an entrenched plutocracy. Here is a land of privilege and rank—a republic dedicated to equality but mired in an archaic system of caste.

Both Imelda and Ferdinand Marcos modeled their public behavior on Jackie and John Kennedy. She organized the "Blue Ladies," a group of younger society women who were given very high publicity doing good works, planting rice, participating in the entourage of the first lady. The president understood the importance of photo opportunities, media leaks, and publicity. Simultaneously, Marcos began a pattern of corruption, buying lavish gifts for both domestic and foreign friends, hiring scores of public relations firms and agents, and bribing outright sycophants and supporters. The use of such money was a long-honored tradition of Philippine politics, but Marcos escalated both his own corruption and that of others to levels unimaginable in the previous administrations. The increasingly bureaucratic outreach of the state was used as a vehicle to put the president, his family, and the government on the take. The schemes and techniques first used during the era of constitutional government were later expanded exponentially during the martial law period.

These were boom years, both because the Philippine economy had a highly trained, sophisticated, English-speaking labor force and also because the Vietnam War pumped dollars into the Philippines. Both Clark and Subic became critical staging areas for U.S. intervention; the department of defense dramatically increased procurement purchases. Lyndon Johnson, in need of finding Asian friends to support the United States' position on Vietnam and hoping to create a broader allied effort that would parallel the prior struggle in Korea, courted Marcos publicly and privately. During these years, the U.S. Embassy lavishly praised Marcos, turning a blind eye to his personal greed and self-aggrandizing efforts. He was celebrated as a key anticommunist leader, a committed friend of the United States.

In 1969, running on the slogan "rice and roads," Marcos was reelected president, the first man ever to win a full second term. During these years, he and Imelda had launched a major worldwide media blitz to put the Philippines on the map. They started a series of public projects—to be expanded ostentatiously during martial law—that led to the building of a monumental cultural center, a new airport, international-grade convention hotels, and other highly visible symbols of national pride and modernity. They gave substantial attention, some of it validly placed, to land-reform projects, strains of miracle rice, and road projects. Although there were constant corrupt practices, there was also a reasonable, if unspectacular, record of governmental action.

A shrewd politician and a brilliant tactician, Marcos had devoted much of his time to building the necessary patron-client relationships to guarantee his power. During his second reelection campaign, he had liberally spent from his own and public funds—estimates range at above $150 million—and he had won with 74 percent of the votes cast. Cemeteries have voted in the Philippines since elections were first held, but there was a new level of professionalism in corruption that boded ill for democracy. Of the eight senatorial seats up for election, Marcos's Nacionalista slate had won seven, and all but twenty-four of the 110 races in the lower House went to Marcos's candidates. But by arrogating power and authority to his own hands, Marcos was driving a tiny but influential group of students at the University of the Philippines, Ateneo, and elsewhere toward violence. Just after his inauguration, a group of radical students marched on Malacañan. In the bloodshed that followed at Mendiola bridge, four student "martyrs" died.

He had become the consummate manipulator of the press, the political system, and the society. But, by 1971, Marcos was a lame-duck president. A constitutional convention was called to review the 1935 constitution and to explore whether the commonwealth structures properly suited the new Philippines. Marcos, an ardent legalist and believer in constitutional structures, was ambivalent about the convention. He was hostile to its potential threat to the existing order but intrigued by the possibility of manipulating the convention so as to change the 1935 prohibition against the president's serving more than two terms. Like earlier Philippine presidents, his prospect was to retire and enjoy his new wealth, leaving the political arena to others who, equally ambitious, had been blocked by his control of the system. But to leave office was to surrender the regalia of power, the luxury of Malacañan, and the opportunity to grow yet richer.

Marcos claimed to fear anarchy, which he said was spreading across the Philippines. In 1971 at a Liberal party electoral rally at Plaza Miranda in Manila, a bomb exploded, wounding 100 citizens and eight senatorial candidates, including Jovito Salonga, Raul Manglapus, and John Osmeña. Benigno Aquino had not yet arrived when the bomb went off. The Liberals accused Marcos; he blamed the left. The Liberals won six out of eight seats in that midterm election. By 1972 political violence, which was always endemic, had reached new heights. Marcos maintained that his serious efforts to reform and improve the social fabric were aborted by a paralyzing political process and a chaotic press. He called for "a new society," arguing that "constitutional authoritarianism" would be necessary to give discipline to the nation, to manage its growth, and to help the Philippines find its way toward that secular utopia of economic progress and social well-being that all modern nations so desperately strive for.

The center seemed unable to hold. Muslims, unhappy that Mindanao had become more Christian, began to wage a war of national liberation. A small group of students made radical by Marcos and the old order and intrigued with Mao, created the New People's Army, reviving a Communist-led insurgency that was openly aimed at overthrowing the existing system.

The failure of the United States in Vietnam and the triumph of communism across the South China Sea suggested a fundamental change in the geopolitical world. The deep domestic tensions tormenting the United States made it less certain and supportive, more introspective and needy of friends who proclaimed unequivocal anticommunism in Asia.

In 1980, during a rare official visit to the United States, Marcos looked back on his decision to proclaim martial law as "crisis management." He added that "no moderates can ever take over a society that is in disarray." But as his key rival, Benigno Aquino, argued, "the real guarantee of freedom is an equilibrium of social forces in conflict, not the triumph of any one force, and surely not the domination of a single man." Aquino, the most likely victor in a presidential election in 1973, had it been held, went on, "for freedom to be safe, no group, let alone a single man, should have unlimited power. Without criticism, no democracy can survive, and without dissent, no government can effectively govern."

MARTIAL LAW

The proof of Ferdinand Marcos's legerdemain was his capacity to win approval from key players, both domestic and foreign, for his declaration of martial law. In that proclamation, he declared, "I, as your duly elected President of the Republic, use this power to protect the Republic of the Philippines and our democracy." The subsequent reality was markedly different from this beginning. In General Order Number 1, Marcos assumed all powers of government and placed all its agencies at his beck and call. That first day he arrested critics and dissenters by the thousands, detaining not only those who advocated the violent overthrow of the government, but also those whose main crime was political disagreement and opposition to him. Torture was used, and thousands were harassed and persecuted. The writ of habeas corpus was suspended and military tribunals established. The right of peaceful assembly was suspended; free speech and free press were totally circumscribed; labor was denied the opportunity to organize and to strike.

Marcos and Secretary of Defense Juan Ponce Enrile had staged an attack on Enrile's limousine to fabricate the claim that the state was at risk. *Mirabile dictu*, Enrile was riding that particular day in the police escort cruiser rather than in his own car (something no Filipino cabinet secretary had probably ever done before or since); the incident was transparent even at the time. The constitutional convention was suspended, its leadership arrested or forced to flee in exile, and the democratic tradition built over the preceding seventy years rudely shattered.

The debate between Marcos and his opponents, radical and moderate, was as old as that between Sparta and Athens. The concept of authoritarianism dated back to the Spanish colonial past and evolved from Roman law, conservative landlords, and traditional Roman Catholic clerics. Francisco Franco and his Falange had strong support in the prewar Philippines.

Apolinario Mabini, the brilliant mind behind Emilio Aguinaldo's Malolos government, had been a seminal political thinker helping to shape indigenous political philosophy. Mabini's writings influenced Manuel Quezon and Jose Laurel among others. Running throughout Mabini's writings was the authoritarian theme of the need for strong centralized control of the state. When, for example, Mabini wrote for Aguinaldo his rejection of the convention's draft submitted at Malolos, he said that "the constitutional guarantees in favor of individual liberty cannot be maintained for the present, since this is the very moment when the necessity of the predominance of the military element is indicated. . . . The ship of state is threatened by great dangers and terrible tempests, and the circumstance in my opinion renders it advisable that the three powers [judicial, executive, and legislative] be to a certain extent combined for the present in a single hand."

During World War II, Laurel saw an opportunity to announce "a national policy, a political ideology, and a moral philosophy." In 1943 he published a short book entitled *Forces That Make a Nation Great,* in which he argued that his "suggested reform is comprehensive and far-reaching and implies a complete renovation of the individual and collective life of the Filipinos." Laurel, fascinated by what he defined as the success of the Japanese educational policy under the Emperor Meiji, wrote that "in education what is needed is not democracy, . . . but regimentation, not liberty but discipline, not liberalism but correct orientation, not flexibility but rigidity in the formulation of the desired mold of citizenship."

Months before the Pearl Harbor attack, Laurel supported emergency powers for President Quezon because he felt that a "constitutional dictatorship" was in keeping with a worldwide trend in which totalitarianism was gradually supplanting democracy. Laurel argued then that "in the interrelationship of powers of government, a center of political gravity must, in the nature of things, be provided. Such a center must necessarily be the executive." Laurel was strongly attracted to the prewar disciplined centralism of Japanese social organization and he saw his nation as paralyzed by its inefficiency and lack of discipline.

Laurel's thinking greatly influenced Marcos. Laurel was his patron and protector both. Marcos may even have helped Laurel draft some of those wartime writings, although there is no hard evidence. But, unlike Laurel, Marcos was a charlatan, a man whose pronouncements did not correspond with his actions. The argument made by Marcos for "constitutional authoritarianism" was skillfully used to play on the anxiety of those, the winners in the Philippines, who feared that they and their privileges were at risk if the society could not be mobilized sufficiently and quickly to protect the status quo. Marcos, arguing that "abrasive politics is borrowed from the United States," maintained in 1981 that political parties are contrary to Filipino culture, since the Malay way is to seek consensus. In effect, Marcos manipulated the anxieties of class war and social conflict—a sense of erosion within the society—to justify his usurpation of political power and the destruction of the freedoms of speech and assembly, an impartial judiciary, and the writ of habeas corpus.

The declaration of martial law won the strong support of the international business community and of President Richard Nixon and his government. The defeat in Vietnam made both Marcos and continued U.S. access to the two giant bases seem critical. Thus, instead of lamenting the destruction of the freedom the United States had granted and its former colony had adopted and adapted, Nixon applauded this suspension of the democratic tradition. U.S. foreign policy has traditionally been based on three objectives: geopolitical concerns, security issues, and a proselytizing belief in democracy and the American way. In the aftermath of Vietnam it was important to maintain allies (Korea and the Philippines, for example) whatever their political repression or internal policies, provided they were anticommunist and pro-U.S. Marcos was one of the beneficiaries of this new policy.

During the first years of martial law, tourism and government revenue tripled and the economy grew at an average annual rate of 7 percent. The private armies of the oligarchs were forcibly disbanded and some half million weapons were confiscated. In those early years, Marcos was often compared to Lee Kuan Yew of Singapore. If he violated human rights, his dictatorship was excused as not as brutal as some others. Many Filipinos in the business community embraced constitutional authoritarianism, willing to trade liberty, especially other people's, for economic development. But it also became slowly obvious that martial law was a vehicle for Marcos's personal aggrandizement. Crony capitalism gave family and close friends of the first family, vast economic opportunity. Sugar and coconut areas were made exempt from the land reform begun with such fanfare in 1973. The obvious and growing greed of the cronies and of Imelda Marcos substituted profit for ideology.

The conjugal dictatorship made Imelda Marcos one of the world's most visible women. She became a symbol of conspicuous consumption and corruption. Known as Nuestra Señora de Metro Manila because, among many other posts, she was also governor of metropolitan Manila and minister of human settlements, she chaired no fewer than twenty-three governmental councils, agencies, and corporations. She controlled hundreds of millions of dollars annually in those budgets alone, and it was during this period that the eleven five-star hotels, the 5,000-seat international convention center, the international film center, and other show projects were built. Her clothes, her jewels, her shoes, and her compulsive need to flaunt her wealth made radicals out of moderates and offended the sensibilities of millions, although she "delivered" patronage very effectively to her supporters, winning much loyalty from those who gained.

As Marcos and his cronies were growing stupendously rich, others in the society were less satisfied. In Mindanao and Sulu, a rebellion within the Muslim community was posing a serious secession challenge to Manila. Based on the age-old hostility between Catholic and Muslim, on economic backwardness, on a sense that Muslim areas were not given their fair share of allocated resources from Manila, and on the grievances over resettlement projects launched by the United States and later by Magsaysay, the Muslim unrest was centuries in the making. It also had a distinct new profile created by avaricious timber and logging operations, the pauperization of the peasantry, and the opportunities for plunder Marcos granted to his friends.

Private bedroom of Imelda Marcos, Malacañan. (Courtesy of the Museo ng Malacañang Foundation)

The formation of the state of Malaysia to include the former British territories in Borneo led to a territorial dispute between Malaysia and the sultan of Sulu—and, therefore, the Philippines—over his claim to legal rights over Sabah. In an ill-conceived military plan prior to martial law, Marcos organized a Filipino Muslim military group with the code name of Jabidah, and planned to train it on Corregidor prior to infiltrating it into Sabah. When the troops learned of their destination and mutinied against the project, they were massacred, although one soldier survived. This acutely embarrassing incident prompted the Malaysian government to summon home its ambassador. It exposed Marcos to much criticism and ridicule in what was then still a free press.

In 1968 Muslim leaders founded the Moro National Liberation Front (MNLF), with full independence as the stated maximum objective, but with the real goal of increased autonomy. During the first years, the organization was relatively peaceful, and at the constitutional convention of 1972, a statement was issued calling for the convention to grant certain Muslim-dominated areas autonomy. After declaring martial law, Marcos moved to suppress the MNLF by requiring Muslims in the South to surrender their firearms. Although negotiations took place in Jidda in 1974 and in Tripoli in 1979, neither side ever observed the terms of the agreements reached.

At its peak in 1974, the MNLF was able to field between 50,000 and 60,000 rebels, according to the estimate of the Philippine military commander and later Islamic Affairs minister, Rear Admiral Romulo Espaldon. The rebellion took on international significance, both because of the resurgent Muslim nationalist pride that has surfaced globally over the past two decades and because of economic and political realities following the 1973 oil embargo and the triumph of OPEC. The MNLF appealed to the wealthy Islamic states and received substantial backing. Muammar Qaddafi of Libya, in particular, was free with money and weaponry, and much of it flowed to the Muslims through Malaysia. The Iran-Iraq war further complicated the Philippine need to purchase oil from Islamic states. Imelda Marcos made herself visible attempting to negotiate with Qaddafi, King Hassan of Morocco, and King Khalid of Saudia Arabia.

In 1977 Marcos granted autonomy to some areas in Mindanao, and the fighting eventually trailed off. At its peak, a large percentage of Philippine armed forces—perhaps as much as two-thirds of the combat units—was tied down in Muslim areas, and the low-grade, sporadic fighting was an expensive drain on the Philippine treasury. The government tried not only to negotiate with local Muslim leaders but often to buy them, both with money and by granting them key positions in the South. The leader of the Muslim hard-liners has been Nur Misuari.

Operating from exile in Libya and Saudia Arabia, he opposed any compromise, even though many of his underlings were bribed. Arguing that there was "no moral basis for peaceful negotiations, let alone a peaceful solution to our problem," Nur Misuari held out for an ideological victory impossible in the face of Marcos's bribery and corruption.

By 1981 the MNLF had only 10,000 guerrillas still active, but the Muslims had won certain political concessions, as Manila agreed to allocate substantially more development aid to the Muslim South and granted the Muslim leadership additional political power. During the heady years when the Arab states were awash in surplus revenue, they hired and imported hundreds of thousands of Filipinos to work in construction and other projects. The hundreds of millions of dollars remitted back to the Philippines became vital to Marcos. As OPEC's monopoly collapsed, Manila was able to buy the oil it needed from other sources and was no longer held captive.

THE COMMUNIST INSURGENCY

If money and political compromise blunted the secessionist fervor of the Muslims, it did nothing to stem the growth of the New People's Army, the radical guerrilla arm of the reorganized Communist Party of the Philippines (CPP). Marcos, who had cited the Communist threat as a key factor in justifying his declaration of martial law, was the best recruiter the NPA could have had. His mismanagement of the economy, especially by permitting his cronies to make a fortune in the agricultural export sector at the expense of the small grower and agricultural worker, his greed and the greed of his associates, and the growing contradiction of a Philippine society polarized between the rich and the poor, drew the hungry, the homeless, and the hopeless to the NPA.

Functioning at first in remote, rural areas and skillfully manipulating local grievances, tensions, and desires, the CPP established armed units and networks of supporters. Over fifteen years, approximately 12,000 to 15,000 hard-core guerrilla soldiers were mobilized; by the end of the Marcos era, U.S. and Filipino military observers felt that the NPA had reached a critical stage of development, one that would permit it to launch larger military engagements. Senior policy planners at the Pentagon prophesied that within a few years the society would be destabilized by the Communist insurgency.

The NPA had a clear antecedent in the Hukbalahap. Both emerged out of the problems of tenancy, poverty, demography, and smashed expectations. The tension between haves and have-nots in key rural areas goes back to well before World War II in ongoing peasant unrest and agrarian revolt. Absentee landlordism and inadequate sharing of the profits from crops was the core of the anger against the friars and by the radical, right-wing Sakdalista peasants during the commonwealth era.

What distinguishes the CPP from these earlier uprisings of both the left and the right was that the CPP began as an intellectual, student-led, highly ideological radicalism based on the teachings and policies of Mao. The origins of the NPA can be found, therefore, in a student movement of the late 1960s, one that surfaced at the Sorbonne, Berkeley, and campuses across the world. The students of the University of the Philippines, Ateneo, and other Manila colleges, adopted an inflammatory rhetoric and violent behavior. Many of these student leaders were the children of upper-middle-class Filipinos, the literal and figurative descendants of the *ilustrados*.

Among the issues on which these Filipino students focused were the questions of imperialism and neoimperialism—the U.S. military bases, U.S. multinational economic power, unequal treaties—the society's seeming incapacity to deal with issues of social justice, economic redistribution, and land reform; and the corrupt, ostentatious, and immensely self-satisfied government of Ferdinand Marcos. These student leaders formed alliances with radical labor and peasant tenant groups and made noisy but marginal impact through demonstrations.

The Cultural Revolution in China and the openly generational conflict in the United States created an environment in which radicalism seemed on the ascendancy, and by the time of the 1972 constitutional convention there were many, including a large segment of the Philippine press, who were prophesizing an apocalypse. The fear of that anarchy, however misplaced, was skillfully manipulated by Marcos, who used the student radicals and their vocal demonstration to establish the legitimacy of his decision to impose martial law, to suspend constitutional, democratic freedoms, and to make himself the defender of the state.

Whereas the Hukbalahap drew support from the CPP, Luis Taruc had been a peasant whose power derived from organizing other peasants in the countryside. The NPA, on the other hand, was more sophisticated and less regional. Initially it reached out to the old Huk areas, the rice-growing region around Clark Air Base. Because this was Benigno Aquino's political turf, Marcos accused Aquino of entering into an alliance with the NPA—something both Aquino and the Communists staunchly denied. In the days just prior to the imposition of martial law, Marcos fanned rumors of Aquino's duplicity, hinting at secret negotiations, especially between Aquino and Jose Maria Sison, a brilliant leader who had founded the CPP in 1968 and had written *Philippine Society and Revolution* in 1970.

Jose Maria Sison. (Courtesy of Jaime Zobel de Ayala)

Marcos understood that he would need the complete support of the Philippine army if he was to rule by martial law. The Philippine army had a long tradition of respect for civilian dominance and constitutional authority. The triumph of William Howard Taft over General Arthur MacArthur was clearly understood by several generations of Filipino officers, many of whom gained combat experience with the Americans during World War II or were trained by at West Point, at Annapolis, or in officer training programs for foreigners at bases like Fort Leavenworth.

Marcos dramatically expanded the army's role in society, tripling its size. The command structure was given opportunites to acquire great wealth, offered a chance to participate in deals at local and national levels and to acquire stock. Inflating the size of the army, however, did not improve its combat efficiency; just the opposite occurred. As the NPA was growing and spreading its challenge over more and more of the archipelago, the Philippine military was becoming less and less combat efficient and more and more corrupt. The brutality of the army helped to radicalize many Filipinos in the provinces. Although the army required ever-increasing supplies and munitions, the opportunities for corruption multiplied proportionally, so that the needed equipment and material simply did not get out to the combat zone quickly.

Marcos placed his most trusted supporters and friends in positions of high power, promoting a cousin and former bodyguard, Fabian Ver, to the highest command. In exchange for personal fealty and acceptance of martial law, the army was freed from many of the constraints of a civilized society, even one engaged in fighting the insurgency of the NPA and the Muslims. Amnesty International and other human rights groups, including those within the church, condemned the state-supported torture, murder, and eradication. The term *salvage* euphemistically described the behavior of an army unit moving into an area of suspected NPA activity. Usually the military acted like a marauding band, wreaking human suffering and misery. The NPA welcomed recruits prodded into radical action by such brutality.

ECONOMIC GROWTH AND DECLINE

When Marcos was first elected president in 1965, the Philippines had a high literacy rate and a large percentage of citizens fluent in English, two characteristics of a culture that put a high premium on education as a vehicle of upward social mobility and status and an economy that remained closely tied to the U.S. market. There were obvious distortions, including too heavy a reliance on export commodities, a gross inequity of the distribution of wealth, a growing population that threatened to outstrip economic development, and obligations in health, education, and welfare that limited the funds available for infrastructure development. The issues of land reform remained unresolved, for the landlords controlled the political process. It was not clear how an entrenched elite would peacefully surrender the source of its power.

There were also serious impediments from foreign business interests. Chinese merchants had a disproportionate control over retail and wholesale marketing and distribution. The Philippines continued to export surplus capital to Hong Kong, Singapore, and the mainland. U.S. businesses, especially giant multinationals, held a stranglehold on key sectors of the economy. Companies like Procter & Gamble, CalTex, IT&T, and Del Monte inhibited local entrepreneurs and controlled both domestic and international markets. The Bank of America, First National City Bank of New York, Manufacturers Hanover, and a substantial cluster of British and U.S. banks were deeply entrenched. By 1963 the Japanese, having reentered the Philippine market through war reparations, had established important trading and export relationships that were to increase substantially over the next twenty years. In mining, timber, and other raw material exports, the Japanese were establishing the Greater East Asia Coprosperity Sphere by peaceful means.

And yet these were the realities of the other newly independent nations of Southeast Asia—Thailand, Indonesia, and Malaysia. All of these nations had to deal with the inflationary pressures of the Vietnam War and, with the exception of Indonesia, the oil shocks of 1973 and 1979. All were scrambling to reorder their economies to be less dependent on industrial imports and raw material exports. All were looking for a growth rate that would meet the rising expectations of the people for material goods and the capital formation needs for infrastructure development. The Philippines entered this era ahead of its neighbors; it ended the Marcos years virtually bankrupt, with a negative growth rate and a chaotic economy.

Marcos declared martial law claiming that the society needed this governmental discipline in order to prosper. Railing against the torpor and corruption of the old order, he presented himself as a viable reformer, someone who could get the economic engine to race. And during the period of 1973 to 1978 he had some success. In his first year, the GNP grew by 10 percent, and there was a surplus in the budget. Marcos had turned to a group of technocrats, many with sophisticated training and experience, to help lead this economic crusade. Even though Marcos was already deeply involved in a longstanding pattern of corruption, his government averaged just under 7 percent per year real growth in GNP from 1972 to 1979. Perhaps even more important, population growth rates came down under 3 percent so that the individual Filipino benefited from the growth of the economy.

During these same years agricultural production exceeded that of Indonesia, Malaysia, and Thailand. Assisted by U.S. and Japanese experts, government technocrats focused on agriculture, especially on the Green Revolution. Irrigation, electrification, fertilizer supplies, and storage facilities were given special emphasis. The Masagana-99 program of 1972, which declared all tenants to be owners of the rice and corn lands they worked (provided that the area of that land was not in excess of certain carefully proscribed limits), led to self-sufficiency in rice for the first time in seventy-five years. Imelda Marcos made the Nutrition Center in Manila a showcase, and the "nutribuses" and the "nutrinoodles" were part of her public relations effort.

Sugar and coconut landholdings, however, were excluded and the corruption that was to destroy the economy was already corroding these advances. The government had no safety net for those at the bottom. Both the Asian Development Bank and the Food and Agricultural Organization (FAO) of the United Nations focused on the daily caloric consumption of the population, which was some 270 calories below the worldwide minimum requirement of 2,210 calories set by the World Bank. As 40 percent of the rural population slipped below the official poverty line of a $200 annual income, an increasing percentage of school children suffered from protein and caloric deficiencies. During the same period from 1972 to 1978, unskilled laborers' real wages declined 30.6 percent and real wages for skilled labor in Manila dropped 23.8 percent. Structural underemployment meant that many Filipinos were dependent on those few members of their families who held regular jobs.

The disparity between rich and poor, so long evident in Philippine society, widened dramatically after 1979. Marcos, secure in his power and position, turned his back on the technocrats to reward the loyalty of his friends and cronies. In his early years, he had been ably served by Rafael Salas and thereafter by Alejandro Melchor as executive secretary. Such men were replaced by what U.S. Congressman Stephen Solarz described as a "kleptocracy." Marcos gave key friends access to sugar and coconut wealth. He permitted the emergence of monopolies that were economically inefficient and ruinous to the small producer. He, his wife, her family, and the circle around them restructured the economy so that no business deal or major transaction took place without their taking a piece of the action. The published official tax payments of the wealthy had no relationship to reality. During the 1970s the president's salary was, in dollar terms, approximately $13,000 a year. By the end of the Marcos era, he had amassed $10 billion.

In the redistribution of wealth he broke the power of former rivals. He removed established management and turned over vast empires to those personally loyal to him. Imelda Marcos's family, the Romualdezes, gained control of scores of major banks, trading companies, and manufacturing opportunities. Eduardo Cojuangco (the estranged first cousin of Corazon Aquino) and Juan Ponce Enrile were given virtually total control over the giant coconut industry. Herminio Disini, a cousin-in-law of Imelda Marcos, built a fortune on tobacco and received huge sums to salvage his company when he ran into trouble. Dewey Dee, a Chinese textile tycoon, eventually had to flee the country, leaving behind $83 million in debts; the resulting run on the banks forced the Central Bank of the Philippines to provide support to the twenty-eight banks and insurance companies that had to absorb the loss. One billion pesos was pledged to bail out the Construction and Development Corporation of the Philippines (CDCP), which had debts estimated at more than $1 billion and was controlled by Marcos's close friend Rudolfo Cuenca.

The list of scandals, bailouts, excessive profits, misplaced construction, and vanity schemes of Imelda Marcos increasingly weakened not only the government's capacity to plan and execute a coherent strategy, but also its creditworthiness. After the 1979 increase in oil prices, other global commodity markets were highly unstable. The worldwide economic recession led to a collapse of Philippine sugar and copra prices and a drop in demand for copper exports. High interest rates also forced up the cost of the national debt. Marcos, trying to spend his way out of recession, funded the deficit by printing money, ballooning a huge external foreign debt.

Some of this debt was offset by remittances from a Filipino diaspora, working on contract in construction and development projects elsewhere in the world. Much more came from nurses and professionals trained in Filipino universities who had left the nation to market their modern skills elsewhere. During the Marcos era, over 300,000 Filipinos emigrated from the Philippines to the United States; Filipinos became the second-largest Asian-American group. The maids at Heathrow Airport in London and the nannies of Hong Kong, the anesthesiologists of the United States and the jazz bands of Asia are all part of the more than 1.5 million Filipinos in diaspora.

Money as well as people drained away from the archipelago, exacerbating domestic problems. Foreign entrepreneurs, Chinese merchants, Filipinos of old or new wealth sent their capital abroad both legally and illegally in order to protect against inflation, economic collapse, a run on the peso. In June of 1983, the peso was devalued by a third to a rate of eleven pesos to the dollar, and the exchange rate eventually fell to twenty to the dollar. The flight of capital was led by the Marcos family, which bought property around the world, including $300 million of New York City real estate alone.

The construction of a nuclear power plant by Westinghouse encapsulates the economic pandemonium that overtook the nation. To help offset the dependence on imported oil, in 1975 Marcos authorized construction of the plant that ultimately cost $2.3 billion. U.S. banks and the U.S. government, eager to participate in this international financing, scrambled to make money available. Westinghouse is alleged to have paid $17.5 million to Herminio Disini, who got Marcos to give the contract to Westinghouse; Marcos is accused of making $80 million in kickbacks. The plant, built at the base of a dormant volcano, lies near several earthquake fault lines and is just 60 miles from Manila. An international team of inspectors visiting the plant after Marcos's fall described it as unsafe, inoperable, and three times the price of a comparable plant Westinghouse built in South Korea at the same time. In 1983 the Philippines defaulted on principal repayments for its foreign loans and subsequently suspended all interest payments on the plant's $1.5 billion of foreign debts—interest payments that cost $350,000 a day. The Philippine government sued the individual banks, Westinghouse, and the Export-Import Bank of the United States for willingly entering into fraudulent contracts.

By the end of the Marcos era, the flight of brains and money, the loss of confidence in the man and the regime, the growing anxiety of international financial institutions, and the anger of the World Bank accelerated economic collapse. The Philippine nation was bankrupt. Inflation was rampant, funds were insufficient to service the debt, and the world monetary system was threatened by the collapse of the Philippine banking structure. The *Economist* predicted in 1985 that the "country's economy may now be locked into a decline that only radical change can keep from ending in complete disaster." During the last years of the Marcos era, the economy declined approximately 15 percent. To raise revenues the government was forced to try to sell, without much success, more than 150 government-owned corporations. When Marcos fled the country in February 1986, he left behind a country with a $27-billion debt. Fourteen sugar mills, built in Marcos's early heyday, were bankrupt and shut. Coconut mills stood empty, and cement plants, automobile factories, and textile mills were foreclosed by the government, which had further jeopardized itself by assuming their debt. Individual Filipinos were, of course, acutely affected: The number of families below the poverty line had grown from 50 percent to 60 percent.

In 1969 Marcos had said that "the new Filipinism represents the discipline and the ethic of independence. It seeks substance rather than the shadow of freedom. It develops independence beyond formality to reality." By 1985 Marcos had sold his nation's birthright for a mess of pottage.

NEW PLAYERS AND OLD

At the beginning of his second term of office, in 1969, Marcos had also noted, "There are those among us who will oppose—probably violently—these ideas. Let us hear them out. The democratic dialogue must be preserved. The clash of ideas is the glory and the safeguard of democracy." That rhetoric fell away after he proclaimed martial law, although Marcos had a sustaining belief that he always needed constitutional authority before he could act. This era was laced with the most involuted, complicated series of plebiscites, constitutional ratifications, emendations, and promulgations.

Following his declaration of martial law, Marcos moved politically to solidify his power by organizing village organizations and citizens' assemblies patterned on the wartime Japanese efforts to create a grassroots, authoritarian, mass party called the Kalibapi. Approximately 40,000 of these citizens' assemblies were hurriedly created to vote upon the 1973 constitution written by Marcos. The government claimed that over 95 percent of the people had ratified this new constitution, but it had made the failure to vote a felony, punishable by law. Even the Philippine Supreme Court, totally a creature of the Marcos presidency, ruled that the 1973 constitution had not been "validly ratified." But the Supreme Court dared not rule the plebiscite illegal, and the revised document went into effect.

Article 17 of that 1973 document, dealing with "transitory provisions" gave Marcos the legal right to remain in office beyond the expiration of his second term as duly elected president. Under the 1935 constitution, December 30, 1973, was to have been the end of Marcos's legal tenure, but Article 17 extended his rule indefinitely. Additional provisions in 1976 further confirmed his overriding power. In 1980 Marcos reversed his position and called for a new constitution, based loosely on the French model, in which the president would hold great power but rule through a prime minister. That new document gave the president powers virtually equal to those he had held since declaring martial law. Among other provisions, the president would be able to serve without limit of term but had to be at least fifty years old to run for office—effectively excluding Benigno Aquino, who was 48 in 1980, from running. This new constitution was hurriedly put to the nation in a plebiscite in April 1981 and passed.

In June 1981 Marcos called a presidential election, which opposition leaders decided to boycott because Aquino had been barred from running.

In that election, Marcos got what he wanted: almost 88 percent of the vote (in Ilocos Norte, his home, he won 100 percent). Nominally, Marcos was opposed by former Defense Minister Alejo Santos, but the most surprising aspect of the 1981 election was the 4 percent of the vote won by one of the fringe candidates, Bartolome Cabangbang, who ran on a platform advocating that the Philippines should become the fifty-first state of the United States. An association with the United States lent Cabangbang a hazy glow of appeal to people who began to remember the colonial era fondly, as martial law became their only political reality. Thus, the technical ending of martial law on January 17, 1981, had really changed nothing, as Marcos had restructured the law to suit his convenience and solidify his total control.

Sycophants and cronies became key players in the economy and in the government. Members of the traditional oligarchy were given an early, tacit choice either to support Marcos actively or to lose out both economically and politically. For example, the Lopez family, one of the richest, most powerful families in the archipelago, was systematically broken by Marcos for its failure to support him. One of the Lopez brothers had been Marcos's vice-president, and the family had owned the Manila *Chronicle*, the Manila Electric Company, and innumerable other properties. Most of these were expropriated, transferred in ownership to Marcos's cronies or run as dummy companies for the president's own profit.

These cronies became the new elite, replacing older money, living on a lavish scale, and servicing an economy that was increasingly devoted to funneling its surplus to the first family. The maze of transactions and deals reached across the economy and included the most venerated companies in the land, including the beer and soft-drink conglomerate San Miguel, the very symbol of corporate Philippines. Billions of pesos were transferred from an older elite to the new rich, who continue to live in great splendor in Forbes Park and mingle with the older families at the polo club.

This reshaping of the social scene not only made students and peasants radical, but also prompted reaction from the old oligarchy, especially the church. The church has remained the most powerful institution in the society, as Marcos ultimately discovered. A complex, multitiered bureaucratic organization, the church was driven toward open opposition by the excesses of the Marcos era. Parish priests, nuns, and lay people saw the atrocities, witnessed the plundering of the countryside, and became the rallying point for opposition. The local priest or bishop could and did intervene to mitigate the harshness of the government, at least from time to time, and the church, politically passive at first and militant later, bore witness. The National Secretariat for Social Action and the association of major religious superiors increasingly spoke out. The archbishop of Manila, Jaime Cardinal Sin, abandoned "critical collaboration" to become a vocal critic Marcos could neither stifle nor exile (see Chapter 5).

As the church moved against Marcos, so too did the oligarchy of the old order. Marcos himself in part brought this on; he felt so secure by the early 1980s that he tolerated a level of dissent he would not have permitted to exist in 1973. Former Senators Lorenzo Tañada, Francisco Rodrigo, Gerardo Roxas, Eva Estrada Kalaw, Jose B. Laurel, Jr., and Jose Diokno became a core group of opponents. They founded a loose umbrella organization, the United Democratic Opposition (UNIDO), under the leadership of Benigno Aquino. Former President Diosdado Macapagal was a frequent critic, although Macapagal lacked any real influence. Raul Manglapus, Ramon Magsaysay's foreign minister and a leader of the constitutional convention of 1972, happened to leave the Philippines the day before martial law was declared. He spent ten lonely years in Washington and elsewhere in the United States attacking Marcos, trying to counter his and Imelda Marcos's public relations blitz on the United States. There was a more shadowy opposition as well, secretly linked to the power elite. The April Six Liberation Movement, for example, resorted to terror and clandestine violence, bombing hotels and international meetings.

At the very epicenter of opposition to Marcos was the one man Marcos feared most, Benigno Aquino. It was Aquino who had been presumed to be the next president of the Philippines had Marcos agreed to yield power peacefully in 1973. It was Aquino who was the first to be arrested by the police when martial law was declared. It was Aquino who was charged in a trumped-up murder case, tried, convicted by a military court, and sentenced to death. He was held by Marcos, often in solitary confinement, for the next seven years—a man too powerful for Marcos to kill, but too dangerous to let go free. It was Aquino in life and then in death who was the symbol of a post-Marcos Philippines.

The last issue of the *Philippines Free Press*, then the leading opinion magazine, carried a prophetic cover bearing the picture of Senator Aquino, standing in the Philippine Senate, targeted through the crosshairs of a riflesight and with the caption, "Senator Benigno S. Aquino: Target?" The date of that issue, never released because of martial law, was September 30, 1972.

Benigno S. Aquino, Jr., was born on November 27, 1932, the son of a prominent prewar politician. During the Japanese occupation his father was hungry for the presidency and angry that the job went instead to Jose B. Laurel. The elder Aquino's early pro-Japanese statements and enthusiasm for collaborating both limited his postwar rehabilitation—

Benigno Aquino and Lorenzo Tañada. (Courtesy of the author)

he died on December 21, 1947, still facing charges in front of the People's Court—and substantially influenced the way his son would respond to greater duress when Marcos had him imprisoned. The war years were thus both formative and traumatic for Benigno Aquino. The years following liberation and his father's death left the adolescent Aquino confronting unresolved issues of identity. The young Benigno (usually called by his nickname, Ninoy) was reared by his mother, Aurora, who played a powerful role in her son's life.

Unlike Marcos, whose grades at the University of the Philippines were superb, young Benigno was bored with school, often cutting classes to work as a cub reporter at the *Manila Times*. Seeking adventure, he volunteered as a correspondent early in 1950, when the Korean War broke out. He was at the battlefront while he was just eighteen. He came back to the university a celebrity but never took learning seriously until he was forced to spend long years in solitary confinement, where he became an avid reader.

He continued as a journalist, traveling across Southeast Asia and filing stories in 1952, and then he became part of the cadre of young Filipinos surrounding President Magsaysay. It was during these years that he met with Luis Taruc, Edward Lansdale, and others. His home and the Aquino power base was in the very stronghold of the Huks, and in later years it was often whispered privately that Aquino was very close to the CIA.

At twenty-one, he married Maria Corazon Cojuangco, a daughter of one of the wealthiest mestizo families with investments in sugar, real estate, banking, and a vast array of other projects. Corazon's cousin, Eduardo Cojuangco, known as "Danding," sided with Marcos and became the crony of cronies, growing stupendously rich. His alliance with Marcos created a family schism that remains to this day. Through his marriage, Benigno Aquino gained access to the power that the Cojuangco wealth automatically generated. He and his wife became the owners of Hacienda Lusita, a vast sugar plantation. At the young age of twenty-two he had already been elected local mayor, the youngest in the islands. In 1957 he became the youngest vice-governor in the country; two years later, at the age of thirty-two, he became senator, again the youngest. From his power base in Tarlac, he became a politician on the make. Like many other regional political leaders, he maintained a private army and arsenal. Although he used modern computers and communications, he also functioned in a classic pattern of patron-client politics. Charismatic, often a compulsive talker, ambitious, shrewd, and suddenly wealthy, Benigno Aquino was, like Ferdinand Marcos, a creature of the old order. Both he and Marcos had belonged to the same fraternity at the University of the Philippines.

But something extraordinary happened during the seven years of confinement and incarceration after martial law. First, Aquino refused to accept the legitimacy of the military courts that tried and convicted him of murder, in effect directly challenging the legitimacy of Marcos and the martial law decree. He refused to respond to duress or entreaty, to accept a pardon and a chance to live at peace with his family. Facing death, confined in very difficult circumstances, and trapped in an environment where Marcos made him a nonperson over the long years of incarceration, he listened to music continuously, read the Encyclopedia Britannica from one end of the alphabet to the other, and devoured books of all sorts. He wrote poetry, for himself and for his wife, one of the few people permitted to see him:

> I am burning the candle of my life
> in the dark with no one to benefit
> from its light.
>
> The candle slowly melts away
> soon its wick will be burned out,
> and the light is gone!
>
> If someone will only gather
> the melted wax,
> reshape it, give it a new wick—

for another fleeting moment
my candle can once again
light the dark
be of service
one more time
and then . . .
goodbye

He became a mature, thinking human being, far more sensitive, far more aware than the brash young politician arrested that first day of martial law. Some people facing adversity are broken by it; others remain more or less the same when the experience is past; Aquino grew in stature.

Having visited his own Gethsemane, he became politically active from jail. In 1978 he ran against Imelda Marcos to be a representative to the Interim National Assembly and would have won by a landslide had the election not been marred by massive fraud.

It was clear that the Marcoses did not know quite what to do with him. They dared not kill him in front of a firing squad for risk of martyring him, and they dared not release him. For some years Corazon Aquino had been attempting to work out a deal by which her husband would go abroad into exile. When doctors reported that he needed a coronary by-pass operation—a diagnosis never fully verified—the Marcoses, especially Imelda, saw exile as the easiest solution. This had been the period when Marcos felt so secure that he permitted opposition news to be printed and broadcast even on Radio Veritas, a station run by the Roman Catholic church. The United States was prepared to accept Aquino, a surgical procedure took place in Dallas, and Aquino settled with his wife and family in a house across the street from Boston College. During those years he studied first at Harvard, then at MIT, and became the center of an interlocking coalition of opponents to Marcos. Running his own political party, Laban (Fight), his home became the center of an obligatory pilgrimage for Filipino dissenters. Later, his wife recalled those Boston years as the happiest in their lives.

DISEASE AND DECAY

In August 1983 Benigno Aquino decided to return to Manila, despite warnings from Imelda Marcos and many others that at the minimum his freedom would be in jeopardy and at the maximum his life itself. He decided to return because Ferdinand Marcos was reported to be dying. It had been increasingly clear for some years that Marcos was suffering from a degenerative illness, lupus erythematosus, that had

Private bedroom of Ferdinand Marcos, Malacañan. (Courtesy of the Museo ng Malacañang Foundation)

attacked his kidneys. Marcos was on dialysis, had kidney failure, and had undergone several kidney transplant operations. Aquino sensed a political opportunity that could not be allowed to pass. Years earlier he had written that "if I have continued this lonely struggle when I had the choice to enjoy my freedom in peace and quiet, it is because I believe that the foundation of democracy is the sense of spiritual independence which nerves the individual to stand against the powers of the world." Having spent these years in exile, he decided, in his own words, "the things that I should not do—that is to submit to dictatorship and to defeat because one is truly defeated only when one accepts it."

The body politic was as sick as its president. Endemic army abuse, a new proliferation of warlordism, rampant corruption, and the collapse of the economy not only gave extraordinary opportunity to the New People's Army and its front organizations but also frightened many in the middle and upper-middle classes. Watching the jockeying for power in the palace became a national obsession. Imelda Marcos, at the center of this palace intrigue, behaved as if she were a Manchu empress. Secretary of Defense Juan Ponce Enrile, among others, lost out to Marcos's cousin and most faithful supporter, General Fabian Ver. The technocratic leadership, including Prime Minister Cesar Verata, was powerless. The oil crises of 1973 and 1979, the collapse of world commodity prices—especially for those export items on which the Philippine economy was so dependent—and a growing tendency of the elite to send capital abroad doubled the nation's foreign debt between 1979 and 1983. Inflation was rampant, and none of those around the president seemed to have either the strength or leadership capacity to steady the ship of state.

The Marcos regime tried to keep Aquino from returning. It even threatened Japan Airlines with a loss of landing rights in Manila if it were to book him a seat. Despite Aquino's efforts to travel incognito, Marcos's security forces and Aquino's supporters both anticipated his return on China Airways. Radio Veritas, the Catholic station that Marcos inexplicably had allowed to broadcast freely, covered the return, and the American song "Tie a Yellow Ribbon Round the Old Oak Tree" became the theme of Aquino's supporters. Aquino himself understood the risks. He anticipated being arrested again and thrown into jail, as his death sentence had never been lifted. He wore a bullet-proof vest.

The security forces boarded the plane to "escort" him. They were his firing squad. On August 21, 1983, Aquino was shot in the back of the head within seconds of leaving the aircraft. He fell dead on the tarmac at the bottom of the stairs.

In the speech he was prepared to deliver at the airport, Benigno Aquino had written that "the willing sacrifice of the innocent is the most powerful answer to insolent tyranny that has yet been conceived by God or man." His martyrdom altered the history of the Philippines. During the next days his death galvanized the nation and dominated the world's attention. The Philippine government claimed that he had been assassinated by a lone radical who had, in turn, been gunned down by Filipino security. The body of Rolando Galman, a petty criminal and thug, had been thrown from a waiting van and shot immediately. No one, however, accepted the government's story.

The still unanswered question is who ordered the assassination? Marcos himself had held Aquino in prison under a death threat for years. Even after he permitted him to leave for exile in the United States, he had both the opportunity and the money, if he wished, to plot an assassination in Boston. Aquino traveled without security, driving his own Volkswagen. Why would Marcos wait almost a decade until Aquino returned to his native land, with a plane full of reporters and an audience of 10,000 supporters, to martyr his opposition? Moreover, Marcos's body was rejecting a kidney transplant. He was ill, bedridden, and in jeopardy of dying himself.

The two who had the most to lose from Aquino's return were General Ver and Imelda Marcos. If they, too, foresaw Ferdinand Marcos's death, Aquino was the one opposition leader capable of challenging their accession to power. The military conspiracy clearly required the direct intervention of the most senior officers. The Metropolitan Command (Metrocom) and the Aviation Security Command (Avsecom) were not units likely to function on their own. What is still unknown is whether Imelda Marcos or Ver alone, or Imelda Marcos and the president had ordered the assassination. It was rumored that on the morning of the murder, she walked into his room where he was on dialysis and asked if he had heard. He is reported to have thrown a glass of water at the first lady.

Benigno's widow flew home the next day to bury him. This woman showed transcendent grace and extraordinary dignity, putting the nation's need to mourn ahead of her own. The widow's instinct is to close the coffin, bury the dead, and retire to seclusion. Instead, Cory, as she was universally called, authorized the coffin to remain open and travel from place to place, permitting an extraordinary outpouring of grief from the people. Millions participated before Aquino was buried. The rituals of death and the symbolic emergence of the color yellow generated the deep structural underpinnings for a revitalized opposition. "*Bayan Ko,*" originally written in 1928 as a nationalist anthem against U.S. colonialism, became a song of defiance and of hope. Its final lines, in translation, are:

> Philippines! My heart's sole burning fire
> Cradle of my tears, my misery . . .
> All that I desire:
> To see you rise, forever free.

Long before Corazon Aquino had any thoughts of involving herself in politics, she merged her grief with the nation's in such a way that the pantheon of Filipino heroes would henceforth include Benigno Aquino alongside Jose Rizal.

Marcos himself, seriously ill, would drop from sight only to reappear seemingly well again. His remarkable physical stamina permitted him to live until September 28, 1989, even though virtually all his vital organs, including heart, kidneys, and liver, had failed. General Ver was under a dark political cloud, although it was obvious that the president relied on him and on the army more and more. Others fluttered like moths around a flickering lamp. Meanwhile, the traditional opposition was attempting to regroup following Aquino's assassination. New groups—businesspeople, upper-middle-class men and women, and others traditionally not motivated to demonstrate—took to the streets.

In February 1984 Marcos called elections for the national assembly, the Batasang Pambansa. The moderate opposition divided between those who advocated an electoral boycott and those who urged participation. Aquino's brother, Agapito (Butz), advocated boycott while his widow and Salvador Laurel strongly supported participation. The burgeoning of NAMFREL; the outspoken activism of the Roman Catholic church, which urged participation; and the emergence of Corazon Aquino altered the outcome so that despite Marcos's political leverage and financial muscle he suffered a substantial defeat. Approximately one-third of the new legislature belonged to the opposition, and, had the vote been fair, it would have won a majority.

Marcos recovered his health sufficiently to reassert control far more completely than even he would have dreamed possible. But politically it was too late. Under extraordinary domestic and foreign pressure, in October 1983 he appointed a commission of inquiry ostensibly to search out who shot Aquino. This commission, chaired by Judge Corazon J. Agrava, issued a report that discounted the army's story, claiming instead a conspiracy of army and air force officers, including General Ver. Marcos was forced to suspend Ver. He organized a sham trial before a special court, the Sandiganbayan, normally a minor administrative court. Ver and the others were exonerated.

This travesty of justice enraged millions of Filipinos and agitated the U.S. government, which saw its security interests endangered by the instability in Manila. Moreover, the world press and the outspoken, sustaining efforts of Stephen Solarz and others in the U.S. Congress renewed the debate over the United States' ideological commitment to democracy. Although President Ronald Reagan remained a friend of the Marcoses, the U.S. government was finally shifting away from its pro-Marcos position. Admiral William Crowe, the commander of the Pacific area, saw Marcos as a threat to retention of U.S. military bases; Congressman Solarz saw him as a threat to the very integrity of the United States.

Twice during this period, Reagan sent his close friend and confidant Senator Paul Laxalt as his personal emissary to Marcos. Marcos decided to call a snap election to restore his mandate. On a U.S. television interview, transmitted via satellite on November 3, 1985, he announced the election, assuming in error that the opposition could not find a unity candidate and that his control of every aspect of governmental power would permit him to rig the results no matter how vocal his critics might be at home or abroad. The world media, especially Japanese and U.S. television, would not let go of the story. Marcos found himself in a difficult bind. Although he had the option to try to reassert censorship, expel foreign journalists, and control information, he rejected this approach in favor of a strategy he believed could recapture White House support.

As soon as General Ver was cleared of the conspiracy charge in the death of Aquino, Marcos restored him to his position of chief of staff of the Philippine armed forces. Almost immediately thereafter, Corazon Aquino announced that she would run for president against Marcos. Many in the opposition rallied to her, but Salvador (Doy) Laurel, one of the sons of Jose Laurel and the opposition leader with the broadest political organization in the country, also announced for president. Had both run, Marcos probably would have been reelected.

After intense negotiations, Jaime Cardinal Sin intervened directly to create a fusion ticket of both candidates (see Chapter 5). Pastoral letters were read from every church in the country, Radio Veritas became an alternate source for news, and thousands of priests, nuns, and lay leaders were mobilized in a struggle couched in moral terms. Corazon Aquino had a remarkable, intuitive sense of politics. She used yellow and a special hand sign in which a thumb and forefinger formed the shape of the letter **L** for her party (Laban), to give millions of people still afraid of the power of Marcos a means to show protest. During the election campaign that followed, the country was swept by a frenzy of rallies. Jeepneys and private cars would sound their horns in rhythmic beat to match the chant "COR-Y, COR-Y, COR-Y." Lacking access to advertising space, functioning with insufficient income, unable to gain television air time, these simple, almost primal political tactics excited the nation. Sections of telephone directories disappeared as millions of yellow pages were shredded to be dropped out of windows during political parades and rallies.

The emergence of this new political force left the Communist party of the Philippines and its fellow traveling front organizations, especially Bayan, nonplused. After intense debate the radical left decided to wait out this election, assuming that Marcos would beat Aquino through corruption and that the resultant cynicism and despair in a postelection era would make it possible for the Communists to advance dramatically. In addition to a political boycott, the NPA ceased most military activities, leaving to the moderate opposition the chance to challenge Marcos.

NAMFREL became the vehicle for middle-class participation. Closely linked to the clergy and the nuns, this secular organization was devoted to free and fair elections. It organized over half a million volunteers to serve at the precinct and provincial capital offices where the official electoral count would take place. They used computers to help assure that a "quick count" could be taken before Marcos and his political organization, the KBL (Kilusang Bagong Lipunan, or the New Society), could perpetuate fraud. Two international observer teams, and over 700

Protecting the ballot box, February 1986. (Courtesy of Tom Gralish and *The Philadelphia Inquirer*)

members of the world press swarmed across the archipelago in the days before the vote.

The level of corruption on election day was stupendous. Where it was possible, the fraud was at the retail level—ballot boxes snatched, fraudulent tally sheets inserted, voting rolls filled with both the living and the dead, and individuals voting early and often. The massive fraud, however, was at the wholesale level, where literally millions of people were moved off voting rolls and denied the franchise. Marcos's operatives had gone across the country putting up posters endorsing Marcos and his slate on the walls of the homes of suspected Aquino supporters. Postal carriers went around a few days later to see which homes had pulled the Marcos posters off their walls. Assuming these people to be Aquino supporters, they deleted their names from the voting rosters. On election day there was a shift from an alphabetical roll to a ward precinct list so that millions of Aquino voters were no longer registered. Despite the efforts of NAMFREL volunteers, including people who literally chained themselves to the ballot boxes during the transfer to the centralized counting sites, the Marcos government claimed a victory. Hundreds of millions of pesos, some with the identical serial number, flooded the countryside as traditional vote-buying took place. The level of corruption was so acute and the moral outrage so high that thirty computer operators at the central Manila Commission on Elections fled their machines, taking refuge at a local church. Both Marcos and Aquino claimed victory.

In the tense days that followed, Aquino announced a strategy of noncooperation, one which refused to accept the very tardy results of the official count. Aquino, claiming to the world press and to the nation that she had a true mandate from the people, was gambling that the momentum in her favor would eventually topple the Marcoses.

A military schism had been building for some years. The intrique at Malacañan, Ver's role in the Benigno Aquino assassination, and the growing sense within certain segments of the military that the corruption was destroying the very fiber of the state prompted a group of middle-level officers to organize the Reform the Armed Forces Movement (RAM). They were scheming to launch a coup of their own when Ver moved to arrest the dissident officers. This, in turn, forced Enrile, their political leader, to open rebellion. Fleeing to Camp Aguinaldo, he appealed to General Ramos, a West Point–trained officer probably not actively involved in the plot, to join him.

On February 22, 1986, Minister of Defense Enrile and the vice-chief of staff of the armed forces, General Ramos, seized the two main military installations in Manila, Camps Aguinaldo and Crame. Enrile, in jeopardy of being destroyed by forces loyal to Marcos, acknowledged massive cheating in the elections and actively sought the help of U.S. Ambassador Stephen Bosworth and Jaime Cardinal Sin. Enrile soon realized that he must endorse Aquino if he had any hope of surviving. Sin went on the radio, calling for the people to gather on the highway that divided the two military camps to protect Enrile and Ramos from Ver's troops.

The cardinal spoke; the faithful responded. The power of the people brought throngs to the potential battle scene. Although Aquino was not a central player during this uprising—she was correctly uncertain that these army officers would support her at all—her moral force was translated by Sin into a new power equation, one that altered profoundly the outcome of the struggle between Marcos and Aquino. Leaving the camp for the first time, General Ramos spoke of the revolution of the people, a revolt that became known as the Edsa revolution, taking its name from the abbreviation for Epifanio de los Santos Avenue, the street the people had blocked.

During these critical days, Ver sought permission from Marcos to crush the rebels. He understood that this military challenge at Camps Aquinaldo and Crame would have to be put down immediately if the Marcos government was to survive. Marcos, however, was tired, befud-

Juan Ponce Enrile (center, wearing glasses) and Gregorio ("Gringo") Honasan (carrying radio), February 1986. (Courtesy of Tom Gralish and *The Philadelphia Inquirer*)

dled, and ill. He lacked the will for decisive action. Marcos's tanks, which had been brought into position, waited rather than attacked. The tens of thousands of people summoned into the streets by Cardinal Sin physically interposed between the two military sides. Nuns and seminarians kneeled by the tanks to pray; citizens put flowers in the gun turrets. And all of this was covered exhaustively by the world media.

By February 24, other units began to defect, and rumors spread that Marcos had fled the nation. One of the government television stations was seized, and rebel helicopters attacked Malacañan. That afternoon Enrile declared the formation of a provisional government with Aquino as president. Aquino, returning to Manila, visited the military camps where she and thousands sang "Ave Maria."

On February 25, Aquino and Laurel were sworn in as president and vice-president by Supreme Court Justice Claudio Teehankee; an hour later, Marcos also took his oath as president. But with the active intervention of Ambassador Bosworth and strong pressure from Washington, Marcos, his family, and key loyalists, including General Ver, fled first to Clark and then to Hawaii. The nation and the world erupted into a celebration of what seemed to be the triumph of good over evil, of decency over corruption. Malacañan was looted as a euphoric nation celebrated this virtually bloodless coup. An all-powerful dictator had been overthrown by people power. During those remarkable three weeks in February 1986, the unfolding drama seemed part television sitcom, part *Picture of Dorian Gray,* part *Macbeth,* and large part passion play.

8

The Age of Aquino

A new era seemed to begin when President Aquino was inaugurated on February 25, 1986, as the Marcoses took abrupt flight to Hawaii. The forces of good had triumphed over the forces of evil. The people had spoken by elevating both figuratively and literally the pious Corazon Aquino to the pinnacle of power. If this had been a myth, if it had been a fable told through literature, the story would have concluded "and they all lived happily ever after."

But history never allows the tale to stop, and the realities of poverty, of hunger, of social polarization, and of staggering debt did not go away with the Marcoses to Hawaii. The nation had been swept up to a fever pitch, believing that it had achieved something truly remarkable. The people had power; moral right vanquished physical might. The world watched and applauded, confirming for Filipinos that this was their nation's finest moment, that this was the point specific in history when insecurities and self-doubts must fall away and a more confident, secure nation appear. The glory of the Edsa revolution, projected nightly across the world by television satellite, created unreal expectations that this moment of euphoria would solve the deep, structural problems—in Marxist terms, the contradictions—of Philippine society.

Was what happened a revolution or a restoration or a reformation? Was a new age dawning or was the old order returning? Was this a conservative, technocratic victory or a radical revolution? Would the emergence of people power shatter elite domination? Would Corazon Aquino empower new sectors of the society or allow continuing oligarchic control? Was the age of Aquino to be part of a long continuity in Philippine history or a clear break with that which had gone before?

Amando Doronila, a prominent columnist and chairman of the editorial board of the Manila *Chronicle,* has described what happened as "an extremely limited and flawed revolution." To Doronila, the Aquino revolution was a "refeudalization" or a "retribalization" in which "the return to political warlordism or tribal politics dominated by the family

The final preelection Aquino rally, Manila, 1986. (Courtesy of Tom Gralish and *The Philadelphia Inquirer*)

dynasties foreshadows the reassertion of the oligarchic tendencies in Phillipine politics." He argued that the alliance formed to overthrow Marcos—one that brought together the rich, the middle class, and the poor—had to fall apart because it "had no ideological motivation to change the social and power structure; it merely sought to change rulers without restructuring society."

Father Joaquin Bernas, the president of Ateneo de Manila University, was less cynical or pessimistic, observing that the initial thrust of the Edsa revolution was a restoration of liberty and in those terms must be judged a success. Democracy was recovered, free and fair elections took place, habeas corpus was restored, the court regained its independence, and freedom of speech and the press were assured. But was it a revolution for equality as well? Was social justice also a consequence of Edsa?

President Aquino in 1987 stated that "the most serious challenge that faces us today [is]: can we have order without tyranny and peace without oppression?" To Corazon Aquino, the restoration of political democracy was her central task. Other tried unsuccessfully to get her to define people power as embracing a social revolution as well. Any evaluation of the Aquino period must ask these historiographical questions, as judgment can only be rendered in the context of expectations and capabilities.

THE FIRST BLUSH

Catapulted suddenly into power, Aquino lacked control over her government agencies and was uncertain about the loyalty of her military. Her vice-president, Salvador Laurel, was clearly a rival, someone whose loyalty was suspect. Her first task was the creation of a cabinet; the coalition she felt compelled to appoint revealed her vulnerability, despite the overwhelming, popular mandate she obviously held.

She named Juan Ponce Enrile secretary of defense and General Ramos chief of staff, even though she was warned the Enrile might lead a coup against her. These initial appointments blurred the break with the past. At the center of power were men who were obviously incompatible with other members of her cabinet. Despite his long association with Marcos, Ramos did give Aquino true allegiance, becoming a key defender of her fledgling government against dissident elements of the army. Enrile, on the other hand, was someone she could never trust, for good reason.

The most powerful positions in her government thus went to men on the right, especially Enrile and Laurel, who became both prime minister—a position that was a carry-over from the Marcos constitution—and foreign minister. To counterbalance these individuals, President Aquino turned to her late husband's associates, people she had known well before. Jaime Ongpin became finance minister. Jose Concepcion, a businessman and the co-chair of NAMFREL, became minister of trade and industry. Aquilino Pimentel, a long-time politician, was given the highly sensitive position of minister of local governments. Jovito Salonga, a former senator and Liberal party leader, became head of the Presidential Commission on Good Government, and Aquino appointed the distinguished but seriously ill former Senator Jose Diokno to head the Presidential Commission on Human Rights. Solita Monsod, a charismatic, chain-smoking economist from the University of the Philippines, became the minister for economic planning. Most important, Aquino named Joker Arroyo, who had long been active in the human rights movement and was her late husband's attorney, to the traditionally powerful position of executive secretary. Trusting Arroyo and distrusting Enrile, she created a cabinet that could never find cohesion.

Her dilemma was compounded by the politically bizarre reality that her claim to legitimacy was based on the 1973 Marcos constitution, under which the election had been held. The bureaucracy and the military had been the vehicles of authority for Ferdinand Marcos. Aquino was suddenly chief executive of a system responsible for her husband's death and the very chaos that led her to power.

On March 25 she issued Presidential Proclamation Number 3, which justified her governmental legitimacy on the Edsa revolt of February 22–25 rather than on the contested election with Marcos. Having claimed to derive authority from revolution, she next proclaimed an interim "freedom constitution," arrogating to herself powers rivaling those exercised by Marcos under martial law. Using this freedom constitution, she abolished Marcos's rubber-stamp legislative body and terminated Marcos-appointed judges, local officials, and senior bureaucrats. To restore democracy, she had to jettison the baggage of twenty years of Marcos's control. Marcos functionaries protested vigorously the assumption of these dictatorial powers.

On May 25 President Aquino created a constitutional commission and appointed its delegates, choosing almost exclusively people in the political center like herself. These forty-eight delegates were remarkably similar to those who gathered at Malolos almost a century before: They were educated, from the upper class, and predominantly lawyers. Many had direct or indirect links to the church hierarchy. And when they reported in October with a lengthy draft of a constitution (it was over 100 pages in its final version), they reaffirmed the traditional, elite verities that have been a hallmark of the Philippines since Rizal.

The constitution established a presidential form of government and returned to many features of the 1935 constitution, including a bicameral legislature. It reemphasized the rights of private property, confirmed a highly centralized governmental structure, and outlined a moderate-progressive vision of social justice, the importance of education, and a bill of rights. The document called for land reform and other measures of social redistribution of wealth but embedded these changes within the existing norms of the society. The draft reflected the world view of a well-heeled, well-educated elite. The ten new justices Aquino appointed to the Supreme Court were likewise people committed to protect those time-honored verities.

There are unique moments in history when it is possible to reorganize the social hierarchy and to redistribute power. William Howard Taft had such a chance at the turn of the century. Douglas MacArthur, as supreme allied commander in Japan, exercised that opportunity to alter in the most profound ways the fabric and structure of Japanese society. During the period when President Aquino had virtually limitless power under the freedom constitution, she had dramatic opportunity to address frontally the social contradictions and economic tensions of her nation. But President Aquino lacked omnipotence. She may have been immensely popular, yet she was constantly at risk of being overthrown in an army-led coup. Although people deified her, she herself felt hesitant and insecure. Some have argued that her personality and upbringing kept her from making any radical changes. Others claim that the army prevented it. Whatever the reason, a chance to redistribute wealth and address issues of social justice was lost. Whether this missed opportunity is of long-term consequence for the nation remains a question.

The Aquino government focused instead on the goals of reintroducing good government, restarting the economy, and restoring traditional political structures. It was deemed essential that Marcos and his cronies be purged, although this raised complicated legal and financial issues. Executive Order Number 1 created the Presidential Commission on Good Government. Executive Order Number 2 dealt with "the funds, moneys, assets, and properties illegally acquired or misappropriated by former President Ferdinand Marcos, Mrs. Imelda Romualdez Marcos, their close relatives, subordinates, business associates, dummies, agents, or nominees." The Presidential Commission on Good government went after the Marcos family and cronies, many of whom had fled to Hawaii with them, in order to regain any possible portion of the vast plunder taken from the Philippine people. The list of defendants included: Alfredo Romualdez, Fabian Ver, Ricardo Silverio, Herminio Disini, Rudolfo Cuenca, and Aquino's estranged and fabulously wealthy cousin, Eduardo Cojuangco. Others, like Manuel Elizalde, were allowed to return to the country provided they paid back to the treasury a solid portion of what they were believed to have stolen—although it is not clear how much money was ever repaid. The magnitude of these thefts, including the approximately $10 billion reportedly stolen by the Marcoses alone, was amazing, and the government understood that it needed these funds to help jump-start the stalled economy.

Equally pressed was the need to gain control of the governmental bureaucracy that Marcos had corrupted and manipulated. More than fourteen thousand local officials were made subject to replacement in the bureaucratic and political hierarchy, especially the operatives of Marcos's monolithic KBL party founded in 1978. Aquilino Pimentel replaced these with "officers in charge." Immediately, local, factional, traditional politics reappeared. Were the "officers in charge" constitutional? Under whose constitution? More important than these abrupt terminations was who would choose their successors. Vice-President Laurel wanted his Unido party to get the patronage; Pimentel wanted the Laban to gain these slots. This scramble for new local power and factional advantage was reminiscent of the 1945 struggle when Sergio Osmeña returned to the newly liberated archipelago. The business of politics was deadly serious; the impetus was restorative. Those people appointed usually had had fathers and grandfathers and great-grandfathers in similar positions in years past. The reestablishment of a pre-1972 local oligarchy made it clear that in upcoming elections the new Congress would look like the Congress Marcos had abolished with the declaration of martial law.

What made 1986 different from 1973 was the NPA insurgency. The new government saw an important tactical and strategic need to break the cycle of violence and counterinsurgency. Aquino's remarkable decency, her belief in the capacity of goodwill to transcend traditional enmity, and her faith in the capacity of all Filipinos to rally collectively led her to reach out to the NPA.

The government released about 500 political prisoners, including Jose Maria Sison, the founder of the CPP, and Bernabe Buscayno, also known as Commander Dante, who was the founder of the NPA. The president promised amnesty to the rebels and called on the NPA to enter promptly into peace talks with her government. Because the CPP had badly misjudged its own role leading to Marcos's fall, it was both divided and defensive about its policy options. The more moderate NPA leadership felt it had to accept Aquino's offer or risk losing thousands of cadres. In early June the NPA agreed to negotiate a cease-fire. Simultaneously, in Mindanao, the Moro National Liberation Front also accepted a temporary truce. These well-meaning efforts to resolve the conflicts of the society nearly destroyed the fledgling government.

THE POLITICIZED ARMY AND THE MILITARIZED PARTY

The tensions within the newly reestablished democratic government of Cory Aquino, a politicized army inherited from Marcos, and a militarized party of the CPP have shaped the complex history of the post-Marcos era. There are many places in the Third World that have witnessed struggles between a militarized party and a politicized army. The colossal struggle between the Kuomintang and the Communist Party of China was one. The yin and yang of the army of South Korea against the party of North Korea was another. The struggle in Indonesia before 1965 and the histories of Burma and Vietnam all suggest that this is a common, explosive contest of two institutional structures, each claiming the mantle of national leadership and the political-military power capable of imposing discipline on the society.

What is distinct in the Philippines situation is the third force, a democratically elected and widely supported government. The Aquino revolution has challenged if not China itself, then the veracity of Mao's dictum that power comes out of the barrel of a gun. Aquino's moral force and the potential of massive civil disobedience turned the linear equation of a struggle between the politicized army and the militarized party into a complex quadratic equation. The historical resolution is not yet clear. If an army pledges full loyalty to civilian authority, if it accepts that the national symbols properly belong to Aquino's government, then the reunited authority of her government stands a strong chance of triumphing over the NPA, provided it can also deal with the existing social and ethnic tensions. If, on the other hand, the army refuses to give full allegiance, threatening or succeeding in mounting a coup, the age of Aquino will have ended calamitously and the struggle between the politicized army and the militarized party will lead the nation into full-scale civil war.

As soon as the then-dominant moderate faction of the CPP agreed to a dialogue with the Aquino government—an agreement that also badly fractured the cohesion of the CPP—there was a sharp reaction from the military. The army, itself factionalized, saw the decision to release political prisoners and to proffer an olive branch as a colossal blunder.

The group loyal to Juan Ponce Enrile included many of the senior officers who waxed rich under Marcos. Aquino's decision to retire twenty-four of thirty-six "overstaying generals," to demote or reassign some fourteen others, and to send lower-ranking officers to "reorientation" courses threatened the existing power structure and prompted most to reaffirm their loyalty to Enrile, who was also vulnerable to inquiries into his wealth and activities during the Marcos years.

Fidel Ramos represented a second major faction; he was the man on whom President Aquino increasingly relied. His own position was problematic, however, both because of his own long association with the Marcos government and because he had been commander of the Philippine Constabulary rather than the regular army. Marcos had skillfully manipulated the tensions between the constabulary and the army, and the jurisdictional lines between these two military commands were blurred and contentious.

Yet a third group was the cadre of younger officers who had created RAM in 1983 after Benigno Aquino's assassination. RAM was led by graduates of the Philippine Military Academy and, in particular, by a group of officers from the class of 1971. These younger captains, majors, and colonels had a different but powerful relationship to Enrile. He had been their mentor in the last years of the Marcos era when Enrile had fallen from grace to be replaced by Fabian Ver. In 1985, at the graduation exercises of the Philippine Military Academy, officers held up signs calling on Marcos to reform the military. These radical younger officers, including Gregorio "Gringo" Honasan, were the most threatening to the fabric of the nation. They were the first generation of officers who had never held command in the pre–martial law era, when the army was

Juan Ponce Enrile and Fidel Ramos, February 1986. (Courtesy of Tom Gralish and *The Philadelphia Inquirer*)

smaller and accepted its subservience to civilian power. At the turn of the century Filipinos had learned a critical lesson from William Howard Taft when he successfully asserted his civilian control over Arthur MacArthur, the commander and chief of the American Expeditionary Forces to the Philippines. Thereafter, the Philippine military had adhered to the U.S. model. The class of 1971 represented a crucial historical break with that tradition. It came of age as the first beneficiaries of martial law.

The fragmented quality of the Philippine military command did not, however, destroy a broadly based consensus that the Aquino government was soft on Communists and hostile to the army. To the military, Aquino's appointments of "leftist" key advisers, including Joker Arroyo and Bobbit Sanchez, were disastrous appointments. The amnesty and release of political prisoners; the openly conciliatory approach to the social concerns of the insurgency; the appointment of a special Presidential Commission on Human Rights, under former Senator Jose Diokno, to explore the military's role in human rights violations; and the effort of the Aquino government to probe military graft and corruption all threatened the army's values, prestige, and power structure. Whoever ordered Benigno Aquino assassinated, it was the army that carried out the deed. Neither the military officiers nor Cory Aquino could forget this fact. Moreover, President Aquino refused to accept the army's new counterinsurgency plan, choosing instead to pursue a political solution by a cease-fire.

On July 6, 1986, Arturo Tolentino, a long-time politician who had run with Marcos as his vice-presidential candidate in 1985, temporarily seized the Manila Hotel, holding a swearing-in ceremony at which he declared himself acting vice-president and called on the people to accept him as their proper leader. Several hundred troops under the command of Brigadier Jaime Echeverria and Colonel Rolando Abadillo joined with Tolentino. After three days, this mock coup, more suitable to a Sigmund Romberg operetta than a real threat, ended peacefully. It seemed a farce (the troops captured were made to do push-ups and sent back to their barracks), but it revealed that Ramos was not completely in charge and that Enrile's role was enigmatic.

The focus of attention next turned to the negotiations with the National Democratic Front, which began in August. Aquino's goal was to coax the insurgents out of the hills into peaceful endeavors through a promise of land reform and amnesty. The Communist delegates to these peace talks, Antonio Zumel and Saturnino Ocampo, were moderates. But neither they nor the Aquino government could control the hard-liners on both sides. Fighting and killing continued. In November there was an agreed-upon cease-fire scheduled to begin on December 10. In the interim the army seized Rodolfo (Kumander Bilog) Salas, a hardliner whose capture threatened to scuttle the compromise. This was a time of assassination; in November the labor leader Rolando Olalia was murdered.

Enrile, by openly breaking with Arroyo, challenged the political legitimacy of President Aquino's government. The fragile consensus of the Aquino cabinet was shattered. Honasan was chief of security to Enrile; rumors of a RAM coup spread. The coup attempt, known as "God Save the Queen" because of the intention to keep Aquino as a figurehead while Enrile became prime minister, produced another crisis. On November 23 Aquino replaced Enrile with General Rafael Ileto, Enrile's former deputy and a former ambassador. The following day, a sixty-day cease-fire with the New People's Army was announced, and Aquino, in a concession to the military, accepted the resignations of four cabinet ministers, including Secretary of Labor Bobbit Sanchez, because they were viewed as soft on the insurgents.

The government appeared weak, Aquino out of control. On January 22, 1987, the Farmers' Movement of the Philippines led a march to Malacañan to present demands for land reform. As the demonstrators marched across the Mendiola Bridge, violence erupted; nineteen were killed and 100 wounded. Triggered either by the far left or the far right, the violence was meant to destroy the cease-fire and challenge a key constitutional plebiscite scheduled the following week. And a few days later air force colonel Oscar Canlas launched a coup effort by seizing a local television station. After a three-day standoff, the action was easily broken. Six officers and 136 soldiers were charged, but the troops again were permitted to keep their weapons. Meanwhile, in Hawaii, Ferdinand and Imelda Marcos attempted to charter a jet to return to the Philippines in open defiance of the terms by which they were granted refuge.

The plebiscite on the new constitution passed overwhelmingly, strengthening Aquino's hand, but the political pollsters also noted that there was much less support from military voters. At the major military bases in Manila, the negative vote against the Aquino constitution was as high as 85 percent; overall negative votes from military installations was about 40 percent.

This continuous pattern of military hostility against President Aquino worried her and the worldwide community of friends watching her efforts. Her army was not loyal; it had the power to topple her. And that reality pushed her toward the right. Aquino agreed to expand the charge to the Commission on Human Rights to include atrocities committed by the NPA as well as by the army. She became increasingly hawkish toward the NPA, saying that it was time "to take up the sword of war," and in the triangular relationship of army, party, and democratic government, it appeared as if the army would be the victor.

This shift to the right was accelerated by the deep divisions within the militarized party of the left. Although the Communist Party of the Philippines claimed to have 25,000 active guerrillas, to control 20 percent of the 42,000 villages, and to have a mass base of 1.7 to 2 million people, there was widespread erosion of loyalty as guerrillas and sympathizers alike turned to Aquino and away from army struggle. Under the six-month amnesty proclaimed by the government, hundreds of guerrillas chose to surrender. The CPP's mass base of support was in danger of crumbling. If Marcos had been the best recruiter the NPA had, Aquino's obvious humanity, idealism, and enthusiam reached directly to the people over a divided Central Committee and Politburo. The internal rectification debate led to savage infighting. The chairman of the CPP since 1977, Rodolfo Salas, was captured by the army because his whereabouts were probably leaked. The secretary general, Rafael Baylosis, lost out to Benito Tiamson and to Saturnino Ocampo, who was himself subsequently arrested with his deputy and wife, Carolina Malay-Ocampo, in late July 1989. In April 1990, Antonio Cabardo, another ranking communist, was caught at the Manila airport; clearly the leadership was unraveling.

The CPP hierarchy had been offstride ever since it had sat out the Aquino-Marcos election. In May 1985 Bayan (the New Patriotic Alliance) was formed as and umbrella organization for mass-based efforts. By 1986 it claimed a membership of over 2 million and created the Alliance for New Politics, or ANP, as its political vehicle. During the senatorial elections the ANP fielded a slate that included Horacio Morales, a former leader of the party; Jose Burgos, the publisher of the mass tabloid *Malaya;* and Bernabe Buscayno. When the elections took place, the ANP's candidates did very poorly.

Assassinations increased (among those murdered was the Bayan secretary general, Leandro Alejandro), and the Politburo imploded into an internecine struggle. Extremists resorted to assassinations by "sparrow" squads, one of which killed U.S. Colonel James Rowe, chief of the ground forces division of the Joint United States Military Assistance Group, in April 1989. Rowe was targeted because of his "direct participation" in counterinsurgency, according to the guerrilla commander Romulo Kintahar. This policy of direct attack on U.S. citizens and installations has been internally divisive, the Communists debating the wisdom of such an escalation of violence.

The local variations in this fluid time have led to a rebirth of regional warlords and the rise of vigilante groups. In Davao City, for example, the NPA was in virtual control in 1985. Since then the NPA has been all but eradicated, even though it once claimed that its power in Davao would be a springboard for conquering the entire country. Deep divisions and factionalism within the NPA led the local commander, Renato Anatalan, to kill thirty of his best soldiers. He, in turn, was shot by his own men. A group of Communists defected to form a self-defense force, assuming the name of Alsa Masa (the Aroused Masses), which, with the blessing of the army, gained control of Davao.

The success of this vigilante group led to a series of comparable movements throughout the country. Terror and intimidation were their key weapons. Like the Mafia in Sicily, these groups further complicated the tensions between party and army, between central government and local authority. Violence, long the scourge of Philippine life, and factional politics, long the bedrock of real power in the country, now had a new, more complicated environment in which to operate. The Alsa Masa movement brought both stability and instability to the country. President Aquino supported these vigilante movements, although the long-term consequences for the society are ominous.

The attempted coup launched on August 28, 1987, by Colonel Gregorio Honasan threatened civilian government. With several hundred rebel soldiers under his command, he attacked the presidential residence, the Manila air base, and a series of other key targets. For a brief period, General Ramos was uncertain which officers were loyal and which had gone over to follow this charismatic colonel. For a few days the entire cadet corps of the Philippine Military Academy threw its support to Honasan. Although the Presidential Guard repelled the attack on the palace and Ramos succeeded in defeating Honasan, fifty-three civilians and soldiers had died and many hundreds had been wounded. A thousand soldiers were captured or surrendered, although Honasan initially escaped. The government was clearly shaken by the scope and severity of this uprising. Aquino, whose son had been injured, lashed out at the "traitors and murderers of unarmed civilians."

Aquino's government survived the challenge but was weakened. Despite her angry rhetoric, the rebellion forced her to placate the military. On September 9, facing an intense crisis of confidence, she accepted the resignation of her entire cabinet. Most important, she eliminated three of her closest advisers, Joker Arroyo, Finance Secretary Jaime Ongpin, and her chief speech writer, Teodoro Locsin. These three had been among her most trusted confidants, and Ongpin had been a vital link to the world banking community. She also forced Salvador Laurel, her vice-president, to step down as foreign minister, although Laurel had never been close to Aquino or played an important role in her government.

The open threat of Honasan prompted the *New York Times* to speak of a "harsh test for Aquino." Honasan, eventually captured, became a major cult figure and escaped with the active collusion of naval officers. The army was also purged. In January, 1988 Secretary of National Defense Ileto stepped down and the president appointed Fidel Ramos to replace him. To the post of chief of staff, she nominated Renato De Villa. Twenty-one colonels were promoted to general and in May 1988 almost a third of the existing generals were retired. The soldiers received pay hikes of up to 60 percent. The government, by taking a continuing conciliatory policy toward the army thought it had bought peace from the RAM officers. For a time it appeared to have succeeded. In March 1988 Rafael Baylosis, the secretary general of the CPP, was arrested in a safe house in Manila. Seized were ninety-seven computer disks that revealed much about the Communist party's organization and about the ideological disputes that have racked the party over the past years. A breakthrough reminiscent of Ramon Magsaysay's success against the Huks thirty years earlier, these disks were an intelligence bonanza.

Corazon Aquino became much less tolerant of the excesses of left and right. In an address in December 1988 in observance of the fortieth anniversary of the adoption of the Universal Declaration of Human Rights by the United Nations, she said, "Respect for human rights is the core value of our bloodless revolution, the single most important reason for the survival of the democracy we installed." But she went on to acknowledge that there have been sporadic violations of those rights, adding that "we are only in the third year of regained democracy. The inhumanity of people obsessed by power or possessed by dogma, whether in the uniform of the regular army or in the casual wear of the insurgency, will be with us for some time yet." President Aquino pledged to win the war against the insurgency as "there will be no substitute for the permanent victory of democracy." And she pledged that she would "not accept the heat of battle as an excuse for brutality—toward the people we are pledged to protect and even toward our enemies." Finally, she stated that although "democracy needs force," she and her government would "not stoop to terrorism to survive."

For the next fifteen months, it appeared that the Aquino government had secured a tacit understanding with the cadre of disaffected army officers who looked to Gregorio Honasan for leadership and to military rebellion for access to power. Despite continuing gossip of plots and conspiracies, it seemed that Aquino had satisfied those officers by a series of concessions. She had not.

On December 1, 1989, yet another coup attempt was launched, this time involving over 3,000 rebel troops, many from the best-paid, elite units of the Philippine military, including the Scout Rangers. Before the coup was finally put down, over ninety-five people were killed and 580 wounded. The coup leaders seized or attacked the major military headquarters installations across Manila, gained access to two television stations, closed the commercial airport, and used Villamor Airbase in Manila to launch aerial attacks on the presidential palace. These attacks were well coordinated and clearly had the passive support of many other military units and officers, even though they themselves chose not to join the rebellion at that point. Army Chief of Staff DeVilla simply did not know which units were loyal to constitutional authority, and in the early hours of the rebellion, there was a clear risk that the rebels would win over their fellow officers.

There were hurried consultations with the U.S. Embassy and with President Bush, Vice-President Quayle, and the Pentagon. To help stabilize the military situation, the U.S. government ordered jet fighters from Clark Air Base to patrol the skies over Manila, forcing the rebels' World War II–vintage T-28 airplanes to stay grounded. This open show of U.S. military might tilted the balance, at least at the time, and sent a signal to those wavering officers that the United States was unequivocally committed to the preservation not only of the Aquino government but of constitutional democracy.

But if this unprecedented display altered the final outcome, it did not end the fighting. It took eight days to quash. In the meantime, the rebels released many military prisoners held from the earlier coups, including those soldiers tried and convicted for killing Benigno Aquino. In Cebu, 350 miles away, the Mactan Air Base was seized. A number of governors and politicians, including Governor Rodolfo Aguinaldo, a former colonel, spoke openly in support of the rebels. Although Colonel Honasan was not visibly in charge, everyone knew that he was at the epicenter of this coup attempt.

A few days earlier, Aquino's estranged cousin, Eduardo Cojuangco, had slipped back into the country. One of the Marcos's closest friends and cronies, he had fled with Marcos to Hawaii. He was widely rumored to have been a key player behind the scenes, along with Honasan's mentor, Juan Ponce Enrile. Money flowed freely. It was a cynical use of pesos and dollars to assure the involvement of those officers who were more interested in wealth than ideology. Vice-President Salvador Laurel was quoted from abroad as saying that the coup was a display of "democracy in its fullest and complete sense." He indicated that he was prepared to serve in a government controlled by the army, and it was widely assumed that there was a cluster of right-wing politicians who were either funding and directing Honasan or, at least, who were working in close collaboration with him and his fellow officers.

A few days into the coup, the rebels seized the modern commercial and residential sector of the city, Makati, trapping literally thousands of foreigners in luxury hotels and homes. They attacked the government at its most vulnerable point: its flabby economic underbelly. The government, unwilling to risk its banking and commercial hub and possible injury to powerful, highly visible foreigners, negotiated a settlement. The rebel troops returned to their barracks, singing regimental songs, carrying their weapons, making **T** hand signs to indicate that this was simply a time out in an ongoing struggle. They claimed they had won, not lost.

The dilemma for General DeVilla and President Aquino was to decide whether finally to crack down on the dissident officers at the risk of alienating others or to permit a charade of a crackdown, a pattern already established by the prior coups. The army chief, Major General Manuel Cacanando, did relieve from command fourteen officers, including Brigadier General Marcelo Blando, a division commander, and Colonel Cesar Elano, chief of army intelligence. But Colonel Honasan had again escaped, as had the rebel commander in Cebu, Brigadier General Jose Commendador. Of the fifteen officers known to have participated in the Makati attack, only four were captured. The five-member commission the president established to uncover the roots of the coup were judged unlikely ever to issue a final report.

The military, including those who had remained passive, closed ranks around the rebels. The government was portrayed in the media as a paper tiger, unable to gain control and discipline its own military. In the aftermath of the coup, there was an increase in terror. A hand grenade blew up in the central post office; it was impossible to tell who had placed it there: Aquino was being attacked vigorously from both the left and the right for calling upon U.S. military assistance. One of the members of the Central Committee of the CCP, Wilma Tiamzon, escaped from prison, perhaps released by the army to further embarrass Aquino.

In the first months of 1990 the government did attempt to crack down, with very mixed results. Captain Pacifico Avenido, who had been responsible for seizing the television station and who had been in hiding for over two years, was captured, as was the helicopter pilot who had "rescued" Honasan. But former Lieutenant Colonel Rolando (Billy) Bibit, who was already in jail, escaped easily, to the embarrassment of the government. When a military unit commanded by the popular Brigadier General Oscar Florendo went to the capital of Cagayan Province, Tuguegarao, to arrest the rebel governor, former Colonel Rodolfo Aguinaldo, he was killed by Aguinaldo's private army troops; Aguinaldo escaped. By April 1990, forty top officers were retired, including twenty generals.

Brigadier General Rodolfo Biazon, a key Aquino supporter in December, was promoted to Deputy Chief of Staff, but Honasan remained free, giving television interviews to CNN and other networks and clearly able to hide behind a wall of protection from his former military colleagues.

On February 27, 1990, the government arrested Juan Ponce Enrile, accusing him of the high crimes of rebellion and murder. These offenses are nonbailable under Philippine law. To the government's acute embarrassment, however, Enrile was placed in an air-conditioned suite in the jail, given a telephone and a computer, and permitted to hold daily news briefings. A few days later, the Philippine Supreme Court, a group of jurists sympathetic to President Aquino, released Enrile on 100,000 peso bail ($4,500). This paltry sum suggests that the case against Enrile was flimsy or that the juridical process was a farce—or both. In the Philippines, charges of high crimes and misdemeanors, the accusation of treason and sedition, are somehow transformed into comic operetta. Enrile, claiming to be a martyr and drawing awkward parallels to how Benigno Aquino was arrested by Marcos in 1973, reveled in the limelight and made President Aquino's efforts to protect the integrity of the nation look foolish.

The threats of the militarized party and of the politicized army continued to erode the fledgling strength of the democratic center. The initial opportunity that existed for Aquino to rework her society, to make the massive structural changes that address issues of wealth and poverty, equality and inequality, became a casualty of this erosion of respect for constitutional authority. As the new decade began, the options for the government narrowed dramatically. If she hesitated yet again, Aquino increased the likelihood of yet another coup, one likelier to succeed. If she struck boldly at the cancer within her army, she risked toppling constitutional government, the very reason she agreed to run against Ferdinand Marcos after her husband's death. Long-term, deep, structural questions had to be swept aside in favor of crisis management. Those questions, however, were, are, and will be at the center of the nation's agenda for decades to come. If the democratic, although oligarchic, center cannot hold, there will be an armageddon, a savage struggle between the militarized party and the politicized army.

PROSPERITY AND STABILITY

The modern state, dependent on the mandate of the people for its legitimacy, defines its primary goal as the delivery of prosperity, a better material life for its people. Force can repress the will of the people, but the second half of the twentieth century suggests that the dream of universal education, improvements in national health, a higher standard of living, and a longer life expectancy are the aims of every society in the world.

After four years in office, the Aquino government was quickly falling behind in this critical task. Conservative by nature, beholden to the military for survival, increasingly snared in corruption, and only precariously in power, the government appeared unable to collect the garbage; deliver electric power without random blackouts; sustain mass transit, telephone, and other vital services; and raise the standard of living for the mass of citizens rapidly enough. During the December 1989 coup attempt, the military used these economic realities to attack Aquino's leadership, even though it was the threat of military opposition that helped account for the government's poor performance. Certainly, the loss of popular support in the opinion polls and the passivity of the people of Manila during that coup attempt demonstrate the critical need to deliver the goods in order to sustain political popularity.

The Aquino government has had to deliver, fairly rapidly, a new prosperity and an economic stability to blunt an insurgency fed by poverty and despair. Jobs and economic security promote democracy. Because the per capita GNP fell about 18 percent from 1981 to 1986 and because prices doubled between 1983 and 1985, the Aquino government had to reverse the downward economic spiral to sustain its popularity. The enormous foreign debt, the need for land reform, rural poverty, unemployment, and inequality of wealth—all transcend the world of economics, reaching to the central issues of the society, its values and the capacity of the government to address them.

The first task was to curb inflation. The general price index rose only 4 percent in 1987 and 9 percent in 1988. The GNP rebounded from the chaos of the last Marcos years, increasing 5.9 percent in 1987 and 6.7 percent in 1988. Many factors helped achieve this turnaround, including a substantial flow of foreign aid, a capacity of the economy to attract investments (which were up 25 percent in 1987/1988), favorable export opportunities (which rose 25 percent in 1988, in large part because of high prices available for copra, sugar, and tin), and a new energy at the top of the government itself.

From its inception the Aquino government was moderately reformist, market-focused, internationally oriented, and technocratic. Jaime Ongpin, the brilliant, wealthy Chinese mestizo, was initially the dominant player shaping economic policy. Forced from government following the August 1987 coup attempt, Ongpin subsequently commited suicide under tragic circumstances. Since his death, the dominant shapers of government policy have been Jose Fernandez, the governor of the Central Bank, and Vicente Jayme, the finance secretary.

Aquino abolished sugar and coconut monopolies among others, and both these large export sectors benefited greatly from a rising world market price. Cronyism as an institutional form of political patronage was abolished, although the task of privatizing the government-owned corporations has been a complex one. During the Marcos era, a whole structure of government-owned or -supported corporations was created. The Aquino government wanted to reduce its active involvement in the economy but faced legal and bureaucratic hurdles and debated the social wisdom of permitting the few who already were rich to acquire these further assets. The counterargument was that such corporations should not be sold to foreign interests.

By the time Ferdinand Marcos fled to the United States, more than 300 corporations were either government-owned or government-subsidized. At its nadir, the Marcos government was committing close to half of its annual budget to these subsidies—often the vehicle for the laundering and plundering of the national treasury by Marcos and his associates—and these companies had massive annual deficits. The Aquino government created an asset privatization trust to sell off these companies, and the Presidential Commission on Good Government was charged to manage this huge economic empire of underperforming or nonperforming government-owned or -controlled corporations. Among them were the Manila Hotel, Philippine Airlines, the National Steel Company, sugar centrals, banks, the oil company, mining corporations, and many others. This task, like the recovery of the assets stolen and taken abroad by Marcos and his cronies, moved forward very slowly, in part because of legal and political constraints, in part because of internal conflicts and new variations of graft.

The renegotiation of the external debt, another crucial part of the Marcos legacy, could not be delayed like privatization. At the end of 1988, the Philippine external debt totalled approximately $28.2 billion, the equivalent of 74 percent of its GNP. In 1987 the nation paid about $2.9 billion in interest payments alone, a sum equal to almost 50 percent of its exports of goods and services. Despite a substantial rescheduling of amortization and of interest payments totaling approximately $4.8 billion since 1985, the country was so in debt to other governments and to itself, foreign banks, and creditors that it could not meet its international obligations and at the same time generate sufficient money to restart the economy. Worldwide there are 483 private banks and creditors that own a substantial portion of the Philippine patrimony. Of the $15 billion owed to commercial banks, approximately $11.5 billion were in medium- and long-term debt. The government owed about $5 billion to multilateral institutions, more than half of this due to the

World Bank, and the balance split between the International Monetary Fund (IMF) and the Asian Development Bank.

The debate over how to handle this debt was a divisive one, echoing similar policy discussions in Mexico, Brazil, and elsewhere throughout the Third World. On the one side there have been those who believe that this debt, or some portion of it, should be repudiated because it was the legacy of a discredited Marcos government and was tied to corrupt projects and practices. The Freedom from Debt Coalition, in an open letter to President Aquino signed by more than 500 economists, businesspeople, and other professionals, argued that "the national debt burden can be reduced by at least deferring payments on the Bataan Nuclear Plant [the Westinghouse project]. We are paying $355,000 a day on interest alone. For 1989, payments for interest and amortization on the nuclear plant will total seven billion pesos." The group advocated the use of that sum as economic assistance to 1.9 million unemployed and underemployed youth.

Economists, both Filipino and foreign, argued that the nation required billions of additional dollars in the next years if the economic recovery was to be sustained. They claimed it was vital to maintain the goodwill and support of foreign governments, banks, and other creditors. Default would doom this effort. After several years of intense negotiation with the IMF, in 1989 the government signed a three-year program that made available $1.3 billion, permitted $1.8 billion of official debts to be restructured, and opened the way for an additional $1.7 billion of credit from commercial banks. This IMF agreement was a precondition of the major international donor nations as they considered the Multilateral Assistance Initiative (MAI), a $10-billion "mini–Marshall Plan" first proposed by U.S. Congressman Solarz and backed by Washington, Tokyo, and other creditor nations.

The government has made some conservative and technocratic assumptions: To sustain growth, to encourage investment, to increase manufacturing exports, and to protect against future oil shocks, the nation needs to heed the external pressure of the major international monetary agencies—which would involve a loss of sovereignty. The Asian Development Bank, the IMF, the World Bank, the Export-Import Bank, and a large number of additional groups could, in effect, tell the Philippine nation what it can and cannot do on the economic front. But if economic progress is the precondition for blunting the insurgency, delivering an improved standard of living for the people, and achieving the priorities of the government, then the Aquino government concluded that there was no choice. It has taken the position that it may need to increase even further the $28.2 billion of foreign debt so that the resultant economic growth generated by the new investment could reduce the amount of debt service as a percentage of export earnings. Toward that end, President Aquino appointed Roberto Villanueva to chair the coordinating council of the Philippine Assistance Plan. This council, composed of representatives of the Philippine cabinet, Congress, and the private sector, was established to formulate policies and guidelines and to facilitate development. The goals of the Philippine Assistance Plan were the reduction of poverty, increased productive capacity, and the transfer of resources to rural areas.

Just prior to the December 1989 coup attempt, Merrill Lynch issued a report predicting that stability in the Philippines had been achieved and that a new wave of investment, especially in high-technology industries, was likely. But shortly thereafter, reflecting nervousness in the international business community, Sony Corporation announced that it was delaying a $40-million investment in a factory to be built near Manila. The attack of the Makati district, an attack that challenged economic revival itself, damaged the confidence that must be a precondition for major investment. The value of the peso weakened, tourism collapsed, the stock market fell. The critical interpenetration of politics and economic development pushed the president to declare a state of emergency so that Congress would grant her special powers to allow her to move decisively to improve services. She had to allay anxieties of domestic and multinational business alike, and to encourage investment or risk seeing her development plans fail.

Right after President Aquino came to power, her government had a much more radical approach to socioeconomic development. The first major government statement appeared under the title "The Policy Agenda for People-Powered Development." At that time, the government argued that "social justice will be the primary consideration in the pursuit of development objectives." The initial goal was to produce a better export performance with an emphasis on the rural areas. At first Aquino was strongly influenced by Minister of Economic Planning Solita Monsod. Monsod was one of the advocates of selective repudiation of "unjust and illegal" foreign debt; she was also the author of the land reform program through which people power development would take place. In the political and economic struggles that ensued, she lost out to Jaime Ongpin and the governor of the Central Bank, Jose Fernandez. But Monsod's defeat did not eradicate the central dilemma for the government: how to address rapidly and aggressively the problems of both urban and rural poverty.

The Philippines has one of the most unequal income distributions in the world. Some 42 percent of Filipino familes in the urban areas and 58 percent of those in rural areas lived below the poverty line in 1989. Malnutrition increased throughout the 1980s. According to a World

Bank report on "The Philippine Poor: What Is to Be Done," approximately 30 million Filipinos live in "absolute poverty, the sense of having an income that did not enable them to satisfy their basic needs." From 1979 to 1989, an additional 12 million people were "recruited into the ranks of the absolutely poor."

Poverty abounds in the countryside. Almost half of the poorest households are made up of landless laborers, small rice farmers and maize farmers often working on marginal land. In Manila 1.5 million families also live below the poverty line. The World Bank report notes that "the urban poor outside Metro-Manila are worse off in terms of income, open unemployment, educational attainment, health care and access to housing facilities."

The population of metropolitan Manila is over 10 million people. In this vast, ever-increasing urban sprawl, the problems of unemployment, underemployment, and the social dislocation of urbanization are most accute. With an annual population increase of 2.8 percent, the society cannot increase the individual standard of living until the number of live births declines. President Aquino's staunch faith and close association with the church have made her unwilling to fund family-planning efforts. But even if she were to reverse herself, the next 15 million Filipino workers are already born and will enter the labor force at approximately 1 million a year. The 15 million Filipinos defined as being in a core poverty group (4 million urban and 11 million rural) are increasing by 400,000 a year. The population, 60 million now, will reach 100 million in under thirty years. To keep pace with current projections of population growth to the year 2000, the Philippines must increase its food production by about 40 percent, expand the school system to handle 300,000 additional youngsters and be prepared to see an additional 16 million new jobseekers joining the 5 million now unemployed and looking for work.

If the future problems are staggering, the current ones also seem intractable. Because there is such a glut of potential employees, it has been difficult for all but the most skilled laborers to organize. Moreover, since the NPA has attempted to coopt and make the labor movement an arm of the insurgency, there has been deep distrust by the government and the corporate leadership of labor's claim to recognition and legitimacy. The Marcos government had manipulated those unions that do exist and had penetrated the union leadership for its own political reasons. Aquino's first minister of labor and employment, Bobbit Sanchez, took a prolabor stance at first, but he ran into sharp criticism from the conservative business elements around the president. Subsequently, some of her most difficult and violent encounters have been with the organized poor, either members of labor unions or rural protesters.

Class, the gap between the rich and the poor, the tension between the haves and the have-nots remain a central friction point for the society. Labor Minister Sanchez was pushed from the cabinet because he was too prolabor and was labeled a leftist. The struggles over the minimum wage and the right of people to picket are the external manifestations of deep socioeconomic fissures within the society.

No issue better demonstrates the tension between the conservative and radical options before Aquino than that of land reform and the government approach to agrarian policy. Unequal asset ownership, which leaves the rich very rich and the poor destitute, is especially obvious in land ownership. More than half of the Philippine farms occupy just 16 percent of the land, while less than 4 percent of the farms occupy over a quarter of the land. The ever-increasing number of rural, landless poor fuels the insurgency. The redistribution of land and therefore of wealth can create a whole new source of economic development, but without adequate compensation or an overwhelming outside pressure, the haves will not surrender readily the privilege that money confers.

Land reform and agrarian policy raise questions that transcend those of simple ownership of land, reaching to ancillary issues of a more effective, rationalized food production and distribution system. Credit, seed banks, access to capital, distribution networks, storage facilities, political stability, the capacity to bring to market or withhold from sale a crop—all these and more must be addressed if any agrarian policy is to succeed.

A prerequisite to land reform is either total authoritarian power, as in North Vietnam, to order without compensation the redistribution of land, or the economic resources, as in Japan and Taiwan, to give the landlords money. Moreover, in a society that no longer has a land frontier, a place for resettlement and new development, the cost of land reform must go up dramatically, as the government must seek to purchase a scarce, increasingly valuable asset. The dilemma for President Aquino was that she came to power committed to agrarian reform but had to accomplish this in a bankrupt economy.

The lack of consensus within her cabinet, the threats from the NPA and her own armed forces, her dependence on the foreign banks, her natural affinity to the entrepreneurial, business-oriented elite of Manila and the landowners of Tarlac pushed Aquino away from her original pronouncement toward a more conservative policy. The internal government debate over land reform delayed both the play's formulation and promulgation.

During the period when she had maximum control, immediately after Marcos fell, Aquino had the potential to move decisively in reordering land ownership. She failed to seize this opportunity, however, perhaps because she felt herself too weak to bring it off, too vulnerable to a coup, too preoccupied with other problems. Or perhaps she failed to act because she was of the landowning elite, because her own, her family's, and her friends' wealth was tied to the land. In any case, by the time her land reform policy was announced, she already had reestablished a new Congress, many of whose members were themselves major landlords. She asked that Congress legislate a social revolution.

The Comprehensive Agrarian Reform Law of 1988 was more sweeping than any of its predecessors, embracing all types of land, but it was a substantially watered down from the plan Monsod and Sonny Alvarez originally proposed. Draft after draft was debated as the Comprehensive Agrarian Reform Program was developed. Whereas originally 11.1 million hectares (27.4 million acres) were to be transferred, the final plan only identified 3.8 million hectares (9.4 million acres); the number of potential beneficiaries declined from 3 million to 2 million tenant farmers.

All public and private agricultural lands became subject to reform, and the government agreed to sell its own surplus land in plots of 1.5 to 2 hectares (3.5 to 5 acres) each to about 1.5 million tenant farmers. Among the most explosive issues debated were the retention limits for land; in a major reversal, sugar and coconut lands were not subject to any upper retention limits.

The final act set a 5-hectare (12.4-acre) limit, allowing 3 additional hectares (7.4 acres) to go to each child of the landowner over fifteen years old who remained actively involved in farming. The ten-year program ultimately will redistribute 2.8 million hectares and reach 2 million tenant farmers. The landlords, in turn, will receive a cash downpayment of between 20 to 40 percent and will receive thirty annual payments with 6 percent interest on their money. The total cost, if it all is implemented, will be over $70 billion across the ten-year span. Without secured sources of funding, however, it remains unclear whether there will be adequate funds made available to see the act through to successful completion.

Whether this land reform act represents a sellout, an intelligent compromise that is fair to landlord and tenant, or, as many landowners claim, a destruction of the values of the society is an issue on which there has been and will continue to be intense debate. An editorial in the Manila *Chronicle* on June 15, 1988, commented that the "recently signed Agrarian Reform Law has confirmed resoundingly an old political truism: no class legislates itself out of existence." The article continued that many leftists and moderates viewed this legislation as crucial to the Aquino administration's agenda on social justice, "a true indicator of how serious this government is in giving priority to the poor." It went on, "Given the outcome, we can only hope that the Department of Agrarian Reform and the farmer groups will do better than our policymakers did." Aquino described the act signed on June 10, 1988, as "a tolerable compromise." Some argued that the reform did too little; others said it did too much. Aquino argued that CARP would create a "radical leap in agricultural productivity," at the same time "uplifting the Filipino masses from their ancient poverty."

Can those two very important objectives both be fulfilled? The issue is not just the ownership of land but rather the potential prosperity to be shared by all in the countryside. Jaime Ongpin had described the land reform program as a "once-in-a-lifetime opportunity to effect a dramatic, positive and permanent change in the course of Philippine economic and political history." Whatever actually happens, that dream of a dramatic approach to the reorganization of society has been abandoned for something much more conservative.

NATIONALISM RESURGENT

"People power" toppled a dictator and brought about a sense of elation and self-confidence long lacking in the Philippine culture. Suddenly, the Filipino national identity was defined to the wonder and applause of the world. In those critical days of Edsa, hundreds of journalists and television photographers confirmed to the world that the Filipinos had done something remarkable. That surge of self-confidence, despite the economic and political disruption that ensued, suffused Philippine society with a new sense of self-worth. In 1990 the ramifications of this change are only beginning to be understood both domestically and abroad, but it is obvious that Filipinos feel better about themselves, feel more empowered, and are willing to assert themselves far more forcefully in the region and the world.

Not surprisingly, the Philippine-U.S. relationship has been the central focus of this resurgent nationalism. Raul Manglapus, the Philippine foreign minister, has spoken of slaying "the American father image," although the government's decision to request the support of the U.S. Air Force during the December 1989 coup attempt suggested that the relationship remains far more complicated than this.

Issues and tensions that date back to the beginning of the twentieth century are being reexamined. Technocrats, the middle class, Manila residents, and the Western-educated elite have shifted away from a previously unqualified pro-American stance. Many Filipinos believed the use of the U.S. jets in the 1989 coup attempt was unacceptable, even though they understood why Aquino had made that decision. The cultural influences remain and the blood ties to diaspora Filipinos living in the United States exist, but there has been a palpable shift.

The lasting support of Ferdinand Marcos by Ronald Reagan clearly contributed to this shift. Despite the gratitude that Filipinos feel for Congressman Solarz, Senator Lugar, and others in the U.S. Congress, Reagan's reflexive support for Marcos left many Filipinos feeling that U.S. policy was based more on its own calculated self-interest than on shared ideals of democracy and peaceful, social change. Filipinos well remembered that George Bush had toasted Marcos in 1981 after a rigged election, saying, "We love your adherence to democratic principle—and the democratic processes." Even after Marcos had fallen, Reagan remained cool to President Aquino, neither calling her by phone nor stopping by when he flew over the Philippines from Indonesia to Japan. These personal slights and the obvious sympathy he felt for the Marcoses, angered and saddened Filipinos. How could Reagan compare the Aquino and Marcos campaigns, speaking of fraud equally on both sides? It was almost as if the United States tried to deny the legitimacy of the Filipinos' finest hour. Speaking before the U.S. Congress in September 1986, President Aquino said, "You have spent many lives and much treasure to bring freedom to many lands that were reluctant to receive it. And here you have a people who won it by themselves and need only help to preserve it." It was something President Quezon might have said.

Filipinos from all sectors of society understood that the U.S. policy of supporting Marcos had been based on retaining the bases. As long as Marcos was a puppet, he would never deny access to them. The United States looked at the bases as part of a chain of key outposts stretching around the world to contain communism and help influence events in the Persian Gulf. For the Filipinos, however, these bases were an issue of domestic concern. The United States refused to acknowledge whether nuclear weapons have been stored in the archipelago or brought in by ship and plane. It is widely assumed that the U.S. nuclear arsenal does come ashore on a carrier or submarine or when a strategic bomber lands. The growing antinuclear movement, especially in Manila, has made much of this infringement of Filipino sovereignty.

The legacy of dependency on foreign creditors, many of whom are American, further exacerbated nationalist tensions. Foreigners, especially the American and Japanese, hold the keys to the future of the Philippines. The United States gave asylum to the Marcoses, and, whatever the complexities of court injunction and due process, it has failed to assist the Filipinos much in the effort to get back desperately needed billions of stolen funds. Decisions of the World Bank and the IMF, taken in Washington, shape the quality of life in the countryside, determining how much interest a Philippine farmer has to pay on a loan to buy seed, whether a road or dam will or will not be built, and the priorities of investments imposed upon the Aquino government. This dependency, a legacy of Marcos and a reminder of times past, has heightened the anger, contributing to a longstanding grievance that the "special relationship" is unequal. Just as foreign aid was given far more generously to Japan, the enemy, than to the Philippines, the ally, in 1946 and 1947, so again the Filipinos' defense of the values of democracy has not been rewarded in ways the Filipinos find appropriate.

By the accident of chronology, in 1988 the Aquino and Reagan governments had to renegotiate a two-year agreement on the bases, understanding that the longer-term lease on those bases was up for review, debate, and possible cancellation in 1991. The economic vulnerability of the Philippines has highlighted the domestic consequences of altering the arrangement. There are 20,000 U.S. personnel stationed on those bases, with an additional 25,000 dependents in the country. The U.S. military directly employ 68,000 Filipinos. The bases pump $28 million a day into the local economy, and the United States spends close to a half billion dollars a year to purchase supplies and services. Almost 3 percent of the Philippine's GNP is credited to military spending on those bases. Second to the Philippine government itself, the United States is still the largest employer in the archipelago. But, as the distinguished Jesuit Father Joaquim Bernas has said, "You do not put a dollar tag on dignity."

To assert national sovereignty is to jeopardize this vital cash flow. Is the country selling out its national heritage for a mess of pottage? But can it afford to do anything else? On November 25, 1987, Congressman Solarz, joined by his conservative colleague Jack Kemp and Senators Alan Cranston and Richard Lugar, wrote to President Reagan, urging the creation of a Marshall Plan for the archipelago. Arguing in favor of a multinational effort, they wrote "there is far more at stake than just continued access to military bases at Subic Bay and Clark Airfield, as important as those bases may be." Instead, the legislators maintained, "at stake in the Philippines is a far more important principle; that peaceful, democratic change succeed in the Third World." They went on to observe that the revolution of February 1986 was an inspiration to others across the world yearning for democracy. Many Filipinos believe that this multilateral assistance initiative is hostage to continued U.S. access to its Philippine military bases.

In October 1988, after a difficult negotiation process, the United States and the Philippines signed an agreement dealing with Clark, Subic, the Crow Valley Range Complex, a bombing run of over 300 square miles, and the other ancillary facilities maintained by the United States. The Filipinos wanted to call the payments "rent," but the United

States refused, speaking instead of economic, military, and development assistance. In any case, whereas previously the Philippine government had received $180 million a year, the new sum was $481 million a year. Foreign Minister Manglapus had fought long and hard for $1.2 billion a year, a sum far beyond anything the United States was willing to pay. Built into the agreement was the opportunity to use some of the $481 million to buy U.S. bonds that could be used to guarantee a new Philippine bond issue and thus help to restructure the long-term debt.

Both Manglapus and President Aquino were accused of selling out by a spectrum of Filipino newspapers from the right to the left and by a cluster of Filipino politicians, many of whom hope to run for president in 1992 if Aquino stays true to her word and chooses not to seek reelection. By September 16, 1990, the Philippine government must declare its intentions, as the existing treaty mandates a one-year renewal notification. Negotiations were to begin in January 1990, but Aquino requested a delay because of the attempted coup. She also refused to meet with Secretary Richard Cheney when he came to the Philippines on an Asian tour in mid-February of 1990. The reasons offered were irrelevant; her purpose was to show that she was not a puppet of the Americans. Her posturing for domestic political reasons backfired.

In 1959, when Nikita Khrushchev banged his shoe at the UN meeting, he was protesting the comments of a Filipino delegate who had compared the Soviet Union unfavorably with the United States. Thirty years later, Soviet leader Mikhail Gorbachev offered to abandon the Soviet bases at Cam Ranh Bay and Da Nang in Vietnam if the United States left the Philippine bases. The autumn of 1989 produced such rapid change on the world scene that the geomilitary balance of power has been totally upset. As the cold war ended, the need and importance of such bases became a legitimate issue of debate at the Pentagon and in the U.S. Congress. The congruence of events, both domestic and global, has changed all assumptions on both the Filipino and U.S. sides. The Philippine nationalist demand to terminate the bases may correspond to a U.S. willingness to contract or withdraw.

The use of U.S. military might in Philippine domestic affairs has also altered the relationship of the Philippine military, especially the RAM faction, to its U.S. counterparts. Because many of these disaffected Filipino officers trained in the United States, there was a camaraderie that was broken when U.S. combat missions altered the outcome of the coup attempt. To be sure, the presence of a massive U.S. military machine always affected Philippine domestic politics to some degree; the U.S. Air Force, for example, organized Marcos's evacuation to Clark and then to Hawaii. But until December 1989, it never figured so boldly in domestic affairs. The decade of the 1990s will bring about a new constellation of relationships, one likely to alter the Philippine-U.S. relationship more profoundly than at any time since independence in 1946.

Redefinition of the Philippine-U.S. relationship is echoed in the resurgence of Muslim nationalism in southwestern Mindanao and Sulu. This ancient tension raises the question: who is a Filipino? The Muslim provinces have the highest infant mortality and illiteracy rates. But Mindanao and Sulu account for 60 percent of Philippine exports of raw materials, including prawns, pineapples, timber, bananas, and copra. This area has gold, substantial mineral deposits, and, perhaps, oil. During the Marcos era the struggle with the Moro National Liberation Front cost approximately 60,000 casualties. The cease-fire with Nur Misuari was an agreement so opaque as to lack any real meaning. Misuari still lives in Libya a guest of President Qaddafi. He and other Islamic leaders have now gained a voice in the Organization of the Islamic Conference and continue to get financial and political support from conservative and radical Arab states alike. Over the past decade the gold rush in parts of Mindanao has helped finance both the Muslim rebellion and the NPA. It has brought hundreds of thousands of Filipinos, Christian and Muslim, into the area to pan for gold. Knowledgeable sources estimate that $1 billion in gold is being mined or panned illegally, virtually all of it smuggled abroad.

President Aquino has insisted that there be a plebiscite to determine what the people in the area want. But because eight of the thirteen traditionally Moro provinces now have more Christians than Muslims, Islamic leaders resist such a plebiscite. If autonomy is to be offered, on what terms? How much tax revenue collected locally will be kept and how much sent to Manila? Which provinces will be included in the autonomous zone? How much will be spent on infrastructure development, on raising literacy and public health standards, and who will make the decision? A "peace panel" of negotiators met in Manila but had only one Muslim out of ten members. Factionalism compounds the problem: In addition to the MNLF and Nur Misuari, there are also the Moro Islamic Liberation Front and the Moro National Liberation Front Reform Movement. Just as Filipinos seek to redefine the relationship with the United States, Muslims are challenging the relationship with Christian Filipinos.

Is there room within the Philippine society for this geographic, religious, and linguistic subgroup? Can Philippine nationalism have a plural face in the twenty-first century or will the society be riven with the tensions that have set Muslim and Christian at war with one other since the sixteenth century?

CHANGE AND STASIS

Speaker of the House Ramon V. Mitra, soon after his election to that post, said, "We cannot afford to squander this second chance history has given us to prove that we can temper political liberty with social reponsibility." Is it true in the Philippines that the more things change the more they stay the same? Has the Edsa revolution altered society fundamentally or restored the old order to power? Has it established a new trajectory for the nation different from the Marcos era and that which had preceded it?

The emergence of people power, the discovery that unarmed civilians could shape their own destiny and could topple authoritarian force by peaceful means, must be one of the most dramatic elements of the age of Aquino. A conscript army was unwilling to fire upon its own people and the Filipinos proved that the ideas of Gandhi and Martin Luther King, Jr., can be carried to their nonviolent extremes successfully, if enough people are mobilized and willing to risk the ultimate sacrifice to pursue political ideals. What happened in the Philippines already has had a tragic echo in the student-led protests in Beijing.

Moreover, the Roman Catholic hierarchy has assumed a unique leadership position in the temporal affairs of the nation. The church, with its broad base of lay and clerical power running through the capillaries of Philippine society, has always had the theoretical capacity to challenge the authority of government. In early history of the archipelago, church and government were, in fact, one. The government required the support and acquiescence of the clergy to transmit its will. In modern times, the church in the Philippines, like the church around the world, avoided political entanglement because it was acutely aware of the risks such intervention could create (see Chapter 5).

Since independence, priests and nuns have increasingly become politically active on behalf of social justice. In the face of the enormous inequities of wealth and poverty, individual clerics found themselves entering into the political arena in order to fulfill the definition of their ministries. In an era in which utopia is to be found by the secular success of a society rather than by assurance of entry into heaven in the world beyond, these clerics and nuns protested when human rights were abused, when poverty and starvation was prevalent, when education and health benefits were denied. After the declaration of martial law, the church was the major source of opposition at the grassroots level. Liberation theology spread from Latin America to the Philippines and was embraced by a whole generation of Filipino and foreign priests.

The Edsa revolution redefined liberation theology, as Jaime Cardinal Sin and the other bishops assumed the lead in articulating the people's rage at constitutional authoritarianism. By assuming this mantle of leadership, by entering into the political struggle, by calling the people into the streets and telling them how to resist threats when voting, Cardinal Sin and his associates called on their enormous moral authority to shape the struggle for succession.

Filipinos of all persuasions have a new sense of national pride and self-worth that will suffuse the nation for decades to come. Unlike the flawed Aguinaldo revolution of 1896, and unlike the ambivalent, bitter legacy of World War II, Filipinos took charge of their own destiny although they lapsed into silence during the 1989 coup attempt. The world's attention and praise created an aura of self-respect and pride that are critical concomitants of mature nationalism.

A corollary to this new national pride is the confidence to reexamine critically the relationship with the United States. "The cobwebs of doubt" raised by U.S. support of Marcos extend beyond that one issue to encompass concerns over the role of the military bases, economic imperialism of multinational corporations, and the condescension and racism that has always been a part of the Filipino-American relationship. To what degree the "special relationship" will be altered in the decades ahead is pure conjecture, but national self-confidence is a precondition for any reconsideration.

To return to the questions raised at the beginning of this chapter, what is the appropriate characterization of the age of Aquino? Is it "a restoration," as in Japan in 1868, a radical movement couched in the name of a conservative tradition? Is "reformation" the right phrase, or is "revolution?" Individuals on the left describe it rather as a "refeudalization," an unequivocal return to a discredited old order. Sheila Coronel, a political columnist for the Manila *Chronicle*, observed soon after the Congress was reelected that the halls of the legislature were full of "politicians of the past, now 15 years older and grayer, resurrected from the mothballs of oblivion, back to the center stage of our political life."

A traditional elite, conservative in outlook, is still in command of the society. This leadership can be traced back from generation to generation for over a century; the leaders of today are the children of the leaders of yesterday. The dominance of the mestizo families remains unbroken. Although there were new faces elected to the Congress in 1987, most members have a long tradition of political power at the local and national level. As always, this oligarchy has had the capacity to incorporate into itself the talented members of newly arrived families, usually those that had already succeeded in the socioeconomic realm.

Factionalism is the reality of the day, just as it was thirty and sixty years ago. Elections today, as in the past, are a form of national sport, and alliances shift with bewildering speed as people change party affiliations and loyalties.

The shifting party structure for personal or factional gain, the concept of jockeying for tactical advantage, and the license to speak, often irresponsibly, from the well of the House and the Senate are continuities of political life. As the 1992 election approaches, the Liberal party leader, Senator Jovito Salonga, Jose Cojuangco, Agapito Aquino, Juan Ponce Enrile, Salvador H. Laurel, and many others are all attempting to position themselves on the left, center, and right in such a way that they might succeed to the presidency, assuming that Aquino means what she says and does not run again in 1992. The interrelationship of personal ambition clouds party discipline or dispassionate, ideological discussion of issues such as the future of the military bases. If Quintin Paredes, Manuel Roxas, or Eulogio Rodriguez were to return from their graves to walk in the halls of the Philippine Senate, they would feel totally at home.

The challenge of the politicized army, of the RAM, is the challenge of a briefly enfranchised new elite against the older oligarchy. These officers, having tasted money and power under Marcos, are not prepared to accept the return of the status quo ante. Beneath the rhetoric lies a bold attack on the social structure that has existed for so long. Just as the priest dominated the pre–twentieth century archipelago, and the lawyer-politico the last hundred years, perhaps the military officer corps will become the voice of the nation in the century to come. When Gregorio Honasan called for a "national reformist government" to replace the Aquino regime, he was speaking in inchoate terms about ending what he saw as the chaotic, civilian, democratic system. But he was also laying claim to a new hierarchy, a new means of upward social mobility, a new group to control the levers and enjoy the Forbes Park estates.

The army officers claim to be both populist and pro–big business. They argue for a conservative approach and maintain that they are the keepers of the nation's ideals, its Holy Grail. They also excoriate the old oligarchy, arguing that they are true to the revolutionary dream of a proud, independent society. The series of coup attempts are an attack on democracy, its seeming wastefulness and inefficiency. The sanctity of constitutional structures and the adherence to the rule of law are viewed as marginal values. They repudiate meliorism, the notions of moderate growth and accommodation to all elements of the society. For them, simple answers exist and solutions are straightforward. Armies do not train officers to explore subtle nuances.

This new military elite does share certain values with the well-established oligarchy. Personal and familial greed are constants, for example. Money is a currency of loyalty in the archipelago. Pesos and dollars bought participation in the coup attempts. Nepotism and corruption remain a universal part of daily life, even though there has been no hint of personal corruption by President Aquino. Members of her family and government have done well in the last few years. Cardinal Sin has become openly critical of the Aquino government's laxness and corruption. Speaking in February 1989, at the third anniversary of Edsa, he observed that "the old politics has come back to the dismay of us all—the positioning for power, the corruption, the grandstanding, the influence-peddling, the petty bickering." The cardinal continued that "the urgent tasks of government . . . were consequently being neglected." Such criticism did sting; Aquino vowed "a relentless effort to weed out the corruption that has resurfaced in our midst," but observers are critical, especially because she is so loyal to her family and so reluctant to fire anyone.

It is estimated that about a third of the nation's budget is lost to corruption and inefficiency every year. The Commission on Good Government, appointed by President Aquino to recover assets and funds stolen by the Marcos family and their cronies, has itself been accused of serious corruption. The solicitor general, Francisco Chavez, accused the chairman of that commission, Ramon Diaz, of "ineptness, incompetence, and corruption." Manila swirls with accusations that members of the Aquino and Cojuangco families have profited by their proximity to the president. Aquino's brother-in-law, Ricardo Lopa, is suspected of cashing in on sequestered assets of the Marcoses. Privatization, the sale of the corrupt, bankrupt government corporations of the Marcos era, has been delayed in large measure because those charged with running these companies temporarily do not want to give up the income and perks that come from that authority. Allegations have been leveled at Aquino's brother, Jose Cojuangco, who with his wife is accused of taking over the gambling casinos and other illicit revenue sources that once had belonged to the Romualdezes. The new justice minister, Franklin Drilon, and the director of the National Bureau of Investigation, Alfredo Lim, have a mandate to eradicate corruption, but few believe that they can accomplish much. And, at the other end of the spectrum, police officers still shake down motorists for a few pesos. The *New York Times* quotes Bishop Francisco Claver as saying, "Imagine if all the money budgeted for roads were actually spent for roads—how the economy would improve."

The litigiousness of the society remains one of its hallmarks. Of the $10 billion Marcos is alleged to have stolen, only about $160 million in assets has been recovered. The judicial process is agonizingly slow, and smart lawyers can delay the recovery of sequestered corporations, the transfer of land deeds, the accusations of fraud and corruption. The society remains dominated by lawyers who use the power of education to widen the gap between the rich and the poor. It remains to be seen whether land redistribution will not fall victim to the manipulation of judicial procedures. When William Howard Taft moved to sell the friar lands in 1907, the Philippine elite used its education and power in the courts to gain most of that property. There is no reason to suppose, given what has happened so far, that the upcoming CARP will not be distorted in the same way. The original draft was sufficiently altered in the legislature to prompt Representative Bonifacio Gilego to vote against it, saying that his colleagues were "foisting the grand deception on our people."

The demographic explosion continues to burn bright hot, but Aquino has dropped efforts of the Marcos government to institute family planning. Aquino, a devout Roman Catholic, does not raise the issue. The population is growing at approximately 2.8 percent per year, one of the fastest population growths in the world. Urban poverty, as calculated by the World Bank, has risen from 24 percent of the city dwellers in 1971 to over 50 percent in 1985. Exact statistics are in some sense meaningless because until the 1990 census, data are suspect. The definition of the poverty line is artificial. But fewer than one-third of the urban poor have piped-in water, sewage systems, or garbage collection. Hundreds of thousands live as squatters in shanty towns, without the most basic protection of police or firefighters, without sanitation or privacy. During the Marcos era, the birth rate went down, but the poverty level increased. As Aquino has restarted the economy, there are now more people above the poverty line, but the birth rate is growing more rapidly.

The balance between the new discontinuities of Philippine life and the traditional patterns and procedures is difficult to assess. If one looks at Corazon Aquino herself, all the tensions and contradictions are present. Is this remarkable, charismatic, devout woman a part of her generation and her class? Or is she, rather, a liberating element, someone who has broken through the normal boundaries of political leadership and social influence to remake profoundly her society and her culture? For many, the answer to the question whether the Philippines has undergone a "revolution" or a "refeudalization" depends on how they assess Aquino. That in itself is a very traditional approach, as Filipinos have always personalized ideology and issues.

Corazon Aquino, as noted, placed the restoration of democracy ahead of social change. In her speech of November 21, 1988, celebrating her first 1,000 days in office, she said, "The first of those aspirations was democracy. Not economic freedom and profits, but democracy—the Filipino's birthright and racial identity." Aquino was not prepared to be a proconsul in the mode of Douglas MacArthur. She did not see her mission as a reordering of the social hierarchy, the redistribution of power, the revolution of the masses. Rejecting both the radical model of leftist revolution and the equally far-reaching reforms imposed upon postwar Japan, the Aquino government and Aquino herself have reaffirmed evolution over revolution. Thus, she is in the great national tradition articulated by Jose Rizal when he wrote that "reforms, if they are to bear fruit, must come from above, for reforms that come from below are upheavals both violent and transitory."

Historians will long debate whether she actually had the power, the authority, the national mandate to face down her violent critics on the left and on the right when she first came to power. Initially, she had the overwhelming support of the people. Her constitution was approved by 76 percent of the 22 million votes cast—and this out of a total of 25 million registered voters. But her ambivalence toward radical change has been an expression of her class at the expense of millions of peasants who would be the beneficiaries of a redistribution of land and wealth. She remains today beloved by many yet beleaguered. The accusations of corruption that continue to plague her government have eroded much of her original popularity. The resignation of Solita Monsod, her original social planner, from the cabinet caused barely a ripple of attention, even though it confirmed her retreat into a traditional, oligarchic posture.

By seeking to appease the military, to win the loyalty of wavering, critical officers because she needed them, Aquino abandoned opportunities to attack frontally the great issues of land redistribution, public sector corruption, and broad-scale venality. It is a classic example of a Philippine anomaly that she is now attacked by the army for her failure to address those very issues. Did she have the power to face down those officers? If her army had been totally loyal, would she have acted differently? Historians will turn over these questions for centuries.

Many Filipinos have seen their president as the suffering Mary Magdalene mourning the slain savior, Benigno Aquino. She herself spoke of "his death" as "my country's resurrection." The religious *pasyon* and the triumph of secular democracy are fused in subtle ways that link the religious element within the society to its secular dimension. The late Robert Shaplen quotes a leading centrist, Jean Trebol, as criticizing Aquino for "not putting her own house in order, for appointing the wrong people to her executive staff, and for condoning a continued corruption." Trebol expressed the common sentiment when, in answer to her own rhetorical question, "Do we believe in Cory?" she said, "We

President Corazon C. Aquino. (Courtesy of Jaime Zobel de Ayala)

have no choice, we have to believe and hope. If we lose faith in her, God help us! She must succeed!"

President Aquino is well aware of the practical questions raised about her governmental skills. Speaking to a group of businesspeople she said, "The question you all really want to ask is: 'Can she hack it? Isn't she weak?' . . . Although I am a woman and physically small, I have blocked all doors to power except elections in 1992." She went on, "I am not sorry that the honeymoon is over. The sooner we get over the fantasy of the honeymoon and face the hard work of marriage—the marriage of president and nation—the better." Stephen Solarz said of her that "this is a woman who has a fist of steel inside a velvet glove. . . . She's a priceless asset of democracy."

And yet, she continues to carry an aura of the sacred, to play a mythical role that cannot be explained by normal political popularity. In 1974 Benigno Aquino, in prison at Fort Bonifacio, wrote a poem on "Maria Corazon":

> You are love
> earnest, genuine, sincere
> womanly, humanly, divine!
> Unruffled by trouble
> undeterred by the burden
> though heavy the load.
> Nothing is impossible
> Uncomplaining, never tired.
> Alarmed but never confused,
> Miserable, scared yet cheerful.
> Giving abundantly
> Expecting no reward. . . .

The nation does see her as "earnest, genuine, sincere, womanly, humanly, divine."

In her speech after 1,000 days in office, she said, "There is not much I regret, not even my failure to strike earlier at the right-wing threat. It was a matter of timing—theirs was wrong and mine was right. The price of delay was, of course, the deterioration of the Philippine image abroad. Yet it gave us the certain survival of democracy." She continued to note that "aside from God, my greatest trust is in the people who never failed me and brought us through the many trials of the past 1000 days. God gave us the gift of freedom; the rest we must work for—keeping our freedom and making progress in the economy." President Aquino blends the meliorist's dream of a secular utopia, a vision closely tied to the twentieth century, with an earlier, more religious link to a deep-seated part of the Filipino past: "For myself, I acknowledge the obligation to show that democracy can work for our people in real terms of effective security for our communities and real progress in the economy, for the greater health and education of our children, and in a greener and richer land where we can fulfill the promises we have made to ourselves and our prosperity."

Claro Recto, one of the most articulate of the twentieth-century Filipino leaders, once wrote that "political independence is not the end, but only the beginning, and in an other sense, not an end in itself, but only the means to an end." Recto observed that "there are those of us who expect too much from independence, and there are those who expect too little from our own people." In the merger of a modern, religious-secular nationalism, "the ideal of national independence became comingled with the dreams of an earthly paradise, in which the Filipinos would live in freedom from fear and want."

The Filipinos are in their symbolic jeepney, bouncing their way toward the next century. It is a fallacy of nationalism to believe that the trip is easy or that the destination can be known in advance. Recto correctly argued that "independence is not a guarantee of freedom and a life of abundance, but only an opportunity to achieve and preserve them through our own efforts and owing little to the magnanimity or suffering of friends or masters." Where President Aquino and the nation will be in a decade or how they will weather the trip are not fruitful speculations. Their jeepney is on its way, and the potholes will not stop it.

Glossary

adat: Malay custom and customary law.

alcaldes mayores: Provincial governors.

Alsa Masa: Aroused Masses, a vigilante group in Davao City.

anting anting: Talisman.

Audiencia: The highest tribunal and the governor-general's advisory council.

bahala na: Accepting one's lot.

barangay: A kinship unit in the pre-Spanish era that consisted of from 30 to 100 families; preserved by the Spanish as the basic unit of local administration.

barong tagalog: Loose-fitting embroidered shirt worn without neck ornaments.

barrio: Village.

bayanihan: Community effort required at harvest and other socially determined moments. The name has been adopted by a dance troupe.

baylan: A spirit medium.

boletas: Certificates of ownership of cargo space in a galleon.

bundok: Tagalog for "mountain"; by extension, the interior, the countryside.

cabecilla: Boss, foreman, or ringleader; a system of distributing and purchasing goods in which a Chinese central agent, and his provincial factors, provided a link between the *indio* producer and the foreign export community.

cabezas de barangay: Spanish term for the hereditary headmen (formerly *datu*) of the smallest unit of local administration.

cacique: Member of the privileged landholding elite.

carabao: Water buffalo.

cedula: Tax certificate of personal registration.

central: Refinery.

chabacano: A patois of Spanish and Tagalog; primarily spoken in Manila during the Spanish era.

Cofradia: A religious brotherhood.

compadrazgo: System of ritual God-parenthood.

consulado: Consulate or guild. Such a guild was established in the Philippines in 1769. It consisted of Spanish merchants in Manila who supervised the galleon trade, subject only to the control of the governor.

Creoles: A term for Spaniards born in the Spanish Empire, in contrast to those born on the Iberian Peninsula (*peninsulares*).

damay: To sympathize, to condole.

datu: Pre-Spanish headman in the *barangay.*

donativo de zamboanga: Spanish levy to help fight against the Muslims.

Filipino: Prior to the nineteenth century, a term applied to Caucasians born in the Philippines (Creoles), as opposed to Caucasians born on the Iberian Peninsula. During the nineteenth century, it came to mean mestizos and *indios* born in the Philippines as well.

galleon: Spanish ship that semiannually carried Asian produce to Acapulco and bullion, goods, and clerics to the islands.

gobernadorcillo: Petty governor; the chief magistrate of a municipality in the Spanish Philippines and the highest *indio* official in the Spanish bureaucracy.

gremio: A district governing council in Manila during the late Spanish period.

hacienda: Estate.

hectare: A unit (2.47 acres) of land measure.

ilustrado: Enlightened one; a member of the indigenous intelligentsia in late-nineteenth-century Philippines, which spoke for the emerging Filipino community.

inaanak: Godchild.

indio: Spanish term for a Malay.

indulto de comercio: Fine paid in advance by the Spanish provincial governors of the Philippines when they expected to transgress the legal proscription on commercial activity.

inquilino: Lessee; an *indio* or mestizo who was given a concession to clear and improve church land. The land remained the property of the church, and the lessee would sublet it to tenants for a percentge of their crop yield.

jihad: A Muslim holy war to convert the infidel.

kalayaan: Independence, redemption, freedom, liberation.

kasamahan: The landholding system whereby an *inquilino* leased land from the church and sublet it to tenants for a percentge of their crop yield.

lakaran: A pilgrimage, a trip, an ascent.

lakas-awa: Active nonviolence.

mestizo: Spanish term for people of racially diverse parents.

Moro: Widely used term for Filipino Muslims.

ninong: Godfather.

obras pias: Church-owned charitable foundations.

pactos de retro: System used by moneylenders to gain ownership of land. A Chinese mestizo would buy land from an *indio* owner, granting the latter the option to repurchase later. Because the original owner rarely was able to repurchase, the moneylender usually kept the land.

pakikisama: The concern to please or satisfy others; a desire to achieve smooth interpersonal relations.

palabas: Exaggerated, fanciful speech, especially political; hyperbole; puffery.

parang sabil: Muslim vow to pursue the holy war even to death (in Spanish, *juramentado*).

parian: The Chinese quarter of Manila.

pasyon: Vernacular folk tradition recounting the death of Christ.

peninsulares: A term for Spaniards born on the Iberian Peninsula, in contrast to those born in the Spanish Empire (Creoles).

pensionados: Filipino students brought to the United States in the early twentieth century.

picul: A variable unit of weight, usually about 60 kilograms (132 pounds).

piezas: The bales or packages carried on a galleon.

polo: A term for draft labor (corvée).

principalia: The village elite.

puhunan: In usage, a favor done for someone else; literally, capital in business.

real patronato: Right granted by the pope to the king of Spain, and by extension to the governor-general, to approve or disapprove religious personnel.

recurso de fuerza: The crown's right to intervene in matters of ecclesiastical jurisdiction.

regulares: Friars; those ecclesiastics who belonged to a religious order, as opposed to the *seculares,* or diocesan priests.

residencia: The judicial and public review faced by all Spanish officials in the Philippines at the termination of their service and prior to their departure from the colony.

sabong: Cockfights.

salvage: The term given for the army's plundering and raping of villages during the Marcos era.

sangleys: Overseas Chinese.

sari-sari: A small general store in a barrio, often owned by a Chinese merchant.

seculares: Diocesan priests; in contradistinction to the friars (*regulares*), who belonged to religious orders.

situado: Annual subsidy sent to the Philippines from the Spanish treasury in Mexico.

swidden: Anthropological term for a worldwide agricultural pattern characterized by slash-and-burn and shifting cultivation. Used in contrast to the wet-rice pattern.

talahib: A tough, commercially useless cogon grass.

tao: Lowland peasant.

tributo: Spanish head tax.

utang na loob: Debt of gratitude; a norm of social behavior. A recipient of a favor is obliged to return the favor with interest in order to discharge his debt of gratitude.

vandala: A forced delivery system that required a peasant to deliver a fixed amount of a crop for a set price.

walang hiya: To be insensitive and thoughtless, to disregard the burdens of friendship and social obligation.

Bibliography

This bibliography is a stepping-stone to scholarly and specialized material available to a Western reader. It is to be hoped that some, if not all, of the books listed can be found in a major urban or university library. Although virtually no library will have everything, good libraries will have a fraction of what follows. It is for this reason that relatively few articles are cited, even though a great deal of the most important research on the Philippines appears in journals of scholarly or special interest. The *Annual Bibliography* published by the *Journal of Asian Studies* (*JAS*), known until September 1956 as the *Far Eastern Quarterly,* is a vital cumulative source of articles and books published. Nearly as important is *Southeast Asia: A Dissertation Bibliography* published by University Microfilms International. Scholarly publishing has undergone a devolution, and it is no longer economically possible for even the best doctoral dissertations to be printed in the traditional manner. Microform, microfiche, and paper copies of doctoral dissertations are the dissemination devices of the present and, alas, the future. Only a relatively few doctoral dissertations are cited below, but any interested student of the Philippines must explore carefully this lode of information.

The bibliography follows the chapter outline of this volume, although it is obvious that this is an artificial device and that in many cases, books listed in one place could easily be cited elsewhere. For example, Peter G. Gowing's *Muslim Filipinos: Heritage and Horizon* (Quezon City, 1979) is cited in the section, "A Singular and a Plural Folk," but Gowing has much to say about Muslim religious practices, dealt with in the chapter "The Religious Impulse," and the Moro National Liberation Front, dealt with in "The Marcos Era." For brevity's sake, bibliographic entries are listed only once.

There are a number of bibliographic reference books, including a *Selected Bibliography of the Philippines, Topically Arranged and Annotated,* prepared by the Philippines Studies Program, the University of Chicago (Westport, Conn., 1973); Shiro Saito, *Philippine Ethnography: A Culturally Annotated and Selected Bibliography* (Honolulu, 1972); E. R. Baradi, *Southeast Asian Research Tools: The Philippines* (Honolulu, 1979); Belen B. Angeles, *A Bibliography of Theses and Dissertations,*

1965–1979 (Quezon City, 1981); and Maria C. Velez, ed., *Images of the Filipina: A Bibliography* (Manila, 1975).

A good factual introduction to the Philippines is *Philippines, A Country Study,* Foreign Area Studies (The American University) (3d ed., Washington, 1983). The Center for Southeast Asian Studies at Northern Illinois University has updated "the state of the art" for each discipline of Philippine studies. Publications to date are Frederick Wernstedt, Willhelm Solheim II, Lee Sechrest, George Guthrie, and Leonard Casper, *Philippine Studies: Geography, Archaeology, Psychology, and Literature: Present Knowledge and Research Trends,* NIU Center for Southeast Asian Studies, Special Report Series no. 10 (DeKalb, Ill., 1974); Donn V. Hart, ed., *Philippine Studies: History, Sociology, Mass Media, and Bibliography,* NIU Center for Southeast Asian Studies, Occasional Paper no. 6 (DeKalb, Ill., 1978); and Kip Machado, Richard Hooley, and Lawrence Reid, *Philippine Studies: Political Science, Economics, Linguistics,* NIU Center for Southeast Asian Studies, Occasional Paper no. 8 (DeKalb, Ill., 1981). See also *Filipino Tradition and Acculturation: Reports on Changing Societies* (Tokyo, 1983), and the anthology of primary sources and scholarly articles with an emphasis on Philippine culture prepared by Cynthia N. Lumbera and Terestia G. Maceda, *Rediscovery* (Quezon City, 1982). Alfred W. McCoy and E. C. de Jesus have collected an important sample of outstanding scholarly articles on several dimensions of culture and society in *Philippine Social History* (Sydney, 1982). William Henry Scott has written *Cracks in the Parchment Curtain and Other Essays in Philippine History* (Quezon City, 1982). See also Damiana L. Eugenio's *Philippine Folk Literature: An Anthology* (Quezon City, 1982).

See also Donn V. Hart, *An Annotated Bibliography of Philippine Bibliographies, 1965–1974,* NIU Center for Southeast Asian Studies, Occasional Paper no. 4 (DeKalb, Ill., 1974); Fred Eggan and Evett Hester, *Selected Bibliography of the Philippines: Topically Arranged and Annotated* (New Haven, Conn., 1956); Gabriel A. Bernardo, comp., and Natividad P. Verzosa, ed., *Bibliography of Philippine Bibliographies, 1593–1961* (Manila, 1968); and Michael Onorato, *Philippine Bibliography, 1899–1946* (Santa Barbara, Calif., 1970). For bibliographies on the Spanish era, see Wenceslao E. Retana, *Aparató bibliografico de la historia general de Filipinas* (Madrid, 1906), and James A. Robertson, *Bibliography of the Philippines,* vol. 53 of E. H. Blair and J. A. Robertson, *The Philippine Islands, 1493–1898* (Cleveland, Ohio, 1903). E. A. Manuel's *Dictionary of Philippine Biography* (Quezon City, 1955) and the less scholarly but more broadly based volume by the National Historical Commission entitled *Eminent Filipinos* (Manila, 1965) offer valuable biographical information.

CHAPTER 1—THE RULES OF THE ROAD

A wonderful introduction to the jeepney is the elegant photo essay by Emmanuel Torres, *Jeepney* (Quezon City, 1979). Richard L. Stone's work can be found in "Private Transitory Ownership of Public Property: One Key to Understanding Public Behavior: I—The Driving Game," in *Modernization: Its Impact in the Philippines,* Institute of Philippine Culture, Paper no. 4 (Quezon City,

1967), 53–63. The multi-volume series published by the Institute of Philippine Culture at Ateneo de Manila University brings together some of the most provocative and stimulating pieces on contemporary Philippine life. Richard L. Stone has expanded his exploration of the use of public and private property in *Philippine Urbanization: The Politics of Public and Private Property in Greater Manila,* Center for Southeast Asian Studies, Report no. 6 (DeKalb, Ill., 1973). An intense debate has been generated, in part by the Institute of Philippine Culture, by the attempt to define Philippine peasant values. A good introduction can be found in the articles by Fred Eggan and George Guthrie that appear in a book edited by George Guthrie entitled *Six Perspectives on the Philippines* (Manila, 1968). The *Four Readings on Philippine Values,* edited by Frank Lynch (Quezon City, 1964), is a most brilliant and controversial work. Other important pieces include Charles Kaut, "Utang na loob: A System of Contractual Obligations Among Tagalogs," *Southwestern Journal of Anthropology* 17:3 (1961), 256–272; Jaime C. Bulatao, "Hiya," *Philippine Studies* 21:3 (July 1964), 424–438; Sidney W. Mintz and Eric Wolf, "An Analysis of Ritual Coparenthood (Compadrazgo)," *Southwestern Journal of Anthropology* 6 (1950), 341–368; George Forster, "Cofradia and Compadrazgo," *Southwestern Journal of Anthropology* 9:1 (1953), 1–28. George M. Guthrie and Fortunata M. Azores have published a fascinating study of "Philippine Interpersonal Behavior Patterns" in *Modernization: Its Impact in the Philippines III,* Institute of Philippine Culture, Paper no. 6 (Quezon City, 1968), 3–63. Donn V. Hart, a dean of Philippine studies, has written *Compadrinazgo: Ritual Kinship in the Philippines* (DeKalb, Ill., 1977). Emma Porio, Frank Lynch, and Mary Hollnsteiner are the authors of a report submitted to the Philippine Social Science Council by the Institute of Philippine Culture, *The Filipino Family, Community, and Nation: The Same Yesterday, Today, and Tomorrow* (Quezon City, 1975).

There is an extensive literature on the cultural impact of U.S. imperialism on Philippine society. A good, and easy to find, introduction is James Fallows, "A Damaged Culture," *Atlantic Monthly* (November 1987), 49–58. A much more extended analysis can be found in the popular history of the archipelago by Stanley Karnow, *In Our Image: America's Empire in the Philippines* (New York, 1989), which won the Pulitzer Prize.

CHAPTER 2—THIS VERY BEAUTIFUL PEARL OF THE ORIENT SEA

A good introduction to the geography and people of the Philippines is F. L. Wernstedt and J. E. Spencer, *The Philippine Island World: A Physical, Cultural, and Regional Geography* (reprint ed., Berkeley, 1978). A much more opulent book is the visually splendid two-volume *The Philippine Atlas* (Manila, 1975), although some of the economic data prepared by the Fund for the Assistance to Private Education was grossly biased in favor of the Marcos administration. Among the more general geographies, see Charles A. Fisher, *Southeast Asia: A Social, Economic, and Political Geography* (London, 1964); Ernest H. G. Dobby, *Monsoon Asia* (Chicago, 1961); and Charles E. Robequain, *Malaya, Indonesia, Borneo, and the Philippines* (New York, 1954). Karl J. Pelzer's *Pioneer Settlement in the Asiatic*

Tropics: Studies in Land Utilization and Agricultural Colonization in Southeast Asia (New York, 1948) is also helpful if very dated.

Over the last few decades there has been a qualitative improvement in economic histories about the archipelago. Perhaps the most important scholar is Norman G. Owen. See, for example, his *Prosperity Without Progress: Manila Hemp and Material Life in Colonial Philippines* (Berkeley, 1984). Owen's approach, like those of many of his generation, is to trace the complex interaction of economic development on social institutions. See also Vicente Valdepeñas and Gemilino M. Bautista, *The Emergence of the Philippine Economy* (Manila, 1977). There are many monographs that focus on a particular industry or economic sector. See, for example, Carlos Quirino, *History of the Philippine Sugar Industry* (Manila, 1974). For a more leftist analysis of Philippine economic development, see Rene E. Ofreneo's *Capitalism in Philippine Agriculture* (1980), and Jonathan Fast and James Richardson's *Roots of Dependency: Political and Economic Revolution in 19th Century Philippine Agriculture* (Quezon City, 1979). See also Robert F. Chandler, *An Adventure in Applied Science: A History of the International Rice Research Institute* (Los Baños, 1982).

A.V.H. Hartendorp's *Short History of Industry and Trade of the Philippines* (Manila, 1953) is a dated but useful introduction to Philippine economic development in the American era. Frank H. Golay's many writings on the Philippine economy are essential reference works. See, for example, *The Philippines: Public Policy and National Economic Development* (Ithaca, N.Y., 1961). See also *The Philippine Economy in the 1960's*, edited by Gerardo P. Sicat (Quezon City, 1964), and George L. Hicks, *Trade and Growth in the Philippines: An Open Economy* (Ithaca, N.Y., 1974). Eliodoro G. Robles has written one of the most detailed accounts of *The Philippines in the Nineteenth Century* (Quezon City, 1969), based primarily on the extensive holdings of the Newberry Collection at the University of Chicago Library. Benito F. Legarda y Fernandez's "Foreign Trade, Economic Change, and Entrepreneurship in Nineteenth-Century Philippines" (Ph.D. dissertation, Harvard University, 1955), remains one of the most important scholarly works on the nineteenth-century Philippine economy. See also Frederick Wernstedt, *The Role and Importance of Philippine Interisland Shipping and Trade* (Ithaca, N.Y., 1957). There are a number of useful firsthand accounts, including W. G. Palgrave, *The Far Off Eden Isles: Country Life in the Philippines Fifty Years Ago, by a British Consul* (Manila, 1929), and the company-prepared *Centenary of Wise and Company in the Philippines (1826–1926)* (Manila, 1926).

Documentary data on the Philippine economy during the American period are extensive and readily available, especially in the annual reports of the governors-general. *The Records of the Bureau of Insular Affairs Relating to the Philippine Islands, 1898–1935*, compiled by Kenneth Munden (Washington, D.C., 1942), and the companion *Preliminary Inventories of the Records of the Office of the High Commissioner to the Philippines*, compiled by Richard S. Maxwell (Washington, D.C., 1963), are introductions to the archival material at the Library of Congress.

The Marcos government suppressed honest analysis and unbiased economic data. Information was manipulated and scholars were denied access to information.

Still, there is much to be learned from the better studies completed during this period. See Robert E. Baldwin, *The Philippines* (New York, 1975), written under the auspices of the National Bureau of Economic Research, and Don Weintraub, Miriam Shapiro, and Belinda Aquino, *Agrarian Development and Modernization in the Philippines* (Jerusalem, 1973). The studies regularly prepared by the World Bank, the Asian Development Bank, the Food and Agriculture Organization of the United Nations are all part of the chronicle of an economic debacle created by a greedy, repressive government.

During the Aquino years there has been a great deal of solid work written. See Pedro Salgado's *The Philippine Economy* (Quezon City, 1985); Filomeno Aguilar's *The Making of Sugar: Poverty, Crisis and Change in Negros Occidental* (Bacolod, 1984), Sally Findley's *Rural Development and Migration: A Study of Family Choices in the Philippines* (Boulder, Colo., 1987); and Niall O'Brien's *Revolution from the Heart: The Extraordinary Record of a Priest's Life and Work Among the Poor of the Philippine Sugarland* (New York, 1987), a firsthand tale of the social injustice of sugar production.

Among earlier monographs that still deserve attention are James A. Roumasset, *Rice and Risk: Decision-making Among Low-Income Farmers* (Amsterdam, 1976); Dennis Shoresmith, ed., *The Politics of Sugar: Studies of the Sugar Industry in the Philippines* (Frankston, Australia, 1977); and Frank Lynch, *The Bittersweet Taste of Sugar* (Quezon City, 1974). A very thoughtful but now dated study on land allocation in the archipelago is Akira Takahashi's *Land and Peasants in Central Luzon: The Socio-economic Structure of a Bulacan Village* (Tokyo, 1969). Jose V. Abueva, one of the most distinguished political scientists in the country wrote an early book, *Focus on the Barrio: The Story Behind the Birth of the Philippine Community Development Program Under President Ramon Magsaysay* (Manila, 1959), that is still historically significant, even though both the economic conditions and the solutions clearly belong to another age.

The contrast between the countryside and its problems and the massive, metropolitan sprawl of Manila is striking. The best pictorial introduction to Manila can be found in Luning B. Ira and Isagani R. Medina, *Streets of Manila* (Manila, 1977). Gilda Cordero-Fernando and Nik Ricio, eds., *Turn of the Century* (Manila, 1978) is a coffee table volume with outstanding illustrations of Hispanized Manila. Aprodicio A. Laquian has studied the problems of the city of Manila in his books, *The City in Nation Building: Politics and Administration in Metropolitan Manila* (Manila, 1966) and *Slums Are for People* (Manila, 1969), a detailed analysis of Manila's urban problem and a development project in its Tondo section. Daniel F. Doeppers, *Ethnicity and Class in the Structure of Philippine Cities* (Ph.D. dissertation, Syracuse University, 1972; Ann Arbor, Mich., 1972), and Jose V. Abueva, Sylvia H. Guerrero, and Elsa P. Jurado, *Metro Manila Today and Tomorrow,* Final report submitted to the First National City Bank by the Institute of Philippine Culture (Quezon City, 1972) are both important sources. Richard L. Stone and Joy Marsella offer insight into Southeast Asian urbanization in their article, "Mahirap: A Squatter Community in a Manila Suburb," in *Modernization: Its Impact in the Philippines III,* Institute of Philippine Culture, Paper no. 6 (Quezon City, 1968), 64–91. See also Mary R. Hollnsteiner, "The Urbanization of Metropolitan Manila," in *Modernization: Its Impact in the Philippines IV*, Institute of Philippine Culture, Paper no. 7 (Quezon City, 1969), 147–174. Donn V. Hart's *The Philippine Plaza Complex: A Focal Point in Culture Change* (New Haven, Conn., 1955) is a dated but interesting study. Robert R. Reed has written on historical Manila in *Colonial Manila: The Context of Hispanic Urbanism and Process of Morphogenesis* (Berkeley, 1978) and his earlier work, *Hispanic Urbanism in the Philippines: A Study of the Impact of Church and State* (Manila, 1967). The comparative scope of Terence G. McGee's *The Southeast Asian City: A Social Geography of the Primate Cities of Southeast Asia* (London, 1967) makes a unique contribution to the literature. For antiquarian pleasure, see Mauro Garcia and C. O. Resurrercion, *Focus on Old Manila: A Volume Issued to Commemorate the Fourth Centenary of the City of Manila* (Manila, 1971).

The best studies of bureaucratic development in the Philippines are still Onofre D. Corpuz, *The Bureaucracy in the Philippines* (Quezon City, 1957), and Joseph Ralston Hayden, *The Philippines: A Study in National Development* (New York, 1942). Hayden deals with the development of the Philippine government specifically under American rule. Also helpful for the early period of U.S. control are James H. Blount, *American Occupation of the Philippines, 1898–1912* (original ed., 1912; Manila, 1968); Dean C. Worcester, *The Philippines Past and Present*, 2 vols. (New York, 1914; rev. ed., edited by J. R. Hayden, New York, 1930); and Eliodoro G. Robles, *The Philippines in the Nineteenth Century* (Quezon City, 1969). Jean Grossholtz, *Politics: The Philippines* (Boston, 1964), is good for the first decades of independence, and *Political Change in the Philippines: Studies of Local Politics Preceding Martial Law*, edited by Benedict J. Kerkvliet (Honolulu, 1974), is useful for the era just prior to the declaration of martial law. See also Carl H. Landé, *Leaders, Factions, and Parties: The Structure of Philippine Politics*, Southeast Asia Studies, Monograph no. 6 (New Haven, Conn., 1965).

CHAPTER 3—A SINGULAR AND A PLURAL FOLK

One of the best general works on peasant society is Eric Wolf's *Peasants* (Englewood Cliffs, N.J., 1966). Among other important general works are the classic three lectures by Cora DuBois in 1947, published under the title of *Social Forces in Southeast Asia* (Cambridge, Mass., 1959), and the numerous writings of John S. Furnivall, including *Colonial Policy and Practice: A Comparative Study of Burma and Netherlands India* (Cambridge, Mass., 1948; 2d ed., New York, 1956). It was Furnivall who coined the phrase "plural society" to describe the social realities of Southeast Asian countries.

There is an extensive literature on what is called "Christian lowland village life." Among the most recent works are Stephen Griffith's *Emigrants, Entrepreneurs and Evil Spirits: Life in a Philippine Village* (Honolulu, 1988), and Lillian Trager's *The City Connection: Migration and Family Interdependence in the Philippines* (Ann Arbor, Mich., 1988). Anthropologists have produced a large body of work. See, for example, F. Landa Jocano, *The Ilocanos: An Ethnography of Family and Community Life in the Ilocos Region* (Quezon City, 1982); Brian Fegan, "Folk-Capitalism: Economic Strategies of Peasants in a Philippines Wet-Rice Village" (Ph.D.

dissertation, Yale University, 1979); and Marshall S. McLennan, *The Central Luzon Plain: Land and Society on the Inland Frontier* (Manila, 1980).

There is an even greater corpus dealing dealing with upland peoples. One of the most recent is James F. Eder's *On the Road to Tribal Extinction: Depopulation, Deculturation and Adaptive Well-being Among the Batak of the Philippines* (Berkeley, 1987). See also R. C. Ileto, *Magindanao, 1860–1888* (Ithaca, N.Y., 1971); William H. Scott, *The Discovery of the Igorots: Spanish Contacts with the Pagans of Northern Luzon* (Quezon City, 1974); Michelle Z. Rosaldo, *Knowledge and Passion: Ilongot Notions of Self and Social Life* (Cambridge, 1980); Renaldo Rosaldo, *Ilongot Headhunting: A Study in Society and History* (Stanford, 1980); and Stuart Schlegel, *Tiruray Justice: Traditional Tiruray Law and Morality* (Berkeley, 1970) and *Tiruray Subsistence: From Shifting Cultivation to Plow Agriculture* (Quezon City, 1979). See also Karl L. Hutterer and William K. Macdonald, eds., *Houses Built on Scattered Poles: Prehistory and Ecology in Negros Oriental, Philippines* (Cebu City, 1982); Felix M. Keesing, *Taming Philippine Headhunters: A Study of Government and Cultural Change in Northern Luzon* (New York, 1984); Yasushi Kikuchi, *Mindoro Highlanders: The Life of the Swidden Agriculturalists* (Quezon City, 1984); and Violeta Lopez-Gonzaga, *Peasants in the Hills: A Study of the Dynamics of Social Change Among the Buhid Swidden Cutivators in the Philippines* (Quezon City, 1983).

Interestingly enough, urbanization has not received as much attention as it should. But see Amaryllis T. Torres, *The Urban Filipino Worker in an Industrializing Society* (Honolulu, 1988). One can get a sense of the traditional barrio in Mary R. Hollnsteiner's perceptive work, *The Dynamics of Power in a Philippine Municipality* (Manila, 1963); Richard W. Leiban's *Cebuano Sorcery: Malign Magic in the Philippines* (Berkeley, 1967); Ethel Nurge's *Life in a Leyte Village* (Seattle, 1964); and Marshall S. McLennan's *Peasant and Hacendeno in Nueva Ecija: The Socio-economic Origins of a Philippine Commercial Rice-Growing Region* (Ph.D. dissertation, Berkeley, 1973; Ann Arbor, Mich., 1974).

The principal minority group of the Philippines, the Muslims, have also received substantial attention over the past two decades. A good introduction is Peter G. Gowing and Robert D. McAmis, *Muslim Filipinos: Heritage and Horizon* (Manila, 1974), and Peter Gowing, ed., *Understanding Islam and Muslims in the Philippines* (Quezon City, 1988). F. Landa Jocano edited *Filipino Muslims: Their Social Institutions and Cultural Achievements* (Quezon City, 1983). See also Samuel K. Tan, *Selected Essays on the Filipino Muslims* (Merawi City, 1982); Michael O. Mastura, *Muslim Filipino Experience: A Collection of Essays* (Manila, 1984); Ruth Moore, "Women and Warriors Defending Islam in the Southern Philippines" (Ph.D. dissertation, University of California, San Diego, 1981); Kenneth E. Bauzon, "Islamic Nationalism in the Philippines: Reflections in Socio-Political Analysis" (Ph.D. dissertation, Duke University, 1981); and Antonio Martel de Goyangos, *The Island of Mindanao* (1977). See also Thomas M. Kiefer's case study, *The Tausug: Violence and Law in a Philippine Muslim Society* (New York, 1972); Cesar Adib Majul, *Muslims in the Philippines* (Manila, 1973); and A. T. Tiamson, *The Muslim Filipinos: An Annotated Bibliography*, 2 vols. (Marati, 1979 and Manila, 1981).

Edgar Wickberg's outstanding book, *The Chinese in Philippine Life, 1850–1898* (New Haven, Conn., 1965), and his article, "The Chinese Mestizo in Philippine History," *Journal of Southeast Asian History* 5:1 (March 1964), 62–100, are seminal studies on those key groups in Philippine life, and both works should be read carefully. The two volumes edited by Alfonso Felix, Jr., *The Chinese in the Philippines, 1570–1770* (Manila, 1966) and *The Chinese in the Philippines, 1770–1898* (Manila, 1969), are useful introductions to aspects of Chinese life in the past. Antonio S. Tan, *The Chinese in the Philippines, 1898–1935: A Study of Their National Awakening* (Quezon City, 1972), deals with a most important era and problem. For relatively recent analyses of the Chinese and Chinese mestizo communities in the Philippines, see Gerald A. McBeath, *Political Integration of the Philippine Chinese,* Center for South and Southeast Asia Studies, Monograph no. 8 (Berkeley, 1973), and John T. Omonhundro, *Chinese Merchant Families in Iloilo: Commerce and Kin in a Central Philippine City* (Quezon City, 1981). See also Andrew B. Gonzalez, *Language and Nationalism: The Philippine Experience Thus Far* (Manila, 1980), and Marr Wai Jong Cheong, *The Chinese-Cantonese in Manila: A Study in Culture and Education* (Manila, 1983).

Education during the Spanish period is the subject of Henry F. Fox, "Primary Education in the Philippines, 1565–1863," *Philippine Studies* 13:2 (April 1965), 207–231. For a general history, see Encarnacion Alzona, *A History of Education in the Philippines* (1932). Joseph Ralson Hayden's monumental book, *The Philippines: A Study in National Development* (New York, 1942), has excellent chapters tracing the development of education and language during the American regime. The annual reports of the American governors-general contain detailed analyses of the school system as it developed after 1900. For a history of the development of Pilipino, see Ernest J. Frei, *The Historical Development of the Philippine National Language* (1959). See also D. E. Foley, "Colonialism and Schooling the Philippines," in P. G. Altbach and Gail Kelly, eds., *Education in the Colonial Experience* (New Brunswick, 1984), 69–95. Renato Constantino has argued that American educational policy was, in fact, miseducation, distorting the Filipino's capacity to see reality clearly. Among his other writings, see *The Miseducation of the Filipinos* (Manila, 1966).

CHAPTER 4—THE SEARCH FOR A USABLE PAST

Over the past decades, increasing attention has been paid to Philippine historiography as scholars, Filipino and foreign, have attempted to assign proper importance to the many players and to create a periodization that accurately reflects the Philippine experience. The emphasis has shifted from colonial masters to indigenous peoples, from "Manilacentric" to regional and ethnolinguistic, from the paramountcy of political periodization and history to socioeconomic and cultural priorities. Historians have debated, for example, whether 1898 represents a historical interruption, a discontinuity, or whether the processes of modernization, economic change, and social integration flowed organically from the late Spanish era into the American era far more smoothly than politics and imperialism would suggest. An excellent place to begin is with Alfred McCoy and Eduardo C. de Jesus, *Philippine Social History: Global Trade and Local Transformation* (Quezon City, 1982). See also *Perspectives on Philippine Historiography: A Symposium,* edited by John A. Larkin, Southeast Asia Series no. 21 (New Haven, Conn., 1979); Norman Owen, "Trends and Directions of Research on Philippine History: An Informal Essay," *Asian Studies* 12 (August–December 1974), 101–107; and Marcelino Foronda, *Some Notes on Philippine Historiography* (Manila, 1972). An important statement of the nationalist argument can be found in Renato Constantino, *The Philippines: A Past Revisited* (Quezon City, 1975).

Philippine historiography needs to be set in the larger context of Southeast Asian and Third World studies. For a discussion of the importance of this comparative area, see Donald K. Emmerson, "Issues in Southeast Asian History: Room for Interpretation," *Journal of Asian Studies* 40:1 (November 1980), 43–68.

In the early 1960s, a series of important pieces appeared in the *Journal of Southeast Asian History* (*JSEAH*), including D. P. Singhal's "Some Comments on 'The Western Element in Modern Southeast Asian History,'" 1:2 (September 1960), 118–123; John R. W. Smail's "On the Possibility of an Autonomous History of Modern Southeast Asia," 2:2 (July 1961), 72–102; F. J. West's "The Study of Colonial History," 2:3 (October 1961), 70–82; and Harry J. Benda's "The Structure of Southeast Asian History: Some Preliminary Observations," 3:1 (March 1962), 106–138. Two other important articles stand out: Lauriston Sharp's "Cultural Continuities and Discontinuities in Southeast Asia," *Journal of Asian Studies* 22:1 (November 1962), 3–11, and Harry J. Benda's "Political Elites in Colonial Southeast Asia," *Comparative Studies in Society and History* 7:3 (April 1965), 233–252.

Nicholas P. Cushner's *Spain in the Philippines: From Conquest to Revolution* (Quezon City, 1970) is an excellent introduction to the Spanish era. Vicente L. Rafael has written a significant monograph, *Contracting Colonialism: Translation and Christian Conversion in Tagalog Society Under Spanish Rule* (Ithaca, N.Y., 1988), exploring the cultural interaction by an analysis of language and meaning. A far more speculative analysis can be found in John Leddy Phelan, *The Hispanization of the Philippines: Spanish Aims and Filipino Responses, 1565–1700* (Madison, Wis., 1959). Cushner has also published a more detailed study, *Landed Estates in the Colonial Philippines* (New Haven, Conn., 1976), as Monograph no. 20 of the Southeast Asia Studies series. See also Dennis M. Roth, *The Friar Estates of the Philippines* (Albuquerque, N.M., 1977), and Martin Noone, *The Islands Saw It: The Discovery and Conquest of the Philippines, 1521–1581* (Dublin, 1983).

A most important, if dated, English-language source for the Spanish era is the fifty-five volumes of documents and footnotes prepared by E. H. Blair and J. A. Robertson, *The Philippine Islands, 1493–1898* (Cleveland, Ohio, 1903). Another dated but important book is William L. Schurz's *The Manila Galleon* (reprint ed., New New York, 1959). Schurz wrote with verve, and the book is full of swashbuckling fun. For a shorter and more recent treatment of the Manila galleon trade, see Benito Legarda y Fernandez, "Two and a Half Centuries of the Galleon Trade," *Philippine Studies* 3:4 (December 1955), 345–372. Pierre Chaunu has edited and elaborated on the records pertaining to Spanish trade with the Philippines in the Archivos des Indes in Seville. His volume, entitled *Les Philippines et le Pacifique des Ibériques (XVIe, XVIIe, XVIIIe siecles)* (Paris, 1960), is particularly relevant to trade in the sixteenth and early seventeenth centuries. *Documents Illustrating the British Conquest of Manila, 1762–1763*, edited by Nicholas Cushner (London, 1971), is a valuable source for understanding this interruption of Spanish rule.

The best short analysis of the economic structure during the Spanish era is Benito Legarda y Fernandez. "The Philippine Economy Under Spanish Rule," *Solidarity* 2:10 (November–December 1967), 1–21. See also Maria Lourdes Diaz-Trechuelo's "Philippine Economic Development Plans, 1746–1779," *Philippine Studies* 12:2 (April 1964), 203–231, and "Eighteenth-Century Philippine Economy: Commerce," *Philippine Studies* 14:2 (April 1966), 252–279. For a brief description of the tobacco monopoly in the Philippines, see Eduardo Lacina's "The Tobacco Monopoly," *Historical Bulletin* (Philippine Historical Association) 8:1 (March 1964), 60–72, and Eduardo C. de Jesus, *The Tobacco Monopoly in the Philippines: Bureaucratic Enterprise and Social Change, 1766–1880* (Quezon City, 1980). Maria Lourdes Diaz-Trechuelo's "Eighteenth-Century Philippine Economy: Agriculture," *Philippine Studies* 14:1 (January 1966), 65–126, is a study of commercial agriculture in the Philippines, and her "Eighteenth-Century Philippine Economy: Mining," *Philippine Studies* 13:4 (October 1965), 763–797, is an analysis of that aspect of the Philippine economy. See also James F. Warren, *The Sulu Zone, 1768–1898: The Dynamics of External Trade, Slavery, and Ethnicity in the Transformation of a Southeast Asian Maritime State* (Singapore, 1981).

Among the most important trends of Philippine historiography since the mid-1970s has been the growth of interest in regional history. Moving away from a Manilacentric focus on national and colonial institutions, a group of younger historians has explored the wealth of regional and local documents, detailing the fascinating mosaic that previously had been all but ignored by both Filipino and foreign scholars. Among the best regional histories, many of which cut across the periodization of this book, are John A. Larkin, *The Pampangans: Colonial Society in a Philippine Province* (Berkeley, 1972); and Robert Bruce Cruikshank, *Samar 1768–1898* (Manila, 1985). See also Bruce L. Fenner, *Cebu Under the Spanish Flag, 1521–1896: An Economic-Social History* (Manila, 1985); Robert R. Reed, *City of Pines: The Origins of Baguio as a Colonial Hill Station and Regional Capital* (Berkeley, 1976); Howard T. Fry, *A History of the Mountain Province* (Quezon City, 1983); Rosario Mendoza Cortes, *Pangasinan, 1572–1800* (Quezon City, 1974); Maria Fe Hernaez Romero, *Negros Occidental Between Two Foreign Powers (1888–1909)* (Negros Occidental, 1974); Marshall S. McLennan, *The Central Luzon Plain: Land and Society on the Inland Frontier* (Manila, 1980); and Willem Wolters, *Politics, Patronage, and Class Conflict in Central Luzon* (The Hague, 1983).

The literature in Spanish is extensive. Many of the friars wrote about their lives and experiences, and Spanish scholars have written much that is of value. One excellent source is Jose Montero y Vidal's *Historia general de Filipinas desde el descubrimiento de Dichas islas hasta nuestras dias* (Madrid, 1887). For a discussion of the changing economic environment, see Maria Louisa Rodriguez Baena, *La Sociedad Economica de Amigos del Pais de Manila en el siglo XVIII* (Seville, 1966).

There are also many firsthand accounts in English. See Thomas R. McHale and Mary C. McHale, *Early American-Philippine Trade: The Journal of Nathaniel Bowditch in Manila, 1796* (New Haven, Conn., 1962), and Austin Craig has edited a volume entitled *The Former Philippines Through Foreign Eyes* (Manila, 1916), in which he has brought together the observations of some of the visitors to the Philippines in the nineteenth century, and in which are included the writings of Tomas de Comyn—the Philippine Company agent in Manila—and of the German scholar Feodor Jagor. Also of value is Sir John Bowring's *A Visit to the Philippine Islands* (London, 1859). In recent years, the Filipiniana Book Guild has done an outstanding job of reprinting many additional memoirs, including Paul P. de la Gironiere's *Twenty Years in the Philippines* (Manila, 1962) and Robert MacMicking's *Recollections of Manila and the Philippines During 1848, 1849, and 1850* (Manila, 1967), among others.

The development of a Philippine political consciousness can be traced in Gregorio Y. Yabes, "The Philippine Representation in the Spanish Cortes," *Philippine Social Science Review* 8 (1936), 36–67 and 140–160, and in Sinibaldo de Mas, *Report on the Condition of the Philippines in 1842*, vol. 3 (reprint ed., Manila, 1963). De Mas was both perceptive and blunt, and his report is essential to anyone studying the collapse of Spanish power in the Philippines.

Among the many works dealing with the late Spanish era and the rise of Philippine nationalism, consult John N. Schumacher and Nicholas P. Cushner, *Burgos and the Cavite Mutiny* (Quezon City, 1969); Josefa Saniel, *Japan and the Philippines, 1868–1898* (Quezon City, 1963); John N. Schumacher, *The Propaganda Movement* (Manila, 1963); Romeo Cruz, "Philippine Nationalism in the Nineteenth Century," *Philippine Historical Bulletin* 6:1 (March 1962), 16–29; Maximo N. Kalaw's classic study, *The Development of Philippine Politics, 1872–1920* (Manila, 1926); Teodoro A. Agoncillo's important if somewhat unsatisfactory work, *The Revolt of the Masses* (Quezon City, 1956); and Eliodoro G. Robles, *The Philippines in the Nineteenth Century* (Quezon City, 1969). *La Solidaridad*, republished by the University of the Philippines Press in 1967, is of great value as a source. The writings of Jose P. Rizal are most successfully translated by Leon Ma. Guerrero as *The Lost Eden* (Bloomington, Ind., 1961) and *The Subversive* (Bloomington, Ind., 1962). The two best biographies of Rizal are Rafael Palma's *The Pride of the Malay Race* (New York, 1949) and Leon Ma. Guerrero's *The First Filipino* (Manila, 1963). See also Eugene A. Hessel, *The Religious Thought of Jose Rizal* (Quezon City, 1983); Pedro A. Gagelonia, *Rizal's Life, Work, and Writings* (Manila, 1974); and an anthology of essays by and about Rizal selected by Gabriel F. Fabella, *Understanding Rizal* (Quezon City, 1963). The publications of the National Heroes Commission in Manila, including *The Minutes of the Katipunan* (Manila, 1964) and the *Memoirs of General Artemio Ricarte* (Manila, 1963), are important source books. Carlos Quirino's *The Young Aguinaldo: From Kawit to Biyák-ná-Bató* (Manila, 1969) is a scholarly examination of Aguinaldo's development, as is Alfredo Saulo, *Emilio Aguinaldo* (Quezon City, 1984).

Cesar A. Majul's brilliant study entitled *The Political and Constitutional Ideas of the Philippine Revolution* (Quezon City, 1967) examines the intellectual assumptions of the Filipino leadership during the Malolos era. The Ateneo de

Manila publications of the *Trial of Rizal*, edited by Horacio de la Costa (Manila, 1961), and the *Trial of Andres Bonifacio*, edited by Virginia Palma-Bonifacio (Manila, 1963), are significant volumes dealing with the executions of those two famous Filipinos. Cesar A. Majul's biography, *Apolinario Mabini: Revolutionary* (Manila, 1964), and Mabini's writings, edited by Alfredo S. Veloso in three volumes for the Mabini Centennial (Quezon City, 1964), are also very important. Leandro H. Fernandez's *The Philippine Republic* (New York, 1926) and Teodoro A. Agoncillo's *Malolos: The Crisis of the Republic* (Quezon City, 1960) both trace the struggle in Malolos and against the Americans. General Aguinaldo's *Memoirs of the Revolution* (Manila, 1967) are of little use as a historical source.

Important source books on the Philippine-American war are John M. Taylor, ed., *The Philippine Insurrection Against the United States: A Compilation of Documents*, 5 vols. (Manila, 1971–1973); John Morgan Gates, *Schoolbooks and Krags: The United States Army in the Philippines, 1898–1902* (Westport, Conn., 1973); and Leon Wolff, *Little Brown Brother* (London, 1960). Milagros C. Guerrero's *Luzon at War: Contradictions in Philippine Society, 1898–1902* (Ph.D. dissertation, University of Michigan, 1977; Ann Arbor, Mich., 1977) is the finest scholarly work on this period.

Peter W. Stanley, *A Nation in the Making: The Philippines and the United States, 1899–1921* (Cambridge, Mass., 1974), is a splendid introduction to the first decades of the American era. There are a number of important new monographs dealing with this period, including, Glenn May's *Social Engineering in the Philippines: The Aims, Execution and Impact of American Colonial Policy, 1900–1913* (Westport, Conn., 1980); Louis Halle's *The United States Acquires the Philippines: Consensus vs. Reality* (Lanham, N.Y., 1985); David Bain's *Sitting in Darkness: Americans in the Philippines* (Boston, 1984); and Russell Roth's *Muddy Glory: America's "Indian Wars" in the Philippines 1899–1935* (West Hanover, Mass., 1981). The essays written for a major conference at Harvard on Fil-American history are excellent; see Peter Stanley, ed., *Reappraising an Empire: New Perspectives on Philippine-American History* (Cambridge, Mass., 1984). William J. Pomeroy, *An American Made Tragedy: Neo-Colonialism and Dictatorship in the Philippines* (New York, 1974), is a Marxist condemnation of U.S. intervention. The motives behind U.S. intervention are analyzed in Ernest R. May, *Imperial Democracy* (New York, 1961); Julius W. Pratt, *Expansionists of 1898* (Baltimore, Md., 1936); and H. Wayne Morgan, *America's Road to Empire* (New York, 1966); and a different point of view is presented in Walter LaFeber, *The New Empire: An Interpretation of American Expansion, 1860–1898* (Ithaca, N.Y., 1963), and Thomas J. McCornick, *China Market: America's Quest for Informal Empire, 1893–1901* (Chicago, 1967). Many of the U.S. participants wrote of their experiences: James A. LeRoy in his *The Americans in the Philippines*, 2 vols. (Boston and New York, 1914), reserved judgment about intervention. Robert L. Beisner's *Twelve Against Empire* (New York, 1968) helps to shatter long-standing illusions about the anti-imperialists. See also Roger J. Bresnahan, *In Time of Hesitation: American Anti-Imperialists and the Philippine-American War* (Quezon City, 1981). Lewis E. Gleeck, Jr., has written extensively on this era. See *A General History of the Philippines: The American Half Century* (Quezon City, 1984); *The American*

Governors-General and High Commissioners (Quezon City, 1986); and *The Manila Americans* (Manila, 1977). See also Arthur S. Pier, *American Apostles to the Philippines* (Boston, 1950), and Peter C. Gowing, *Mandate in Moroland: The American Government of Muslim Filipinos, 1899–1920* (Quezon City, 1977).

The controversy over the friar lands can be followed in W. C. Forbes, D. C. Worcester, and F. W. Carpenter, *The Friar Land Inquiry, Philippine Government* (Manila, 1910); in the "Report of the Committee on Insular Affairs, No. 2289," 61st Congress, 3d session, March 3, 1911; and in "Disposition of the Friar Lands," a speech by Manuel L. Quezon to the U.S. Congress, May 1, 1912.

An excellent way to sense the political tensions and fights is to enjoy Alfred McCoy's and Alfredo Roces's *Philippine Cartoons: Political Caricature of the American Era, 1900–1941* (Manila, 1985). Among the best books analyzing the development of a political consciousness in the islands are Bonifacio S. Salamanca's *The Filipino Reaction to American Rule, 1901–1913* (n.p., 1968) and the very dated study by Dapen Liang, *The Development of Philippine Political Parties* (Hong Kong, 1939). See also Norman G. Owen, ed., *Compadre Colonialism: Studies on the Philippines Under American Rule,* Michigan Papers on South and Southeast Asia no. 3 (Ann Arbor, Mich., 1970). See also Emily Hahn, *The Islands: America's Imperialist Adventures in the Philippines* (New York, 1981).

In addition to the works already cited, there are many books that study the Harrison and Leonard Wood regimes. Michael P. Onorato, in particular, has written often of these decades. See his *Brief Review of American Interest in Philippine Development and Other Essays* (Berkeley, 1968). For an analysis of the Democratic party years, see Roy W. Curry, "Woodrow Wilson and Philippine Policy," *Mississippi Valley Historical Review* 41 (1954), 435–452, and Francis Burton Harrison's *The Cornerstone of Philippine Independence* (New York, 1922). The protracted struggle between Governor Leonard Wood and the Filipino leadership produced a great deal of polemical literature. See, for example, Jorge Bocobo's *General Leonard Wood and the Law* (Manila, 1923) and Manuel L. Quezon and Camilo Osias, *Governor-General Wood and the Filipino Cause* (Manila, 1924). Bruno Lasker's *Filipino Immigration* (original ed., 1931; reprint ed., Chicago, 1969) and the Institute of Asian Studies, *The Filipino Exclusion Movement 1927–1935* (Quezon City, 1967), examine the problems of the Filipino migration to Hawaii and the United States. See M. P. Onorato, *Philippine Bibliography, 1899–1946* (Santa Barbara, 1968) for additional sources.

The most literate and perceptive analysis of the transition from U.S. rule to Commonwealth status can be found in Theodore Friend's *Between Two Empires* (New Haven, Conn., 1965). See also four *Philippine Studies* articles by Friend that deal with sugar and the independence question: "American Interests and Philippine Independence, 1929–1933," 11 (1963), 505–523; "Philippine Interests and the Mission for Independence, 1929–1932," 12 (1964), 63–82; "Philippine Independence and the Last Lame-Duck Congress," 12 (1964), 260–276; and "Veto and Repassage of the Hare-Hawes-Cutting Act: A Catalogue of Motives," 12 (1964), 666–680. See also Bernardita Reyes Churchill, *The Philippines Independence Mission to the United States, 1919–1934* (Manila, 1983). Manuel L. Quezon's autobiography, *The Good Fight* (New York, 1946), is far more revealing than most of the scholarly literature dealing with the commonwealth president. Daniel F. Doeppers, *Manila, 1900–1941: Social Change in a Late Colonial Metropolis* (New Haven, Conn., 1984) is a fascinating study of this era.

CHAPTER 5—THE RELIGIOUS IMPULSE: GLOBAL AND LOCAL TRADITIONS

There is, not surprisingly, extensive literature about the Roman Catholic church in the Philippines, much of it written by clerics, past and present. An excellent place to begin is with *Readings in Philippine Church History,* edited and introduced by John N. Schumacher (Quezon City, 1979). See also Pablo Fernandez, *History of the Church in the Philippines, 1521–1898* (Manila, 1979). Another important volume dealing with the church in the Philippines is *Studies in Philippine Church History,* edited by Gerald H. Anderson (Ithaca, N.Y., 1969). Horatio de la Costa's *The Jesuits in the Philippines, 1581–1768* (Cambridge, Mass., 1961) is a classic. The casual reader, however, might prefer Gregorio F. Zaide's *Catholicism in the Philippines* (Manila, 1937), despite its very dated approach.

The artistic and architectural impact of the church can be studied in Richard Ahlborn, "The Spanish Churches of Central Luzon," *Philippine Studies* 8:4 (October 1960), 802–813; Benito Legarda y Fernandez, "Colonial Churches in Ilocos," *Philippine Studies* 8:1 (January 1960), 121–158; Armengol P. Ortiz, *Intramuros de Manila de 1571 hasta su destruccion en 1945* (Madrid, 1958); and Fernando Zobel de Ayala, *Philippine Religious Imagery* (Quezon City, 1963). Also of value is Winfield Scott Smith III, ed., *The Art of the Philippines, 1521–1957* (Manila, 1958), and Alicia M. Coseteng, *Spanish Churches in the Philippines* (Quezon City, 1972). E. G. Gatbonton, *A Heritage of Saints: Colonial Santos in the Philippines* (Manila, 1979), is a good source on these religious artifacts.

The literature attacking and defending the friars is extensive and usually polemical. A good example of antifriar writing can be found in M. H. del Pilar, *Monastic Supremacy in the Philippines* (Barcelona, 1889; reprint ed., Quezon City, 1958). For a sympathetic defense of the friars, see Vicente R. Pilapil, "Nineteenth-Century Philippines and the Friar Problem," *Americas* 18:2 (October 1961), 127–148. One of the best volumes is a monograph by the prolific and scholarly Jesuit, John N. Schumacher, *Father Jose Burgos: Priest and Nationalist* (Quezon City, 1972).

One of the best introductions to the Iglesia Filipina Independiente, or Aglipayanism, is, ironically, in a multivolume work by two Jesuits, Pedro S. de Achútegui and Miguel A. Bernad, vols. 1–2, *Religious Revolution in the Philippines: The Life and Church of Gregorio Aglipay, 1860–1960* (Quezon City, 1960), and vol. 3, *The Religious Coup d'État, 1898–1901: A Documentary History* (Quezon City, 1971). See also Daniel F. Doeppers, "Changing Patterns of Aglipayan Adherence in the Philippines, 1918–1970," *Philippine Studies* 25 (1977), 265–277, and Frank H. Wise, *The History of the Philippine Independent Church (Iglesia Filipina Independiente)* (Dumaguete, 1965). See also Jaime T. Licamco, *The Magicians of God: The Amazing Stories of Philippine Faith Healers* (Manila, 1981).

The best study of the *pasyon* and its role in shaping the religious life of the people is Renaldo C. Ileto's *Pasyon and Revolution: Popular Movements in the*

Philippines, 1840–1910 (Quezon City, 1979). Ileto's thesis has generated a debate with people who hold the position advanced by David R. Sturtevant in his many articles on millennial movements, and this dialogue is one of the most interesting in Philippine studies. See David R. Sturtevant's numerous works, including *Agrarian Unrest in the Philippines: Guardia de Honor,* Southeast Asia Studies no. 8 (Athens, Ohio, 1969); Popular Uprisings in the Philippines, 1840–1940 (Ithaca, N.Y., 1976); and "Sakdalism and Philippine Radicalism," *Journal of Asian Studies* 21:2 (February 1962), 199–213. R. M. Stubbs, "Philippine Radicalism: The Central Luzon Uprisings, 1925–1935" (Ph.D. dissertation, University of California, 1951), and M. C. Guerrero, "The Colorum Uprisings, 1924–1931," *Asian Studies* (Manila) 5 (1967), 65–78, are also good.

A related scholarly debate has examined whether Philippine masonry is distinct from other and rural movements of the local tradition. Ileto has placed masonry in a local context; others have stressed its alien, Spanish origins. Consult John N. Schumacher, "Philippine Masonry to 1890," *Asian Studies* (Manila) 4 (1966), 328–341, and Teodoro M. Kalaw, *Philippine Masonry* (reprint ed., Manila, 1956). The impact of Christianity in its various sectarian manifestations is analyzed somewhat less successfully by Richard L. Deats in *Nationalism and Christianity in the Philippines* (Dallas, Tex., 1967).

Among the more interesting analyses of modern religion in the Philippines are Jaime Bulatao and Vitaliano Gorospe, *Split-Level Christianity* (Quezon City, 1966); Marcelino Foronda, "The Canonization of Rizal," *Journal of History* (Philippines) 8 (1960), 1–48; and Vitaliano R. Gorospe and Richard L. Deats, comps., *The Filipino in the Seventies: An Ecumenical Perspective* (Quezon City, 1973). See also F. Landa Jocano, *Folk Christianity: A Preliminary Study of Conversion and Patterning of Christian Experience in the Philippines* (Quezon City, 1981).

CHAPTER 6—COLLABORATION AND RESTORATION

The war years are among the most controversial in Philippine history. The meaning of collaboration, the debate over definition of national obligation, the role of the United States, both during and after the fighting, the special position of Douglas MacArthur, the reaction to Japanese imperialism, the politics and ideology of the Hukbalahap are all elements of controversy. My book on collaboration has been argued over ever since. See David J. Steinberg, *Philippine Collaboration in World War Two* (Ann Arbor, Mich., 1967). Teodoro A. Agoncillo, the late professor at the University of the Philippines, disagreed most sharply, first in his two-volume work, *The Fateful Years* (Quezon City, 1965) and again in his final publication, *The Burden of Proof: The Laurel-Vargas Collaboration Case* (Manila, 1984). Mauro Garcia published a valuable source book of documents, *The Japanese Occupation of the Philippines* (Manila, 1965). Alfred W. McCoy, who also challenges my interpretation, has an important essay in *Southeast Asia Under Japanese Occupation: Transition and Transformation,* Southeast Asia Series no. 22 (New Haven, Conn., 1980). Theodore Friend III has also written an important book on this era, *The Blue-Eyed Enemy: Japan Against The West in Java and Luzon, 1942–1945* (Princeton, 1988).

Many of the principals have written memoirs, apologia, or autobiographies. Jorge Vargas, Jose Laurel, and Claro Recto are only the most important figures to attempt to justify their wartime involvement. The literature on World War II is so extensive it is almost impossible to know what to cite here. Ronald Spector, *Eagle Against the Sun: The American War With Japan* (New York, 1985) is a good beginning point. The literature on Douglas MacArthur is almost as extensive. See Carol M. Petillo, *Douglas MacArthur: The Philippine Years* (Bloomington, Ind., 1981) for a candid, nonhagiographic analysis, including the issuance of $500,000 to MacArthur by Quezon, a clear violation of ethics and law. Finally, the literature on the guerrillas is also extensive, both as a piece of the military history and by participants. See Carlos Quirino's *Chick Parsons, America's Master Spy in the Philippines* (Quezon City, 1984) for a fun read about one of the most remarkable men of this era.

The old order restored by MacArthur and confirmed by the election of Manuel Roxas is best introduced by Ronald K. Edgerton, "The Politics of Reconstruction in the Philippines, 1945–1948" (Ph.D. dissertation, University of Michigan, 1975). There are several biographies of Sergio Osmeña, including Resil Mojares, *The Man Who Would Be President: Sergio Osmeña and Philippine Politics* (Cebu, 1986); Vicente A. Pacis, *President Sergio Osmeña: A Fully Documented Biography* (Manila, 1971). See also Jose V. Abueva, *Ramon Magsaysay: A Political Biography* (Manila, 1971), and Marcial P. Lichauco, *Roxas: The Story of a Great Filipino and of the Political Era in Which He Lived* (Manila, 1952), which is flawed as a work of scholarship. Francis L. Starner, *Magsaysay and the Philippine Peasantry: The Agrarian Impact on Philippine Politics, 1953–1956* (Berkeley, 1961), is useful. See also Emerenciana Y. Arcellana, *The Social and Political Thought of Claro M. Recto* (Manila, 1981); Carlos Quirino, *Amang: The Life and Times of Eulogio Rodriguez, Sr.* (Quezon City, 1983); the many books of essays by Nick Joaquin, for example, *Reportage on Politics* (Manila, 1981); and Carolina G. Hernandez, "The Extent of Civilian Control of the Military in the Philippines, 1946–1976" (Ph.D. dissertation, State University of New York at Buffalo, 1979). The best works on the Hukbalahap are Benedict J. Kerkvliet, *The Huk Rebellion: A Study of Peasant Revolt in the Philippines* (Berkeley, 1977), and Eduardo Lachica, *Huk: Philippine Agrarian Society in Revolt* (Manila, 1971). Luis Taruc, the leader of the Hukbalahap, wrote a number of books, the most important of which is his first, *Born of the People* (New York, 1953). There have been a number of recent works dealing again with this rebellion, in part because of the high success of the NPA and also because of the deaths of several of the principals. See D. Michael Shafer, *Deadly Paradigms: The Failure of U.S. Counterinsurgency Policy* (Princeton, 1988), and Cecil B. Currey, *Edward Lansdale: The Unquiet American* (Boston, 1989). Among the best of earlier studies are Thomas C. Nowak, *Class and Clientist Systems in the Philippines: The Basis for Instability* (Ph.D. dissertation, Cornell University, 1974; Ann Arbor, Mich., 1974); Renze L. Hoeksema's "Communism in the Philippines: A Historical and Analytical Study," (Ph.D. dissertation, Harvard University, 1956); Alvin H. Scaff's *The Philippine Answer to Communism* (Palo Alto, Calif., 1955); and Uldarico S. Baclagon's *Lessons from the Huk Campaign in the Philippines* (Manila, 1960). William J. Pomeroy's *The Forest: A Personal Record of the Huk Guerrilla Struggle in the Philippines* (New

York, 1963) is an interesting account of guerrilla life in 1950–1952. In his book *Communism in the Phiippines* (Manila, 1969), Alfredo B. Saulo has written a brief introduction to the growth of the Communist party in the Philippines.

CHAPTER 7—THE MARCOS ERA

Literature on the Marcos era must be divided between what was written while Ferdinand Marcos was in power and what has appeared since. After martial law was declared, it was difficult for any Filipino to publish anything critical of the president, until late in his regime, when he abandoned strict censorship. For scholars abroad, it was often nearly impossible to get reliable information, especially statistics.

To understand Marcos, it is essential, but far from sufficient, to read from his own voluminous publications. See, for example, *Today's Revolution: Democracy* (Manila, 1971); *Toward a New Partnership: The Filipino Ideology* (Manila, 1983); *Progress and Martial Law* (Manila, 1981); *In Search of Alternatives: The Third World in an Age of Crisis* (Manila, 1980), and *An Ideology for Filipinos* (Manila, 1980). There was also a cottage industry of hagiography. See, for example, Jose M. Crisol, *Valor: World War II Saga of Ferdinand Marcos* (1983), and Cesar T. Mella, *Marcos: The War Years* (Manila, 1981). There were, as well, a whole genre of books explaining, justifying, and defending the constitution, edicts, and laws of martial law. Jose Aruego, *The New Philippine Constitution Explained: Including the Constitutional Amendments* (Manila, 1981), is a good example of this type of work. In contrast, see Alex D. Brillantes, *Dictatorship and Martial Law: Philippine Authoritarianism in 1972* (Manila, 1987) to see what was written after Marcos fell.

Imelda Marcos also had published material prepared for her delivery. See, for example, *Identity and Consciousness: The Philippine Experience* (Quezon City, 1974); *A Humanist Approach to Development and Other Selected Speeches* (Manila, 1981) and *Paths to Development* (Manila, 1981). This fascinating, mercurial, and often mawkish dragon lady has been a subject of fascination to many writers since she fled to Hawaii. Carmen Pedrosa's *Imelda Marcos: The Rise and Fall of One of the World's Most Powerful Women* (New York, 1987); Katherine E. Ellison's *Imelda: Steel Butterfly of the Philippines* (New York, 1988); and Beth Day Romulo's *Inside the Marcos Palace* (New York, 1987) are all studies of a woman who will be written about for decades to come.

Among the many monographs that analyze the Marcos era see David Wurfel, *Philippine Politics: Development and Decay* (Quezon City, 1988); Belinda Aquino, *Politics of Plunder: The Philippines Under Marcos* (Quezon City, 1987); Charles C. McDougald, *The Marcos File* (San Francisco, 1987); Lewis E. Gleeck, Jr., *President Marcos and the Philippine Political Culture* (Manila, 1987); Filomen Rodriguez, *The Marcos Regime: Rape of a Nation* (New York, 1985); and Robert Stauffer, *The Philippines Under Marcos: Failure of Transactional Developmentalism* (Sydney, 1986). Sterling Seagrave, *The Marcos Dynasty* (New York, 1988) is a highly readable, muckraking attack on Marcos and his myths. Raymond Bonner, *Waltzing With a Dictator: The Marcoses and the Making of American Policy* (New

York, 1987), by a former *New York Times* correspondent, is an interesting study of how Marcos manipulated and, to a remarkable degree, controlled U.S. policy toward the Philippines during his tenure.

There are a number of anthologies of essays, many with somewhat uneven quality, analyzing these two decades. See *Crisis in the Philippines*, John Bresnan, ed. (Princeton, 1986); John Lyons and Karl Wilson, *Marcos and Beyond: The Philippine Revolution* (Kenthurst, Australia, 1986); David A. Rosenberg, ed., *Marcos and Martial Law in the Philippines* (Ithaca, N.Y., 1979); and R. J. May and Francisco Nemenzo, eds., *The Philippines After Marcos* (New York, 1985).

The Muslim struggle for autonomy and challenge to national unity can be explored in Eliseo Mercado, "Economics and Revolt in Mindanao: The Origins of the MNLF and the Politics of Moro Separatism," in *Armed Separatism in Southeast Asia*, Lin Joo Jock, ed. (Singapore, 1984) and in Lela G. Noble's many writings, including "Muslim Separatism in the Philippines, 1972–1981: The Making of a Stalemate," *Asian Survey* 21 (November 1981), 1097–1114; "The Philippines Autonomy for Muslims," in *Islam in Asia—Religion, Politics & Society*, John Esposito, ed. (New York, 1987); "The Moro National Liberation Party in the Philippines," *Pacific Affairs* 49:3 (1976), 405–424. See also T.S.J. George, *Revolt in Mindanao: The Rise of Islam in Philippine Politics* (Kuala Lumpur, 1980), and Samuel K. Tan, *The Filipino Muslim Arms Struggle, 1900–1972* (Manila, 1977).

There is a full literature dealing with the Philippine-American relationship, including the issues of neocolonialism, the charge of U.S. economic dominance, the role of the military bases, and the feelings that define the "special relationship." Claude A. Buss, *The United States and the Philippines: Background for Policy* (Washington, D.C., 1977), is a good place to begin, since Buss was a senior U.S. colonial officer before World War II and has followed Philippine-American relations for half a century. Garal A. Grunder and William E. Livezey have revised their standard text of the 1950s, *The Philippines and the United States* (Westport, Conn., 1973). Willard S. Thompson's *Unequal Partners: Philippine and Thai Relations with the United States, 1965–1975* (Lexington, Mass., 1975) is a book by a Fletcher School professor with a strong anti-Communist bias. An opposing attitude can be found in Walden F. Bello and Severina Rivera, eds., *The Logistics of Repression and Other Essays: The Role of the United States Assistance in Consolidating the Martial Law Regime in the Philippines* (Washington, D.C., 1977). Among other works, see Alejandro M. Fernandez, *The Philippines and the United States: The Forging of New Relations* (Quezon City, 1977), and G. D. Loescher, "Human Rights and United States Foreign Policy: Idealism and Realism in Conflict," *Round Table* 276 (1979), 332–342. Robert L. Youngblood's "Philippine-American Relations Under the New Society," *Pacific Affairs* 50:1 (1977), 45–63, is one of the best overviews of the subject. See also Stephen R. Shalom, *The United States and the Philippines: A Study of Neo-colonialism* (Philadelphia, 1981); Jose D. Ingles, *Philippine Foreign Policy* (Manila, 1982).

A good introduction to the economic chaos created by the Marcos government is Gary Hawes, *The Philippine State and the Marcos Regime: The Politics of Export* (Ithaca, N.Y., 1987). Much additional information was published by the Asian Development Bank, the IMF, the World Bank, and similar agencies. The several hearings of the House Subcommittee on Asian-Pacific Affairs chaired by Congressman Stephen Solarz and the less frequent but important hearings in front of the Senate counterpart committee offer much primary material on the Philippines in general and on the economic state of the nation in particular.

The Reports of an Amnesty International Mission to the Republic of the Philippines, November, 1981 (London, 1982) and *The Philippines, a Country in Crisis: A Report by the Lawyers Committee for International Human Rights* (New York, 1983) both chronicle in detail the selective use of terror by the Marcos government. Alfred McCoy, *Priests on Trial* (Ringwood, 1984) is an important study to be reviewed. For an unusual insight into martial law see Jose Maria Sison's *Prison and Beyond: Selected Poems, 1958–1983* (Manila, 1984); Sison, one of the founders of the New People's Army, is also one of the most interesting, talented Filipinos of his era.

There was an extensive literature produced by those who fled into exile to escape Marcos. From Washington, President Aquino's foreign minister, Raul S. Manglapus, wrote extensively in newspapers and journals; see his *Philippines: The Silenced Democracy* (1976). Stephen Psinakis, *Two Terrorists Meet* (San Francisco, 1981), describes in fascinating detail his and Benigno Aquino's encounters with Imelda Marcos in New York. Psinakis, a son-in-law of the Lopez family, reveals how the elite interacted, even though they were mortal enemies. One of the most eloquent and passionately written attacks on the Marcos government came from a martyr of the resistance, Reuben Canoy, *The Counterfeit Revolution: Martial Law in the Philippines* (Manila, 1980).

The literature on the assassination of Benigno Aquino is extensive and uneven. Gerald H. Hill has written *The Aquino Assassination: The True Story and Analysis of the Assassination of Philippine Senator Benigno S. Aquino, Jr.* (Sonoma, 1983), and Nick Joaquin has written a very interesting book, *The Aquinos of Tarlac: An Essay on History as Three Generations* (Manila, 1983). See also reports of the *Fact Finding Board of the Assassination of Senator Benigno Aquino, Jr.* (Manila, 1984), and the journalistic work of such people as the late Robert Shaplen, who published a series of "Letters from Manila" in *The New Yorker* from 1983 until early September 1986.

William Chapman, *Inside the Philippine Revolution* (New York, 1987), and Bryan Johnson, *The Four Days of Courage* (New York, 1987), are both good introductions to the fall of the Marcos government. There are a number of dramatic photo volumes chronicling these same days. See, for example, *Bayon Ko! Images of the Philippine Revolution of 1986* (Hong Kong, 1986)

Finally, there is a fascinating exchange in *Orbis* between the distinguished historian Theodore Friend and the exiled Marcos in Hawaii. Why Marcos chose to answer in print Friend's essay is pure conjecture, but it was perhaps the only time he spoke out in self-defense. See Theodore Friend, "Marcos and the Philippines," *Orbis* 32:4 (1988), 569–586; Ferdinand E. Marcos, "A Defense of My Tenure," *Orbis* 33:1 (1989), 91–105; and Theodore Friend, "What Marcos Doesn't Say," *Orbis* 33:1 (1989), 97–105.

CHAPTER 8—THE AGE OF AQUINO

The drama of the fall of Marcos and the triumph of Aquino spawned some fascinating literature. Robert Manning's "The Philippines in Crisis," *Foreign Affairs* 63 (1984), 392–410, and Carl H. Landé and Richard Hooley, "Aquino Takes Charge," *Foreign Affairs* 64 (1986), 1087–1102, are good brief introductions to this period. Lucy Komisar, *Corazon Aquino: The Story of a Revolution* (New York, 1987); Isabelo Crisostomo, *Cory: Profile of a President* (Quezon City, 1986); Alfonso Policarpio, *Ninoy, the Willing Martyr* (Manila, 1986); and Sandra Burton, *Impossible Dream: The Marcoses, the Aquinos and the Unfinished Revolution* (New York, 1989), all cover the same general material. M. A. Mercado, ed., *People Power: An Eyewitness History of the Philippine Revolution of 1986* (Manila, 1986), and Douglas J. Elwood, *Philippine Revolution 1986: Model of Non-violent Change* (Quezon City, 1986), are also worthwhile reading. There are also a number of specialty monographs; see, for example, Richard L. Schwenk, *Onward Christians! Protestants in the Philippine Revolution* (Quezon City, 1986).

Political philosophers and scientists have been intrigued with "people power," the nonviolence of the Philippine revolution, and the personal grace of Corazon Aquino. The distinguished Jesuit priest and president of Ateneo University, Father Miguel A. Bernad, has collected a group of writings into a volume, *The February Revolution and Other Reflections* (Quezon City, 1986). See also Carolina Hernandez, Winifreda Evangelista, and Edgardo Maranan, *Issues in Socio-political Transformation in Asia and the Pacific: The Recent Philippine Experience* (Quezon City, 1987); Lela G. Noble, "Government in the Philippines: The Privatization of Politics," a publication of the *Asia Society* (New York, 1989); Raul de Guzman and Mila Reforma, *Government and Politics of the Philippines* (New York, 1988); Peter Krinks, ed., *The Philippines Under Aquino* (Canberra, 1987). M. Rajaretnam, ed., *The Aquino Alternative* (Singapore, 1986), has papers delivered at a June 1986 conference, including writings by Jose Maria Sison, Arturo Tolentino, and Joaquin Bernas among others. The Philippine government publishes Aquino's official speeches and documents; Corazon Aquino, *Speeches of Corazon Aquino* (Quezon City, 1987).

There are a number of interesting studies on the struggle between the military and the NPA. See Gareth Porter, "The Politics of Counterinsurgency in the Philippines: Military and Political Options," Center for Philippines Studies of the University of Hawaii, Occasional Paper no. 9 (Honolulu, 1987). Richard Kessler has written a perceptive article, "Development and the Military: Role of the Philippine Military in Development," in J. Soedjati Djiwardono and Young Mun Cheong, eds., *Soldiers and Stability in Southeast Asia* (Singapore, 1988), and has expanded it into a monograph, *Rebellion and Repression in the Philippines* (New Haven, Conn., 1989). Gregg Jones has written a very good piece on the revolution entitled, *Red Revolution: Inside the Philippine Guerrilla Movement* (Boulder, Colo., 1989). Amnesty International published a report, "Philippines: Unlawful Killings by Military and Paramilitary forces" (New York, 1988), and the Lawyers Committee for Human Rights issued "Vigilantes in the Philippines:

A Threat to Democratic Rule" (New York, 1988). Newspapers and magazines have extensively covered the several coup attempts against Aquino's government, including the serious rebellion of late 1989. It will be some years until enough can be known for scholarly examination of the military rebellion and internal tensions within the several units of the army, navy, and Philippine constabulary. It is worth going back to Juan Ponce Enrile's *Toward New Horizons* (Manila, 1974) to get a sense of his political philosophy.

There are a number of studies exploring the economic dilemmas of the post-Marcos world. See Robin Broad, *Unequal Alliance: The World Bank, the IMF and the Philippines* (Berkeley, 1988). Robert Dohner has written "Aquino and the Economy: An Assessment of the First Three Years," *Pilipinas* 11 (Fall 1988), 1–33; and "Philippine External Debt: Burdens, Possibilities, and Prospects," *Asia Society* (New York, 1989). Mahar Mangahas has written *The Political Economy of Land Reform and Land Distribution in the Philippines* (Quezon City, 1986). When Solita Collas-Monsod was the chief economic planner for Aquino, the government published the *Medium-term Philippine Development Plan, 1987–1992* (Manila, 1986), which detailed one vision of where the society ought to be pointing.

There are a number of earlier works that are well worth reading. Bernardo M. Villegas, one of the most prominent economists of the country, wrote *Strategies for Crisis* (Manila, 1983) and *Readings on Philippine Economic Development* (Manila, 1981), and Walden F. Bello, *Development Debacle: The World Bank in the Philippines* (San Francisco, 1982). See also Remigio E. Agpalo, *Philippine Interest Groups and Their Role in Modernization and Development* (Quezon City, 1977), and Harry T. Oshima, *The Transition to an Industrial Economy in Monsoon Asia* (Manila, 1984). Both trace the tension between economic development and political interaction. See also Brian Fagan, *Rent Capitalism in the Philippines* (Quezon City, 1981), and his *Land Reform and Technical Change in Central Luzon: The Rice Industry Under Martial Law* (Manila, 1982). Edmund K. Oasa studied "The International Rice Research Institute and the Green Revolution: A Case Study on the Politics of Agricultural Research" for his doctoral dissertation at the University of Hawaii in 1981. John F. Doherty has explored *The Philippine Urban Poor* (Honolulu, 1985).

There has been much scholarship exploring the military bases agreements. Fred Greene prepared a short book, under the auspices of the Council on Foreign Relations, entitled *The Philippine Bases: Negotiating for the Future* (New York, 1988), and Evelyn Colbert wrote *The United States and the Philippine Bases* (Baltimore, Md., 1987). Prior to his appointment as ambassador in Washington, the distinguished Filipino politician and statesman Emmanuel Pelaez wrote "The Military Bases and the Philippines: The Past and the Future," *Foreign Relations Journal* 1 (January 1986), pp. 1–39, which was published under the auspices of the Philippine Council for Foreign Relations. Carl Landé edited the papers of a conference in May 1986 for the volume *Rebuilding a Nation: Philippine Challenges and American Policy* (Washington, D.C., 1987). For the historical background, see Claude A. Buss, *The United States and the Philippines: Background for Policy*

(Washington, D.C., 1977). See also Eduardo C. Romualdez, *A Question of Sovereignty: The Military Bases in the Philippine-American Relations 1944–1979* (Manila, 1980); Romualdez, Imelda Marcos's brother, was a principal player in Washington during that earlier period. A good book to close this bibliography is Glenn A. May, *A Past Recovered* (Quezon City, 1987).

About the Book and Author

A unified nation with a single people, the Philippines is also a highly fragmented, plural society. Divided between uplander and lowlander, rich and poor, Christian and Muslim, between those of one ethnic, linguistic, and geographic region and those of another, the nation is a complex mosaic formed by conflicting forces of consensus and national identity and of division and instability.

It is not possible to comprehend all the recent changes in the Philippines—such as the rise and fall of Ferdinand Marcos or the revolution that toppled him—without an awareness of the religious, cultural, and economic forces that have shaped the history of these islands. These forces formed the focus of the first edition of *The Philippines.* Of that 1982 edition, the late Benigno Aquino, Jr., noted that "anyone wanting to understand the Philippines and the Filipinos today must include this book in his 'must' reading list." Now the author, a student of the Philippines for over thirty years, has revised the book extensively and added chapters on the Marcos era and the ascension of Corazon Aquino, making even more valuable the study Benigno Aquino called "endlessly readable and illuminated by penetrating insights into the complex character of the Filipino."

David Joel Steinberg is president of Long Island University. He first became interested in Philippine history in 1957 and has conducted extensive research in the country. His book *Philippine Collaboration in World War II* won the University Press Award in 1969. With a group of other Southeast Asian specialists, he coauthored *In Search of Southeast Asia,* most recently revised in 1987. He was a member of the International Observer team during the Marcos-Aquino election of 1986. He has consulted for the Ford Foundation, the United Nations Fund for Population Activities, and the United States government and has testified often before Congress on Philippine matters.

Index